COME TO
THE TABLE

COME TO
THE TABLE

Louise Luiggi

A PASSION FOR
EATING AND
FRENCH LIVING

PORTRAIT

Visit the Portrait website!

PORTRAIT Portrait publishes a wide range of non-fiction, including biography, history, science, music, popular culture and sport.

Visit our website to:

- read descriptions of our popular titles
- buy our books over the internet
- take advantage of our special offers
- enter our monthly competition
- learn more about your favourite Portrait authors

VISIT OUR WEBSITE AT: www.portraitbooks.com

First published in 2004 by **Portrait**
an imprint of
Piatkus Books Ltd
5 Windmill Street
London W1T 2JA
e-mail: info@piatkus.co.uk

This edition published 2005

The moral right of the author has been asserted

**A catalogue record for this book is available
from the British Library**

ISBN 0 7499 5065 X

Text design by Goldust Design
Edited by Ian Paten
Illustrations by Martha Reynolds

This book has been printed on paper manufactured with respect for the environment using wood from managed sustainable resources

Typeset by Action Publishing Technology Ltd, Gloucester
Printed and bound in Great Britain by
Bookmarque Ltd, Croydon, Surrey

For Stéphane who has inspired me all the way.

Contents

Acknowledgements

Big thanks go to the following: Mum for always being there to read and encourage, my intuitive agent Judy Chilcote for telling me to keep going, Nina and Pierre who patiently allowed me to use the computer and the team at Piatkus for recognising and understanding my passion.

Prologue

'*Bonjour, monsieur dame!*' My jovial greeting alarms another reserved couple hoping for a quiet coffee. They retreat to a safe corner and huddle around the foreign menu, fearing even worse to come. They will soon loosen up, be drawn into the spell. Many years of calming suspicion and anxiety, sometimes even scorn and prejudice, have built my confidence to unprecedented levels. I will not be thwarted. I grasp the challenge, and to settle their nerves ease off with the *bonjour*s and *merci*s, softening the approach. A soothing sip of our ever-popular *grand crème* coffee breaks through the resistance. I recognise the signs. Before long they'll leave the safety of their corner, inch their way along the illuminated cheese cabinet, heads bowed low, avoiding the hazardous basket handles trailing trap-like in front of the counter. As they confront the glass jars of ready-made dishes, lined up like laboratory test samples, labelled in a most unhelpful way '*civet d'oie*' and '*enchaud Périgourdin*', timidly feeling their way along the row of alien tins, I am still uneasy, sensing possible defeat. Just one happy jolt of memory – 'Oh, look at this, do you remember, we ate this in Normandy last year!' – and I can relax. Another victory.

I consider myself one of the lucky converts to the French cult. It's taken years of gradual transformation, my life choices moving me closer and closer to French living while keeping me surrounded by the comfort and reassurance of my English heritage. I am insistent that the move towards a French lifestyle, in culinary terms, came from within and was not thrust upon me by *la famille*, although I will admit to coming dangerously close to conforming to the traditionally silent model of the French daughter-in-law, seething tensely for many years, yearning to take the freedoms of French living and make them my own. Happily this is exactly what I achieved, and this is where I now find myself – proprietor of a shop-cum-café-cum-restaurant in the heart of Nottingham, the shop a capsule of Frenchness encased in Provençal blue protecting the secret of our cosy haven of chequered tablecloths, friendly French waiters and well-executed *plats du jour*, hidden below in the dusty red-brick cellar.

French Living transforms customers for five minutes of their busy lives; they loosen up, drift into holiday mode, talk food and, most surprisingly, reveal a therapeutic urge to chat and air their troubles over a slice of Brie or a frothy *chocolat chaud* and a flaky butter croissant. Immersing themselves, however briefly, in the eclectic blend of *café, boulangerie, épicerie fine* and restaurant ensures that the calming uniqueness of French food and culture works its magic, and yet I still feel a curious sadness once everyone has left and the doors are locked, the music silenced – a glimpse of a lifestyle, a transitory pleasure, quickly dissipates once the doors close.

I have travelled a long way, in England as well as in France, searching and learning with my Gallic husband, adapting my beliefs, traditions and opinions as children have appeared, families grown and the business has thrived. I'm still on my journey, growing and learning, unaware of where it will all end. I have listened to people's desperate searches for the ultimate French cookbook in the belief that this will unlock the secrets of the French Living charm, help them move closer towards living the idyllic French dream, and I have been overwhelmed by a chivalrous need to help. Having adequately matured, assimilated and digested, I am now ready to unpeel a layer from the French Living exterior and expose the realities of living *à la française* under grey English skies, among the sterile aisles of impersonal supermarkets and the confusing media-chef messages unique to our fair isles.

I have no detailed revolutionary recipes, sophisticated cooking skills or flashy kitchens and trendy gadgets. There are only experiences, memorable meals, shrewd kitchen observations and temperamental chefs to help guide you towards renewed culinary inspiration. There are no simple answers. A love of food, cooking, eating and mealtimes comes from within, once the intimacy of family life and a friendly circle of companions has been gently nurtured and lovingly developed. The strange metamorphosis of raw food into a dining experience, whether alone or in company, is a complex and powerful process, a human necessity but one imbued with an inexplicable fascination. Once the full potential of food, its miraculous ability to bring people together, to resolve upsets, even to control relationships, is understood, then and only then will cooking become a real pleasure and a fulfilling part of life.

I have stumbled my way through family relationships, hindered and frustrated by the complexities of a foreign language, cultural differences and inborn stubbornness, and at every step my feelings about nourishment and the kitchen have evolved and changed. Ultimately my transformation has culminated in my embracing food as an integral part of my life and in my understanding its role as an initiator of ultimate well-being.

I think I may just have found the answer to a cherished dream.

ONE

La Salade

SUNDAY LUNCHTIMES WERE warm, sleepy, happy times – a plate piled high with well-roasted grey beef, a multitude of chopped vegetables, at least two sorts of potato, mashed and roasted, all harmoniously united by a smooth, tepid traditional gravy. I loved these meals, everyone cosily ensconced in domestic bliss, still holding on to weekend high spirits, protecting each other from the inevitable slide towards Sunday teatime melancholy. These gatherings around a copious table – to laugh, cry, debate and shout – were sacred throughout my years growing up at home.

We were a close-knit unit – Mum, Dad, me, my sister and brother, us children securely enveloped in a protective, sometimes smothering, parental love. Cuddles, hugs and explosive displays of emotion united our secret world. We rarely mixed with other family members, obediently shadowing Dad in his crusade for freedom. He had a desperate need to create a loving family of his own, to be surrounded by innocent, childlike devotion, an embittered protest against the cold upbringing inflicted upon him by his own parents. This detachment from our extended family became irreversible following a particularly volatile exchange of opinions. Not the greatest diplomat, Dad had an irrepressible tendency to speak frankly, often cruelly, unable to control or articulate his emotions and so, as is often the case with all family arguments, with blame on both sides, forgiveness and tolerance were scrunched tightly into a crumpled ball, never to be unravelled again, and permanent family breakdown ensued. How strange that my own life, my own family relationships, should take such a similar turn. I was not to blame – it was obviously in my genes. I had no experience of handling a big family or coping with well-intentioned individuals who longed to guide me, to show me the way to fit in sensibly and politely, to conform to traditions, long-established methods that should never be questioned. No, I was not to blame. I grew up in isolation, my independence encouraged, leading to inevitable embarrassing mistakes, wept over and then instantly forgotten, lessons learnt.

One summer my adventurous father decreed that we would seek novelty by holidaying in barren campsites tucked away within the quaint villages of Normandy. Touched by the plump yet authoritative *madame*, by sparsely decorated restaurants with tables of *toile cirée* serving crunchy raw-vegetable starters, he led us deeper into France's great heartland, the Dordogne and the Ardèche, finally coming to rest in overvisited, fashionable Provence. It was fun, momentous, an adventurous era. We were tourists, sampling the specialities yet imposing our English manners and peculiarities on the food, requesting a plate for the bread, don't forget the butter please, and where are the vegetables? Piling the plate high, a distinctive English tradition. And yet I perceived a burning desire within my father to embrace this indefinable Gallic appeal. Year upon year we marvelled at his choice of bouncy cars, the inimitable Citroën CX, a monster of a vehicle, but at least the camping gear would fit. Six o'clock 'tea' was unceremoniously dropped and replaced by dinner at seven thirty, with a bottle of wine and proper coffee; subtle innovations progressively modifying our intrepid middle-class household.

Childhood holiday memories full of scents, flavours and happiness are frequently rekindled thanks to my overexcited customers. Their holiday tales take me back to my early French discoveries, and I cannot resist a giggle at the innocence of our beliefs then. My life has wormed its way deeper and deeper into the soul of a ridiculously extended family, ranging from the isolated traditions of Tulle veal farming via the suburban, concrete monotony of life as a Parisian *fonctionnaire* to the cloistered, controlled existence of the inhabitants of Corsica. Not surprisingly, much of my early understanding of what it means to be French has been extinguished and replaced with an astute knowledge of family life across the Channel. I now realise the extent to which I apply this wisdom, like an unworldly revelation, to everyday living. I have unwittingly extracted the most relevant French attributes, particularly anything food-related, and unconsciously applied them to my life in England.

The gathering of this 'insider' knowledge began with the impulsive yet perfectly natural desire to escape home. It came as no surprise when the daughter inherited her father's wanderlust and imitated his brave travelling initiative by moving to the chic Paris *8ème arrondissement* as au pair to a respectable family, the father an English banker, the mother a Catholic journalist of aristocratic Normandy origins. My stay began with me enclosed with three young children in a grandiose, high-ceilinged apartment, requiring essential after-school trips down in the rickety iron lift to the neighbouring Parc Monceau; by Christmas three young children had become four, all under the age of six. The routine was monotonous and confined, far removed from the liberty and space of my own childhood. As a child, I was free to wander in and out of the garden, jump the fence to join the fun next door, sometimes braving the toothless rage of the neighbouring farmer by disturbing his tempting castles of golden hay soaking up the sun in the field adjoining our garden (a prickly adventure playground, impossible to resist). In contrast, my poor Parisian charges waited impatiently for adult agreement before being let free, wrapped up tightly in smart, velvet-collared coats and marched hand in hand to the *parc*, where they were turned loose like frantic wild dogs, fired by boundless pent-up energy suddenly released as in a coiled spring, immediate, intense action calming gradually to soft, gentle play. Even within the park I did not feel that this release was complete or satisfactory as we were obliged to politely conform to park rules – *pelouse interdite*, play neatly restricted to the areas allocated for such unruly activity. Unsurprisingly tension did sometimes spill over back at the *appartement*. One rainy evening I witnessed a dramatic, uncommonly fierce tantrum that was finally and abruptly quenched by Monsieur using the sharp impact of a cold shower to shock

lovely

4

the screams into a dripping, remorseful bundle of sobs. I felt sympathy and a little sadness, yet these children were on the whole happy. They knew no different.

I found city living claustrophobic, felt myself hemmed in by the tall, classical, elegant architecture of Parisian buildings rising up on either side of the narrow streets, minimising the sky, pulling my eyes down to the uneven, hazardous pavement, where I jostled for space. Occasionally I could breathe again and walk more confidently, my head raised, as the streets widened to form expansive tree-lined boulevards, but this was not enough – I craved green open space in which to walk, run, cycle and be free of the incessant hum of traffic buzzing around in my head.

Luckily there were numerous weekend escapes to Normandy, visiting the grandparents' noble château, which helped me survive and fully appreciate life in Paris. This was a fairy-tale castle with heavily timbered towers, attached to a symmetrically formed country house sitting on a gentle embankment of well-kept lawn, neat rose beds and formally clipped trees. Reached by crossing the creaking heavy wooden planks across the moat, this home was a working property, gathering, sorting and processing the apples from the vast orchards which filled our nostrils with their potent scent. Inside, the house was musty, with nicotine-yellowed wallpaper, peeling and damp, framing the solid pieces of antique furniture crammed into every room, all in need of some tender loving care. This was a relic of a bygone era, a glorious home left to wither away in the hands of a tired, wilting couple without the strength or desire to maintain this former rambling palace.

Mealtimes, however, were a chance for the proud grandparents to flaunt unashamedly Normandy delicacies and specialities, many of them home-made wares from their own land, to the amazement and delight of the foreign au pair. The men would leave early in the morning, scrambling excitedly into the forest undergrowth with guns casually slung over their shoulders, ready for action. They were in search of *sanglier,* wild boar. Majestically simmered in red wine for hours, even days, until moist, tender and flavour-some, the captured beast was truly sumptuous. Normandy cheeses I had already discovered in Paris, but the unpas-teurised farmhouse Pont l'Evêque and Camembert presented at the Normandy table were of a far superior quality and intensity of flavour. I was also introduced to the intoxicating apple liqueur Calvados, by having the bottle routinely thrust under my nostrils at the end of each meal with the lordly command to *sentez.* They explained that Calvados was often used during long, exhaustingly rich dinners to help revive the appetite. Downed in one, a swift shot of Calvados will apparently give you the strength and space in your belly for the courses to follow. I did not have the opportunity to try this *trou Normand* technique, but I eventually built up enough courage to put glass to lips and savour the infamous combination of classic apple tart and eye-wateringly puissant Calvados.

Under a dusty blanket in the barn, almost buried under an unsteady stack of apples, I discovered a rusty cycle. One swift wipe and this was the perfect solution for free-wheeling the heaviness from my pounding, sleepy head. The Normandy countryside reminded me of England and home – lush green fields filled with lazy grazing cows and apples everywhere. I was rejuvenated, cleansed, fresh and ready to face another week of demanding children, the monotonous school run, eager to investigate the bustling maze of Paris *centre ville*. With no real childcare skills apart from those derived from regular babysitting duties, my cool, innocent approach to such a hefty responsibility amazes me.

In Paris Madame would frequently cook dishes flavoured with the scents of her Normandy roots. This dish was special because it not only introduced me to the surprising delicacy of pigeon but always reminded me of my bike rides through the apple-rich Normandy countryside:

PIGEONNEAU POÊLÉ AU CIDRE

Soak a handful of sultanas in cider overnight.

Ask your butcher to prepare 4 wood pigeons into 8 breasts (this will feed 4 to 6 diners).

Preheat the oven to 230°C/450°F/Gas Mark 8.

Make a stock by roasting the carcasses with 2 onions and 2 leeks (or any vegetable trimmings) for 15 minutes in the oven, then cover with water and cook slowly for at least an hour until the water has absorbed the colour and taste of the ingredients. Strain and reserve.

Peel and cut one Granny Smith apple per person into wedges, cook in a frying pan with a knob of butter until they start to turn gold and reserve.

When you are 20 minutes away from eating this dish, heat a frying pan, add oil to coat the pan, cook the breasts briskly without overcrowding the pan for 2 minutes, turn over, season, cook for a further 2 minutes and remove the pink breasts.

Add 350ml of cider and 350ml of your stock to the pan, bring to the boil, reduce a little for 5 minutes and add 100ml single cream, season, whisk in 25g butter (you can thicken with roux if you like a richer texture). Put the

sultanas and apples into the sauce for 1 minute to reheat
and warm the breasts in a separate pan.

Cut the pigeon breasts into slices to reveal the luscious
dark pink colour, fan out onto plates and coat with the
sauce.

Similarly, I had no useful cooking talents, no real interest
in food preparation, and yet this bourgeois Parisian family
sparked within me an uncontrollable fascination with
mealtimes. My letters home spilled over with excruciat-
ingly detailed menus, far outnumbering the anticipated
descriptions of elegant Paris landmarks. What had
happened to me? To write with so much animation you
would have thought I was living with a couple of master
chefs. This was certainly not the case. Madame was a
gentle, caring lady, controlled and serene, but rather
absent-minded in the kitchen. I can recall a handful of
charcoal-blackened *tartes tatin* once imbuing the *appartement* with invasive, choking smoke. Monsieur revelled in
the weekend march to market and lovingly extolled the
culinary skills of his adored wife to guests, visitors and au
pair, but he personally did not cook.

As au pair I became a member of the family, dining *en
famille* and sharing confidences. However, Parisian apartments were not designed to embrace the modern home
help completely, and so every evening I would tentatively
climb up the steep external spiral staircase to my quarters.
This grim and sad reminder of an earlier age of servants was
the other side of the coin of an environment that welcomed
you in with one hand and abruptly rejected you with the
other.

Wrapped in a warm, cosy robe, I descended each

morning to the bright, coffee-filled kitchen, where Madame, identically robe-clad and sleepy, would be spreading runny jam along buttered lengths of toasted baguette, piling the centre of the table high with ready-to-eat *tartines*. Large round bowls of steaming, aromatic coffee and *chocolat chaud* proudly awaited the inevitable plunging of a neatly prepared *tartine*, once slurped dry shamefully revealing the telltale soggy chunks clinging to the bottom of each *bol*. Breakfast was a messy affair, the long, solid, unprotected oak table, plate-free, thoroughly jam-stained in spite of the extremely practical long spoons with discreet hooks at the top, cleverly designed to stop their annoyingly frequent disappearance into the sticky oversized jars of home-made *confiture*. The chaotic freedom of breakfast created a glorious display of crumbs, drips and *tâches*, all swiftly washed away until the next morning with a series of firm wipes.

The children would all come home from school for a lunch of popular *steak haché*, flash-fried dry on a multi-purpose cast-iron grill, with *haricots verts* tossed in garlic or cubed potatoes sautéed in goose fat, a natural yogurt with a measured sprinkling of additional sugar stirred furiously until smooth and maybe fruit to finish. We would eat the same as the children, but the yogurt would be replaced by cheese and a green-leaf salad with vinaigrette dressing. Oh, how I loved this salad! I experienced many new things in Paris – the underground world of the Métro, invigorating, bouncy bus rides across the vast cobbled Place de la Concorde, the spaceship plumbing of the Centre Pompidou, eating hot chestnuts along the romantic Champs-Elysées – and yet a simple 'green' salad of purple-tinged lollo rosso, spiky bitter *frisée*, softened with deep green lettuce, copiously coated with a sharp mustard vinaigrette, managed to conquer all in the radical breakthroughs I made at this youthful time of my life. Interestingly, to this day it is the French concept of salad which creates the most controversy and fascination among my customers. Once they have tried it, they are eternally convinced of the refreshing, palette-cleansing properties of a pure, unadulterated salad.

Vinaigrette is a great French mystery that seems to confuse and bewilder the English, who apparently struggle to recapture the flavours of holiday restaurant salads. The most successful vinaigrette recipe uses Amora, strong Dijon mustard, mixed with some red wine vinegar and then blended with a combination of olive oil and vegetable oil, seasoned and whisked to a homogeneous sauce. It is ready to be shaken and enjoyed immediately, or can be kept in a screw-top jar in the fridge.

Try making your own *salades composées* by using a mixed green-leaf salad tossed in vinaigrette as your starting point.

SALADE ROQUEFORT ET NOIX
Add cubes of Roquefort cheese and then sprinkle with crushed walnuts.

SALADE AU CHÈVRE CHAUD
Halve a Crottin de Chavignol goat's cheese and heat under the grill or in a pan until bubbling. Place the golden cheese on top of toasted croutons and position on top of the dressed leaves.

SALADE NIÇOISE
Chop some tomatoes, sprinkle over the salad, place a
mound of tuna in the centre, and quarter a cooked egg
and position around the tuna. Top with tiny, highly
flavoured Niçoise olives kept in Provence herbs and grape-
seed oil, pouring some of this aromatic oil over it all to
achieve a quick Niçoise salad.

FRISÉE AUX LARDONS
Use spiky, chewy and slightly bitter *frisée*, perfect when
combined with cubed *poitrine fumée*. Blanch the *poitrine
fumée*, or *lardons*, as they are more frequently known, in
boiling water and then sauté in hot oil until crisp and
golden. Sprinkle over the leaves, together with some
chopped herbs such as parsley and chives. I also love this
salad with a poached egg proudly placed on top.

SALADE PAYSANNE
Sprinkle some chopped tomato and cubed Comté cheese
over the leaves, quarter a cooked egg and arrange around
the side of the bowl. Position thin strips of Bayonne ham
across the top and finish off with Niçoise olives and a
drizzle of their herby oil.

SALADE D'AUTOMNE
Try an autumn combination of cubed Cantal cheese,
chopped apple and walnuts. Cantal is one of the oldest
French cheeses and has the texture of Cheddar but a more
intense, woody flavour. Good delicatessens and supermarkets should stock it.

11

Evening meals in the Paris household were lighter, quieter and civilised, just the three of us catching up on the day's news in a peaceful child-free atmosphere. We would enjoy simple healthy combinations such as cooked, chopped and seasoned spinach with a runny yet crisp fried egg delicately placed on top, varied sometimes by replacing the spinach with ratatouille or lean slices of mildly salty ham and maybe a poached egg. Artichokes with vinaigrette dressing were a favourite with Madame, and she patiently tutored me in the art of dismantling these. I was fascinated by the hands-on, sensual, almost erotic practice of sucking each leaf free of its goodness, creating a mountain of chewed and broken leaves until the sought-after heart comes cleanly away, to be triumphantly relished on its own, in all its simple glory.

Only eighteen and yet perceptive enough to realise that this overtly in-love couple required their own space, I appreciatively ate my food and then hastily disappeared up to my sombre *grenier*.

With a new baby disturbing the night's peace and upsetting the daily routine, confusion reigned as the children struggled to understand their revised position within the family, and as everybody tried to come to terms with this intrusive new guest. Stability was called for, and I was asked to stay on over Christmas. This would be my first time away from my traditional family celebration and I was naturally upset at missing familiar Christmas customs. Distance suddenly emphasised a sentimental longing for the most unusual festive memories: bowls of mixed nuts – Brazil, walnut, pistachio – with dates and dried fruits scattered around the house to proclaim the beginning of festivities; the deep, sensual odour of a living tree lifted from the forest, made to shine and glisten, displaying its natural glory within the confines of our four walls; spicy mince pies bubbling over, hot currants escaping from the protective pastry lid, the profuse baking steaming up the kitchen windows as the endless production of tantalising Christmas appetisers continued throughout the days and evenings leading up to the big day. I would miss this homely, comforting familiarity, but at the same time I was intrigued to know what a French Christmas would bring.

There was no tree, but Madame carefully pieced together a moving, beautifully crafted crèche filled with lifelike *santons* depicting the classic birth scene, recalling distinctly my naive, hesitant performances at the school nativity play. There was not a great focus on Papa Noël, which had a lot to do with Madame's religious beliefs; she preferred to encourage her children to remember Christmas as the birthday of our Saviour and not as an excuse to embrace the materialistic trappings of overzealous gift-buying. Everything seemed calmer and understated compared to the frenetic Christmas rush I was used to. It was a fresh, thought-provoking time, but it did lack a little of that overexcited anticipation of a miraculous visit bringing a glorious spectacle of toys, fulfilling your secret hopes and dreams. Memories of lying in bed, stomach churning, heart hammering, squeezing the eyes closed, refusing to even glimpse the red-coated visitor in case it all disappeared and the spell was broken, were not a part of this family's Christmas. The children went to bed peacefully, as on any other night, maybe a tad more excited because Auntie Grace and *Tonton* from Normandy were coming for dinner. This was a religious festival, appropriately respected.

Christmas was celebrated on the evening of the twenty-fourth, a sophisticated family gathering around the long table reserved for special guests and important celebratory feasts. I felt honoured and yet a little out of place, strangely awkward, as if I were somehow intruding on this intimate, convivial dinner. It was all timed perfectly, each course carefully presented and leisurely perused, each fragrance relished, with 'hmm's and 'ah's filtering across the table, each detail discussed at length. 'Hmm. This is good. Which do you prefer, duck or goose foie gras?'

After the admiring, smelling and identifying of each ingredient, everyone would then eat, the initial silence brusquely broken by a cross-fire of animated conversation which tested my inadequate school French to the full, building to a loud crescendo as the dinner continued and the wine flowed. The meal was designed not only to satisfy our appetites but was also an essential element of the Christmas proceedings, keeping us occupied and awake until midnight, when the champagne could be ceremoniously popped. Only then would the kissing, hugging and exchange of gifts be allowed, the whole proceedings recalling our New Year's Eve celebrations.

Numerous tasty entrées were the key to extending the evening, contrasting with the single huge Christmas dinner plateful I had always known hitherto. In fact it is the special, luxurious food, together with the reserved *vendange tardive* wine, which characterises the French Christmas celebration. This is what everyone looks forward to – a lengthy, belly-filling feast to savour and remember, and a chance to be merry: round mirrored platters tantalisingly gleaming with fragile orange slivers of smoked salmon, layered flatly across the plate, interspersed with lemon wedges ready to be firmly squeezed or crushed, releasing their citrus flavour over the smoky, salty fish; grey-white oysters smelling strongly of the sea, decorated with shaggy green seaweed, hesitantly sucked from their sharp shells with doubtful appreciation; *boudin blanc*, a typical French Christmas speciality, like a white black pudding, a sausage made from a *béchamel* mixture combined with finely minced chicken, grilled until browned and served warm on a plate, simply, proudly on its own; *foie gras de canard*, rich duck's liver spread on warm wholemeal toasted bread, pleasantly complemented by a chilled sweet Sauternes, followed swiftly by the meat – roast duck, served with nutty wild *cèpe* mushrooms, roast chestnuts and *haricots verts*. The slow, easy pace helped with digestion, but I had never before experienced such a gastronomic marathon. A refreshing salad accompanied a varied display of cheese: goat's cheese pyramids, some pure white, others coated in ash; marbled, mouldy blue Roquefort; the bitter, orange-coated rind of a Pont l'Evêque; a creamy soft, indulgently ripe Camembert. I loved the cheese and could easily have ended my meal with this gratifying contrast of flavours. I struggled with sweet foods. I am not really sure when my sugar incompatibility began, but I simply could not relate to the lure of rich dark chocolate, lashings of whipped cream and sickly-sweet sugar. Physically my body seemed to want to reject the desserts, particularly after a long-drawn-out, copious dinner. However, I picked politely at the traditional *bûche*, a log-shaped ice-cream dessert, chilled and slipping over the tongue with ease and sliding down, almost refreshingly easily, thankfully helping to hide my awkward secret.

With Christmas over, the routine of escorting the children to and from school and the relentless trek to the park in all weathers started again. It was a lonely existence, made harder by my shortage of vocabulary. Unable to eloquently express my feelings, I was obliged to keep any anguish or uncertainties to myself. I longed for a good chat, someone with whom to share my experiences over a *chocolat chaud* or to enjoy a Sunday afternoon wander around an undiscovered corner of Paris. I met other au pairs sitting primly on the park benches exchanging experiences and family gossip and realised how fortunate I was not to have to iron my way through mountains of creased laundry or clean and polish the house from top to bottom. No, I was one of the lucky few.

I resorted to writing long letters, losing myself in words, hopes and dreams, and then impatiently waiting for the arrival of the post, nervously knocking at the *concierge*'s door to check for UK-stamped letters, parcels, postcards – any form of warm human contact. I read my way through my Parisian family's bookshelves, losing myself in the aristocratic world of Nancy Mitford. The final chapter completed, with no sequel to follow, I decided it was time to return home.

Three meals a day, not counting the children's obligatory after-school *goûter* of home-made *pain au chocolat*, a roughly torn baguette filled with a couple of dark bitter chocolate squares; ceremoniously laying the table, washing the salad, bringing the cheese to room temperature and the fruit bowl to hand, followed by twenty minutes of self-indulgent solace, digesting, indulging in carefree pleasure – I was beginning to understand the power of food, its indefinable role in forging strong relationships, encouraging communication, discussion, laughter and love. Suddenly there's time to see each other, to reach out over a warming, comforting bowl and listen, to just be there. This surprisingly straightforward eating routine, three times a day, became an essential part of my life, unexpectedly surviving my return to the familiar world of impulsive English temptations and solitary snacking, resolutely prevailing as a fond and powerfully influential memory of my first French family.

TWO

The Convivial Cassoulet

THE PULL OF France was inexplicable, a powerful inner
need to change, to speak another language, a romantic quest
for independence. Quite simply France just seemed considerably more alluring than my quiet, predictable English
village life. And so I returned, this time to the smaller,
dynamic university city of Toulouse, *La Ville Rose*, so called
because of the abundance of distinctive red-brick buildings
and monuments turning the city pink under the glare of the
balmy midday sun.

For a year I became a student at the Ecole Supérieure de
Commerce, which was housed in the most run-down,
charming maze of buildings, typifying a grand *hôtel
Toulousain*; this was the original *école*, situated in the
beautiful rue de la Dalbade before the school made the
monumental error of moving to a life-threateningly busy

boulevard a good ten minutes' walk away from the bustling *centre ville*. I spent a considerable amount of my time in the *cave*, a magnificent subterranean student refuge, the French equivalent of a student union blended with a sixth-form common room, with the essential buzzing bar serving intoxicating Pelforth beer alongside syrupy arabica espresso. This damp, mouldy *cave* was indeed an essential refuge where I could savour more typically challenging student behaviour away from the formal classroom atmosphere of this prestigious school. I hated the lessons, and despised the condescending tone of the teaching staff, who spooned out their precious wisdom to obediently unquestioning pupils, and I equally resented the young for their conservative, conformist and strangely dutiful behaviour. If only I had fully heeded these early warning bells that ring out so loudly to me today, demonstrating so explicitly the huge gap between the generations in France, and their old-fashioned ways of relating to one another, the older generation expecting respect, warranted or not, exercising control and influence over the young, deaf to the remotest avant-garde suggestions or fresh contemporary thoughts. Maybe, just maybe, I would have handled my second French family with more tact, understanding and restraint.

Nevertheless, hiding away in the *cave* empowered me with some useful and novel life skills, including the addictive passion of French rock and roll and the more practical skills involved in running a proper French café.

In truth my increase in caffeine consumption had much to do with my growing obsession with the recently elected *Président de la Cave*. Stéphane Luiggi, swarthy and sociable, possessed an edgy, angry, almost exciting rebellious potential. Externally he seemed content, and yet I could sense his desire to break free from the tight adult hold of the Ecole de Commerce. This moody, dark side to his temperament is most certainly linked to his Corsican origins, to the island's association with the Mafia and the passionate struggle to liberate it from French control. These passions were raised to explosive levels at the end of the first year; narrowly failing his exams, and unfairly forced to repeat the entire first year's course, Stéphane was enraged, particularly at having to explain this failure to his fee-paying parents. I couldn't help but feel partially responsible for this irreversible disaster, having wantonly distracted Stéphane from the classroom, consequently becoming absorbed in the fight against the bitter unfairness of this cruel institution.

It was during this emotional time that I was introduced to my future parents-in-law. They had decided to confront the school's director, determined to fight for a little compassion and understanding, trying to avoid the financial drain of paying for an extra year. These were clearly not ideal conditions in which to meet my boyfriend's parents. I felt guilty, the unquestionable culpability written all over my face. I should really have stayed away, hidden safely within the confines of my *appartement* until the drama had been forgotten and the new school year had got underway. But no, I decided to confront the family and face the parents head on.

We shook hands politely, smiling and over-friendly, trying too hard to be liked, exchanging uncertain pleasantries. They were evidently dubious about my linguistic abilities, undecided whether I could actually understand a word they were saying. I could understand perfectly, but my ability to articulate a reply in time and with impressive grammatical perfection was thwarted by severe premarital nerves. They compensated by speaking with slow, exaggerated precision, articulating each sound in a ridiculously comical way, like an English holidaymaker trying to communicate with a bemused Spanish waiter.

I know they were both taken off their guard, confronting for the first time in their lives plain speaking and unrehearsed views offered straight from the heart, as I tried to explain in my limited French vocabulary my feelings of injustice and anger at the school's decision to make Stéphane repeat his first year. I now know this offended them deeply, particularly as I was still an outsider, not part of the clan, so not entitled to air my opinions in such a forthright tone. As everyone knew I was the real reason Stéphane was in this mess, I must have looked mildly ridiculous standing there in front of these strangers defending my new-found love. Unfortunately this would not be the last time my blunt, passionate tone would cause offence. I had a long way to go before I understood that in France the young do not express their emotions, particularly in front of adults they have barely met. In some ways I consider myself lucky that I was innocently unaware of such etiquette and continued unabashed and true to myself for many years, unknowingly upsetting the family with my fiery tongue. These were still the early days – I hardly knew Stéphane and had only met his parents formally on a couple of occasions – but already I could detect a subtle difference in the way they spoke to each other and dealt with tricky emotional situations as compared to my experiences with my own parents. They seemed fiercely possessive, almost scared to let go, clinging on to a little boy who had left them many years ago.

Thankfully, as students in Toulouse Stéphane and I were blissfully free, far from any parent's watchful eye, making decisions together, wandering aimlessly around the Sunday morning St Sernin flea market, warming ourselves with piping-hot *chocolat chaud*, casually choosing our Sunday dinner at the Marché des Carmes – a metre of Toulouse sausage, a ripe, yellowing Camembert, a wet, muddy lettuce stuffed unceremoniously into a plastic bag, a couple of baguettes.

We became inseparable very quickly, enclosing ourselves snugly for long hours in Stéphane's intimate studio flat, talking, whispering, sharing music. We would greedily devour bowls of pasta sprinkled heavily with ready-grated Emmental cheese bought from the local late-night shop, only emerging briefly to replenish our cupboards. We were enraptured by each other's scent, touch and compatibility. At first we communicated in both languages, flitting from one to the other, mixing the two irreverently, helping each other out whenever we were paralysed by an irretrievable word or phrase or were just too tired to express our feelings in another language. Increasingly, maybe a little self-ishly, Stéphane preferred to speak in English, and I lazily indulged him, laughing at his errors, giggling at his twisted pronunciation and incorrect vowel sounds, his enunciation of silent letters, despairing at our impossibly complicated rules and irregularities. This fun didn't last long as his mistakes soon became few and far between – he was a natural linguist, understanding the origins of words and always ready to recount tales, riddles and anecdotes to help him remember. He knew he was good, practising reli-giously, uninhibited, unashamed and ready to make mistakes, to use phrases heard only a few minutes earlier. He grasped the challenge of a new language and culture with enthusiastic vigour. I recall watching him improvise his own unique tea-making routine. I found his attempts to make me feel more at home charming and considerate, watching as he laboriously boiled some water in a tiny battered pan, adding the tea bags directly to the boiling water and stirring vigorously before pouring his dark, bitter concoction into his minuscule espresso cups. I slurped appreciatively.

It was here in this cosy studio that Stéphane told me about his origins. As a child, he had divided his time between the dull, ugly Parisian suburbs and spectacular, colourful Corsica. His parents were both teachers and had taken the path followed by so many educated islanders direct to the mainland, their only real hope for successful careers. Outside tourism there is little scope for professionals on the island and the mainland continues to lure away the young and spirited, leaving the abandoned islanders in disillusion and despair, particularly during the silent grey-sea months.

He had an enormous map of France pinned on the wall which covered one whole side of his tiny neat room. Immensely proud and passionately enthusiastic, he used this dominant feature to highlight his island. The name was familiar but geography had never been a strong subject, and so I always made a point of admitting this weakness to all new acquaintances to eliminate any embarrassment when reading maps or made to answer tricky board-game questions. I was secretly surprised to learn that Corsica was French. I arrogantly considered myself an expert on France, having lived and worked there; my experience as a Parisian au pair and regular family holidays had expanded my knowledge of all things French, and so I felt cheated to discover a part of France that I knew absolutely nothing about. Corsica. *La Corse*. Even the name did not sound French. I associated this place with exotic long-haul destinations, a ten-hour flight to a secluded beach hut, with palm trees and coconut cocktails, certainly not cafés, Ricard and garlic. Located as it is above Sardinia, it is easy to see how it can become lost, blending smoothly into its Italian neighbour. And it is not such an easy holiday destination when you consider the immense volume of sea that has to be negotiated to get there, possibly dissuading those brave Northerners who manage to complete the long trek down the efficient and expensive *autoroutes* from venturing any farther. And so Corsica remains a treasured secret, a glorious holiday haven for the select few, for those discerning travellers who have taken the trouble to find out more about this lonely island.

I was fascinated by Stéphane's island tales, which only made him more alluring, more exotic, but this life, these people, were all very far away, not part of our existence as a couple. I loved this man for his humour, his gorgeous smiling face and loud, free guffaw, his fun-loving embracing of life, his appreciation of good food and wine, and his gentle, caring, sensitive devotion, which made me feel exceptionally special and loved. We were able to love each other for who we were, what we represented as individuals, without the burden of family, associations and background that can unwittingly influence feelings.

As time went on we socialised more, crawling out of our studio, meeting others, yet always wrapped up in each other. Our student socialising was not the typically English endless bar crawl, but always something food-centred, such as our group soirées at Chez Fazoul, an atmospheric, cellar-like restaurant with distinctive pink-bricked walls and a cheap set menu with a litre of house wine thrown in.

Coarse, grainy terrine roughly decorated with unchopped gherkins would welcome everyone to the candlelit table, followed by a classic *salade Fazoul* of mixed leaves tossed in mustard vinaigrette, sprinkled with crispy fried *lardons* and *gésiers*, a main course of simply prepared *steak au poivre vert* and the best fries ever, finishing with the *Toulousain* speciality, *gâteau Basque*. With all this for sixty francs, you could easily understand why it became increasingly difficult to get a table.

Stéphane and I also began to entertain at home once we had found our new, bigger rooftop *appartement*. We were extremely lucky to come across an incredibly spacious apartment perfectly designed to cope with calm, candlelit dinners raucously degenerating into noisy rock and roll classes. Its parquet floor swept elegantly towards two perfectly styled French doors, with the traditional window-closing mechanism that typifies French charm and character. Opening these revealed our splendid backdrop of a multi-coloured stained-glass window belonging to the awe-inspiring Eglise St Augustin. An eerie yet calming light would wash over our living room, sometimes accompanied by distant choir harmonies and the solemn tones of church organ chords. Rooftop views over the red-brick city could be admired from our fifth-floor balcony, perfect for intimate dining and observing the world bustling by.

These informal meals, casual student entertaining, were the best cookery lessons ever for me, a novice and recipe book addict with no recollections of protected culinary secrets, precious tips or homely parental advice. I shadowed Stéphane closely like an overenthusiastic infant, revelling in the freedom of his creativity, finally grasping with an overwhelming sense of relief that there is no strict code, no divine French cookery gospel to memorise and adhere to religiously. Individual interpretation was allowed; indeed, in most instances it was obligatory, imposed upon us when money ran out or at the mere thought of another muscle-wrenching climb back up the five flights of icy-cold marble stairs for an ingredient that could easily be replaced.

Fresh, glistening cod steaks, neatly rolled pork loin expertly parcelled in string, dirty mounds of potatoes, powdery *saucisson* – inspiring, magical objects luring Stéphane like bait, drawing him closer to his eventual mouth-watering decision. This was real, liberated, pressure-free shopping, appreciating food for its true colours, celebrating its flavours and shapes and the raw embryonic potential of each component. I absorbed these moments, threw away my pitiful collection of cookery books and proudly stepped into the kitchen, for the first time confident and cheerfully impervious to criticism.

We were free spirits, skipping early-morning classes, both uninspired by the *école*'s aim of turning us all into *directeurs d'entreprise*, future managerial dictators to lead, make profits and be boringly unhappy and mundane. No, not for us this commercial formula for wealth and bitter success; we were more interested in finding the best café, the smoothest arabica espresso, in choosing the *pain aux raisins* with the most raisins and the creamiest centre squeezed full of oozing *crème pâtissière,* in hunting down the late night *tabac* to satiate Stéphane's hankering for tobacco, rolled or otherwise; it had to be found. Thankfully, one Sunday afternoon, after a fruitless, exhausting search for cigarettes through the silent streets of Toulouse, he declared the end of his smoking career. And from that day he never smoked, nor was he ever tempted to veer from this courageous, determined decision.

My father also fell in love with Toulouse. He now had a great excuse to travel, to drive the length of France to visit us, providing a gastronomic opportunity to savour the culinary delights on offer from the plethora of *Toulousain* restaurants surrounding our apartment. Place St Georges was a pretty square packed with chair-filled terraces, inviting parasols and a narrow, cosy restaurant serving the best cassoulet ever. This was Chez Emile, and we relished numerous speciality dishes at this delightful establishment whenever my parents were in town. We leisurely wandered the cobbled *centre ville* and just loved sitting on the terraces, sipping a golden, frothy *demi*, watching the world go by. I recall vividly Dad's self-satisfied grin as he sat on a terrace around the Place de Capitole, wallowing in the mid-morning heat of the sun, and I knew he would love to swap places with me and live here. Having never travelled as a young boy or been allowed even to leave home and go to university, he had studied at evening classes while working through the day and coping with three babies at night, struggling financially and physically for many years. I suddenly felt a profound pang of sympathy for him, watching his ridiculously gummy smile, realising he had never been given such an opportunity, and I loved him intensely at that moment, deeply grateful that he was allowing me to live my dreams, not tempted to selfishly deprive me of the opportunity of following my own fantasies, hopes and ambitions.

Dad relished his food, had a healthy appetite and grew increasingly knowledgeable about many French dishes. One day Stéphane thought he would surprise him by introducing him to a speciality he was sure he had never tasted before. We stepped through the doors of a shabby, plain restaurant, leaving Toulouse behind to enter the Germanic, heavy-timbered, doll's-house atmosphere of the Alsace. This is the heartland of the *choucroute*, a hearty, filling meat dish, centred around that rather unromantic vegetable, the cabbage, requiring an immense appetite, stamina and a love of meat. This cabbage is certainly special, not at all like the soggy, boiled-to-death varieties I suffered at school. This cabbage undergoes a very precise process to achieve the final flavours, which are unusual and not at all cabbage-like. This is what I so admire about the French and their attitudes to food; they have an imaginative ability to transform the least inspiring ingredients and achieve incredible results. *La choucroute* is a superb example of this ingenuity. First the cabbage is shredded into fine strips and placed in a large container with sea salt added to drive the liquid out. It is then pressed firmly down and the container hermetically sealed to avoid any contact with the air. Nothing else is added and nothing else is done, and amazingly a perfectly natural lactic fermentation happens, giving off a pungent smell. The fermentation lasts from two to eight weeks, depending on the outside temperature. The cabbage is washed and is then ready to be eaten.

Here we were in this cluttered, folksy restaurant, await-ing the arrival of our very first *choucroute*. Apart from Stéphane, we were all unsure about the exact nature of our order, and so our faces, particularly Mum's and even round-bellied Dad's, paled significantly as huge salted hocks of pork kept finding their way from the kitchen to our table – platefuls of bone, covered thickly in pink, salted pork, squeezed on to every inch of the table, with sausages, fat and thin, thick slivers of aromatic bacon and a mountain of pale, shredded, spicy cabbage. It was all mouth-wateringly delicious but it was far too much – an overwhelming feast reducing us all to a giggling huddle. Our childish laughter degenerated into loud belly laughs as Dad stood up to leave and the absurd rustic triangular chair remained steadfastly wedged on to his spongy buttocks. This was a hilarious yet fitting end to our visit to the land of *la choucroute*.

Living as students in Toulouse often left us short of cash, particularly as most of our assets were invested in our lush, extravagant *appartement*, but there was absolutely no way we would give up this rooftop paradise – it was an essential component of our lively, entertaining parties, and of our desire to shop, cook and feast with fellow students and friends. I decided to take on a part-time job, conveniently finding the ideal post with the cosy, very English Laura Ashley shop ideally located two minutes away from our *appartement*. Perfect. I was transformed into an 'English rose', clothed in romantic floral gowns with puffed sleeves and floating skirts, the sort of dresses I adored to spin round in when I was seven. Playing a starring role as the heroine from a Charlotte Brontë novel, I managed to sell with ease to the bourgeois *Toulousain* ladies all the prerequisites for achieving a longed-for English charm and style: the oh-so-English fabrics, designs and clothes and the fragrant flowery perfumes. With my quaint accent, I embodied Laura Ashley Englishness and brought this quiet little corner of England alive. I was a wow. Customers were coming in just to gaze, chat and discover for themselves what all the fuss was about. Sales rose and I was rewarded with a precious booklet of *tickets restaurant*. These are similar to luncheon vouchers, and I could use them at lunchtime or in the evening at any restaurant in Toulouse participating in the scheme. I was euphoric; this was the most sublime gift.

Consequently, Stéphane and I dined out like kings, pampering ourselves in the warm night air, relishing the intimate walk to the restaurant and the anticipation of returning home satisfied and content. Naturally we soon discovered a favourite restaurant, hidden away in the grubby backstreets. It had an ornate iron gate that opened on to a tiny square courtyard with draping ivy and fiery red geraniums bursting out of window boxes, decorating all four walls. This was the memorable Louis XIII. They operated with an extremely simple, unembellished home-cooked menu of dishes, verging almost on plain. However, it was exceptional value, faultlessly executed and we never had any reason to complain; in fact we returned regularly, becoming familiar friendly faces. François would greet us with a welcoming intimacy – *'On fait des bises'* – and a cosy *camaraderie*. We felt special, unique, as he cleared away our favourite corner, bringing our wine and carafe of water, no instructions required. Stéphane revelled in making François recite the dessert menu in his singsong, melodic *Toulousain* accent, his fast chanting a poetic delight. *'Mousse au chocolat, crème caramel, gâteau Basque, gâteau Basque aux pruneaux . . .'*

GÂTEAU BASQUE

I love to make this simple cake as a fond reminder of our Louis XIII days. You can adapt the filling by adding prunes or soft moist fruits such as plums.

The filling is *crème pâtissière* which is a very simple custard of flavoured milk, flour and egg yolk.

Put 300ml of full fat milk in a saucepan, add 1 split vanilla pod and bring to just below boiling point over a low heat. As soon as small bubbles appear, turn off the heat and leave the milk to infuse for at least 15 minutes.

Sift 1 level tablespoon of flour and 1 heaped teaspoon of cornflour into a bowl, then tip in 3 tablespoons of caster sugar. Use a whisk to combine the flour and sugar until well blended. Add 2 large egg yolks and continue whisking vigorously until the mixture becomes paler and starts to thicken.

Remove the vanilla pod from the milk and gradually pour it into the flour and egg mixture, whisking as you go until the mixture is smooth. Strain the mixture through a sieve into the saucepan.

Bring the custard to the boil over a low heat. Once it bubbles, keep it boiling gently for about 5 minutes to let the flour cook through completely.

Take off the heat, whisk in 10g of chilled butter and 1 tablespoon of rum (optional) and leave to cool.

Preheat the oven to 190°C/375°F/Gas Mark 5.

For the pastry, break and beat 3 eggs. Mix in 300g of caster sugar. Add 300g of plain flour and 2 teaspoons of baking powder as well as 200g of melted butter. Mix in the juice of an orange and its zest.

Butter and flour a tart dish big enough for 8 servings. Cover the dish with about two-thirds of the pastry.

Spread a layer of *crème pâtissière* over the pastry (and the fruit if you have chosen to add it) and then cover with the rest of the pastry. Bake in the oven for 45 minutes. Sprinkle with icing sugar.

Our new-found wealth not only enabled us to satisfy our gastronomic appetites but also led us to purchase our very first car, opening up the city boundaries, making us free to roam the *Toulousain* countryside. I loved this car; reliable, solid and bouncy, it could only be a Deux Chevaux, the 2CV, a work of French creative genius, an inspired design whose fan-spinning growl, a noise that is uniquely French, takes me instantly back to Paris as an au pair and to the Toulouse Ecole de Commerce. Our car was an original design with the front seats in the form of a bench, great for cuddling up close to one another as we ricocheted along with the sunroof folded back, hair flicking annoyingly over eyes and nose, looking out for a weekend *chambre d'hôte*.

On one occasion we stopped before a cluster of buildings on the way towards Limoux, having spotted a fading triangular sign that Stéphane assured me indicated *chambre d'hôte*. It was getting late, and however much I adored our new toy I was not particularly enamoured at the thought of spending a chilly, cramped night in this vehicle.

We had once again fallen on our feet, tumbling into the home of M. et Mme Monnier, the owners of this rambling farmhouse, which had been tastefully renovated and adapted into a magnificent weekend escape. A small yet refreshing swimming pool greeted us, reviving our senses preparatory to joining the other guests for dinner. We all dined together around a long, unstable trestle table. We had a variety of compelling dinner partners: a Dutch couple with their two children, a German businessman and a French family of four who apparently spent a week here every June. I remember this meal vividly because it was so delicious, lovingly prepared and presented by this couple, who clearly rejoiced in bringing their guests together, watching and listening, entranced by the simplicity of it all. The company was so animated and engrossing that we sat up until the early hours, sipping tisane, others cognac, until we finally drifted off to bed.

Our meal began with a perfect thirst-quenching summer soup, *soupe au pistou*, a magnificent combination of summer vegetables, *pistou* being the name for the blend of crushed garlic, olive oil, basil and grated cheese which gives this soup its distinctive summer flavour. This was followed by a sublime *sauté d'épaule d'agneau aux aubergines*, a well-chosen dish for a large gathering of hungry guests because it had been made in advance and simmered enticingly during our tour of the premises, benefiting incontestably from this lengthy amalgamation of flavours. To finish, a superb *clafoutis*, made with my favourite fruit, the cherry.

This menu sits alongside a growing collection of memorable meals, some there just because of the occasion and the characters invited, others, like this one, because of the complete picture – a balanced, exquisite menu enjoyed by a fascinating, eclectic mix of people.

SOUPE AU PISTOU

For 6–8 people, soak 250g of red and 250g of white haricot beans overnight.

Peel an onion, cut into four and insert a clove into one piece. Fill a large pot with 2.5 litres of water and place on a warm heat. Add the red and white haricot beans, the pieces of onion and 250g of sliced runner beans.

You should also add a bouquet garni which you can buy or make by tying together 4 branches of fresh parsley, 2–3 sprigs of fresh thyme and 1 bay leaf.

Cook gently for 25 minutes. While this is simmering, peel

3 carrots, a small slice of pumpkin, 250g of *haricot vert* beans, 2 potatoes, 1 big turnip, 3 tomatoes and 2 leeks. Wash 3 courgettes, do not peel but remove the ends and cut into 2cm slices. When the haricot beans are cooked, cut the carrots, turnip and 1 stick of celery into cubes and add them to the haricots; 10 minutes later add the *haricots verts* cut in half, the potatoes cut in four, the sliced courgettes, the tomatoes (chopped), and salt and pepper. Leave this to simmer gently and then add 150g macaroni and cook for 15 more minutes. While this is cooking prepare the *pistou*. Crush 6 cloves of garlic with a little salt. Add at least 20 large basil leaves and crush firmly to achieve a smooth paste. Add 150g grated cheese (parmesan or dried Dutch cheese or a combination of the two) and mix well with a fork, gradually pouring 1 tablespoon of olive oil into the mixture.

Remove the bouquet garni and the onions from the pot. Pour in the *pistou* and whisk it into the soup, stirring well.

SAUTÉ D'ÉPAULE D'AGNEAU AUX AUBERGINES

For 4–6 people, peel and cut 5 aubergines into cubes. Poach 10 tomatoes in boiling water, rinse under cold water and then peel, remove the pips and cut roughly. Heat some oil in a casserole dish and sauté 800g–1kg of trimmed and boned shoulder of lamb, cut into 5cm pieces, for about 15 minutes. Take the meat out and place on a plate. In the same oil sauté 1 chopped onion and 3 shallots for about 10 minutes. Add the aubergines and 5 chopped garlic cloves, leaving them to cook for a further 10 minutes. Remove everything from the casserole dish and put to one side with the lamb. Pour away $3/4$ of the oil and add about $1/2$ glass of white wine and a little sugar and rub the bottom of the pan well to deglaze (remove the tasty bits from the bottom of the pan). Let this simmer for a minute before adding the chopped tomatoes, lamb, onion, garlic, a bay leaf, some chopped thyme and parsley, salt and pepper. Cover the casserole dish and let it simmer for 20 minutes on a gentle heat and then 10 more minutes on the lowest heat.

CLAFOUTIS

Preheat the oven to 200°C/400°F/Gas Mark 6

For 6 people, lightly beat 4 eggs. Add a small pinch of salt and 55g of caster sugar. Mix in well. Sift 1 heaped tablespoon of self-raising flour over the egg mixture and whisk in well, then trickle in 3 tablespoons of melted butter. Work in until smooth. Gradually pour in 225ml of milk, stirring well. Flavour with 1 tablespoon of rum or kirsch. Butter an earthenware tart or gratin dish (about 24cm diameter). Arrange 550g of ripe black cherries (remove stalks and stones) in the dish. Cover with the custard mixture and bake for 40–45 minutes until set and golden. Leave to cool before dusting with icing sugar and serve.

Deliriously happy and utterly besotted with each other, Stéphane and I announced to our incredulous families that we were getting married. Stubbornly defiant in the face of any objection or hurtful doubt concerning the suitability of our union, we created perhaps the biggest upset of all by taking control of proceedings and organising the wedding ourselves in Toulouse. We were unbelievably young, naive and impetuous, and wanted immediate action. With Stéphane not yet released from the *école*, but with my own degree freshly and gratefully received, we undauntedly set about organising our day.

We had to fill an entire day with ceremony, celebration and festivities, drawing in family from all directions – from Paris, Limoges, Tulle and Aix-en-Provence to Corsica and England. We would need to accommodate and feed them all. The proceedings were consequently organised to extend throughout an entire day to make sure everyone was happily entertained. This was how the dual ceremonies of town hall and church primarily developed – a civil service in the morning followed by a religious ceremony in the afternoon – the perfect plan for prolonging our day. Neither of us were brought up as devout church-goers or educated under one faith although Stéphane had almost succeeded in cele-brating his first communion. Attending Catholic Sunday school, *le catéchisme*, he reported back to his parents one day that the following Sunday was to be his big day and he would be celebrating his first holy communion. His parents were not particularly au fait with Church procedure and so simply followed their son's instructions, happy to believe that the time had come for his inauguration into the Church. They prepared the champagne and planned a simple party to mark the event. The day came and everyone went along to church. Front-row positions were keenly fought over and they sat expectantly waiting for Stéphane to step up with the other children, somewhat bewildered by the fact their son was not dressed like the others in an angelic white gown. I don't really know what happened that day, but I think Stéphane must have misunderstood the priest because he was not ready, it was not his turn and there would be no communion. Perplexed and even more confused about Church procedure, his parents decided to celebrate anyway by taking everyone for a slap-up meal in an expensive restaurant. Unfortunately there was to be no happy ending to this unfortunate day because it was the 1st of May and all the restaurants were closed, so, forced to abandon any hope of celebration, they reluctantly settled for a slice of ham and *purée Mousline*.

This is how Stéphane has remained – a logical, ordered, no-nonsense thinker who struggles with the spiritual, unscientific dimensions of the Church. The reflective atmosphere of an ancient building did, however, appeal to both of us. The moral contemplation involved in a religious service would reinforce the depth of our feelings, the seriousness of our commitment, without our having to be faithful followers of religion. We both felt that a church service was a vital component of our day in order to fortify the vows we would be making to each other. We now had to find a priest who would carry out this service for a non-Catholic couple who were not from Toulouse and who wanted to use his church only for its ambience and location.

After a lot of research Stéphane found a name and a telephone number. The priest's instant answer was no, out of the question, completely contrary to Church rules. Couples marrying in his church must have family in the area. Stéphane began to use all his powers of persuasion, pleading the fact that we both currently lived in Toulouse and even had distant family connections who lived here, which was true. Stéphane had a second cousin who lived in Blagnac and helped us out with laundry, ironing and repairs to the 2CV on numerous occasions. After long sessions of polite supplication, requesting that he make an exception and bend Church rules, the priest agreed to meet us.

We drove to the grey, rambling village of Le Castera,

winding around the back of the church to find his house. We had to clamber over messy mountains of torn and faded books, scraps of paper and important-looking documents written in Latin to reach the spacious kitchen, which was equally overflowing with clutter. Dirty pots, with days-old dried food stains, piles of papers and leather-bound books covered every available surface. He offered us tea and I shuddered as he rummaged through the disarray – never before had I experienced such a stupendous level of untidiness. This was supreme mess, a colossal muddle, yet he managed to pull out three cups, stained and chipped, and proceeded to make tea. He was a man in turmoil, struggling to find his way through the clutter of his life. His surreal story explained a lot about the state we found him in at home that day. Our Catholic priest was in fact a Jew! During the war a Catholic family had saved his parents from the Germans and, in relief and overwhelming gratitude, they promised to give their son to the Catholic faith. And so this was how our disturbed and confused Jew became a reluctant, anguished Catholic priest.

He finally agreed to carry out our wedding service, explaining the procedure that would guide us towards the spiritual awareness necessary to cope with the events of our big day. This would involve a certain amount of preparatory work, and so we would need to meet again. He volunteered to call in on us in Toulouse, around teatime, almost every other week, insisting that we required a little extra religious care and attention.

And so our holy visits began. He would sit formally on the edge of his seat, starting the meeting with discussions about life as a couple and the obligations and promises we were about to make to each other, often leaving behind interesting reading material for us to peruse once he had gone home. As he relaxed, he moved deeper into the comfort of his chair and started to drift away from the issues at hand, gradually releasing his anguish, his bitter resentment of his parishioners, who, he lamented, would selfishly lead their narrow lives, often in sin, and then come to church on Sunday to pray and confess, ready to recommence their lives of hypocritical faithlessness. He would groan and growl, exposing his tormented soul and frustrated anger to our fascinated ears. One evening, as the harrowing lament was beginning to lose its appeal, our stomachs also started to growl. Stéphane suddenly remembered that he had baked a *gâteau au yaourt*, a Sunday treat we shared whenever I became homesick and needed a reminder of something typically English, like tea and cake.

A slice of cake and hot milky tea miraculously did the trick, abruptly ending the priest's tortuous chain of thought, calming the man just long enough for him to savour the rich, sweet temptation of a moist, spongy *gâteau*.

GÂTEAU AU YAOURT

I later discovered that this simple, ingenious cake is excellent for calming overzealous children, not just priests. The fun lies in using the yogurt cartons to measure the ingredients, making this the ideal baking recipe to share with children.

Preheat the oven to 180°C/350°F/Gas Mark 4. In a large bowl mix the contents of one plain yogurt carton with two yogurt cartons of caster sugar, three of plain flour, a teaspoon of baking powder, 3 eggs, half a yogurt carton of milk, half of vegetable oil, half of lemon juice, and some finely chopped lemon zest. Stir the mixture well until a smooth consistency is achieved.

Butter a cake tin (20–24cm) carefully and pour in the well-mixed cake mixture. Bake in the oven for 50 minutes until a knife comes cleanly away when piercing the centre of the cake.

Allow to cool before removing from the tin. Serve cold, on its own or with jam.

It was during these nerve-racking days that I started to fully grasp the extent and importance of Stéphane's family. This was something new. I was totally inexperienced in the handling of extended family matters and just could not understand why they were making such a fuss. Just leave us to organise our party, I thought. Let's have friends, relatives we love and talk to often, all those we cherish and really want to gather around us for this precious, personal day.

The full weight of *la famille* bore down heavily on the delicate, all-too-familiar problem of the invitation list. Trust in our ability to get this crucially vital component right was sorely lacking, and so my wedding day featured quite a few unfamiliar faces. Yet I was immune to this impersonal gathering of strangers, affectionately sheltered as I was by just five of my intimate family. This was all I needed, all I saw during the fast-moving, eventful day. I wanted to slow it down, rewind and play parts of it over again – not because it did not go to plan, but simply to relive my happiness, to experience repeatedly how it felt to be fulfilled, to smile until it hurt.

There was nothing flamboyant about our wedding – we were able to control the mood fully, and for this I am grateful. We allowed some details to be amended once Stéphane's parents arrived in Toulouse. I was tired, uncertain as to what was expected of us and simply too emotional to care. So Stéphane ended up wearing a black dicky bow instead of the tie I had lovingly chosen, ironically looking more like a smart restaurant waiter than a groom on his wedding day. But at least we complemented each other, with neither of us out-dressing the other. I was certainly not swathed in expensive luxurious fabrics, economising by recycling my bridesmaid's dress worn just a year before at my sister's wedding. With the addition of a delicate *voile* veil and ivory heels to bring me up to a comfortable height in anticipation of the Wedding Kiss, I felt sophisticated, serenely beautiful and ready to be married.

Events were timed to perfection as we moved from the majestic, opulent Place de Capitole town hall register-signing to the sharply contrasting Le Ratelier, an isolated, rural *gîte*-cum-restaurant, solid and rustic, where we drank and ate our way through a three-course lunch, loosening ties, settling nerves, ready for church. This religious monument was sadly shabby and neglected, perched on top of a lonely hill with splendid wedding-photo views over the *Toulousain* countryside. But the tapering, uneven steps sweeping up in front of the doors gratifyingly enabled us to capture the entire wedding party, squeezed closely together on successive steps, a permanent record of who had attended, what they wore and how young everyone looked all those years ago. There was Stéphane's grandmother, proudly, dogmatically refusing to smile or show her true emotions, standing solidly at the bottom of this uncoordinated frame, holding a magnificent bouquet still protectively enveloped in its cellophane wrapping.

We haphazardly snailed our way back again, beeping car

following beeping car to Le Ratelier, with just enough time for a swift game of *boules* before aperitifs and dinner. I hitched up my ivory party dress, not wanting to miss out on the boys' fun.

We broke all the rules of French celebratory menu planning, dismissing the *foie gras*, casting aside the noble meats and sophisticated *légumes*, deciding to treat our guests to a regional feast, an enduring flavour of Toulouse and our wedding. This could only be achieved with a cassoulet, our *pièce de résistance*, a delicious, rich, garlicky combination of preserved duck, Toulouse sausage and haricot beans topped with a crusty lid of toasted breadcrumbs. Followed as it was by lively rock and roll and an inspired, rhythmic Mediterranean tango from Stéphane's father and my mum, the cassoulet, as well as the party, was an unprecedented, if controversial, success.

I learnt that the French use preserved quality dishes very discerningly, always keeping a jar or two in the cupboard in case of unexpected guests dropping in for dinner.

Try these liberating, controversial ideas for a stress-free convivial dinner:

Treat yourself to the ultimate 'ready meal' by buying a jar of cassoulet from a reputable supplier. Empty the contents into an ovenproof dish, and sprinkle with breadcrumbs (2–3 slices of bread should be enough) and warm through in a hot oven until bubbling and golden. As cassoulet is very rich, serve on its own, followed by a refreshing green salad.

Buy a jar of *confit de canard* or *d'oie*. Remove the duck or goose legs and place in a heavyweight pan to warm through on the top of the stove. Cover with some, not all, of the goose fat from the jar and monitor carefully while on the heat to make sure the meat does not become dry. The fat will help to keep it moist, so don't be tempted to remove it. Use the remainder of the fat to sauté cubed potatoes, or smother some potatoes in the goose fat with your hands and then roast in the oven. Serve the *confit* with the potatoes and a helping of crunchy *haricots verts* tossed in a little chopped garlic.

For a special occasion – Christmas, birthdays, anniversaries or weddings – buy a tin of luxuriously rich *foie gras de canard* or *d'oie*. Keep the tin or jar in the fridge for at least an hour before serving. Remove and place on a serving plate. Warm a knife by dipping it in a jar of boiled water and slice the *foie gras*. Serve with warm toasted wholemeal bread accompanied by a sweet wine such as Sauternes, or a not-so-sweet option such as Gewürztraminer or a Tokay Pinot Gris.

Breaking the rules, letting go, escaping routine, convention and order allowed me to start cooking. I began to enjoy the wonders of food itself, savouring harmonious flavours, confident in my personal development.

Discarding my despotic cookery books and banishing the lists they breed was the most liberating feeling ever. No one can cook well while tightly controlled, whether by books, lists or judgemental friends and family. Menu planning, shopping and cooking flow more naturally and instinctively when you allow yourself the privilege of dipping your fingers into a sauce and licking the bowls clean, when inspiration emanates from the bountiful, food-rich market, from like-minded friends and from the occasion itself.

THREE

Stews, Soup and Pasta

I SOMETIMES FEEL rather sad when I think back to those free-spirited, carefree Toulouse days and wonder why I could not hold on to my individuality, creativity and confidence. The power of the family now overwhelmed me. I was a Luiggi. I had the name and total integration ensued; instantly I was invited to all family do's and expected to behave according to family norms. Refusing a dinner invitation, for example, was not a good idea, as this could prompt the gossiping lines of communication into action, stimulating any amount of inaccurate scandalous comment.

I had the name, but I felt my difference immediately. I was certainly not a Luiggi, with their swarthy Mediterranean complexions, stocky, well-built frames and concealed round tummies. Here was an intruder, indefinably strange, and so I suppose they had every right to be suspicious. No doubt my alienness prompted their caution: light golden hair, a pale, fragile skin, a frail frame. Ethereal and waif-like, perhaps I was just too delicate to touch, and like a young branch I would easily snap if carelessly handled. No one was certain what I was going to bring to the family, how I would fit in.

The role of food and mealtimes took on new meaning during the early years of my marriage and those long hot Corsican summers. Dinners were essential tools for getting to know everyone, a drawing together of individuals around a table to share delicious food while listening, watching, gradually acquainting myself with the characters that made up my new family. There were dozens of them – aunties, uncles, cousins, second cousins, their children and children's children, with a confusingly high number of Antoines or derivations of this name. So many characters, backgrounds and histories to absorb – it was clearly going to take some time to acclimatise myself to their ways and their foibles, to unravel the Luiggi network and figure out swiftly who was who. It was fun, particularly when the characters and their stories started to fit into place. I almost looked forward to the next reunion when I would hear the following episode. These were exciting times, sorting out the clues to the family jigsaw handed out unwittingly in Toulouse, the photos, the brief meeting with his parents, helping me establish a few of my own ideas about this new world. I was, however, surprised by how much I revelled in the reality of these characters and their lives. Maman was particularly keen for me to meet everyone, also revelling in the family gatherings and the organisation of dinners, perhaps a tad too enthusiastic in her desire to be surrounded by guests. It almost felt as though she were frightened to be alone, with her own thoughts, with her own life. Stéphane's father, however, did not appear to suffer from this dedicated focus on family, their comings and goings, intrigues and gossiping circles. He frequently escaped out to sea, closely followed by his old schoolmate, the two of them leaving in the early hours of the morning with a box of Corsican treats – charcuterie, melon and figs, some wine – ready to disappear into the calming expanse of the gentle sea. I identified with his need to abandon civilisation and bond more closely one to one with a special friend, with the power and intensity of nature, the very soul of this island, the sea itself – something that Stéphane's dad understood better than anyone else I knew.

I did appreciate the reasons for this generous sharing of meals with my new family members, having experienced the power of food to bring people together and encourage communication. My language skills were probably not as well developed as I would have liked, making this discovery process more frustrating and fatiguing, and so food helped enormously to divert attention away from my inarticulate silences. We could communicate with food, sharing pleasure, relaxing with soothing wine, giving me space to listen without any pressure to perform.

Soon I began to feel uneasy at some of these gatherings, something I did not particularly like. I wondered whether these people were acting out a role to please, to gain respect, out of duty, not necessarily accepting the invitation for pleasure, for themselves? It was clear that some of our family members, who had been hastily, perhaps unfairly, summoned for an early evening commitment, did not really want to be there. They would sneak sly glances at their watches, shuffle uncomfortably in their seats, waiting for a silence, a break in the noisy chatter, in order to drop a few hints about work the next day: 'I've got a busy day tomorrow, you know. I think it might be wise if I headed off now.'

These forced explanations, the apologetic stuttering and mumbling, enraged me during these early days. I was naively, boldly, of the opinion that life was too short to be sitting around a table with people you really did not particularly want to be sharing the experience with, and the specific concepts of duty, respect and honour had not featured in my upbringing, making me incapable of relating to this behaviour.

I was not yet completely sure why I felt such growing apprehension about family dining. I seemed unable to put my finger on the cause of my misgivings. However, my first inkling of the source of these concerns came from Stéphane's parents. They clearly loved their food and looked forward to lunch, dinner and unexpected guests – any excuse to cook, eat and drink. Their days seemed to be planned around meals. Having not yet finished their breakfast coffee, barely swallowed the last mouthful of heavily coated *tartine*, they would begin to plan in detail the next meal.

At *midi* precisely the table would be laid, the aperitif tray prepared with a clanging of bottles, a clatter of ice cubes brusquely thrown into the awaiting bucket, the flame lit under the *cocotte*, ready to serve, no delay. Even if we had enjoyed a *grasse matinée*, leisurely slurping our coffee and flicking through the papers, easing ourselves into the day, lunch would still be served at midday precisely.

I felt that there was a game being played. Mealtimes were being shrewdly used to control us and bring us into line, selfishly keeping us within parental view, particularly during the early years of our marriage. I believed that this peculiar, indeed somewhat unhealthy, relationship with food derived from a powerful desire to ply, gorge and satiate guests, an insecure longing to feed to secure attachment and admiration. This obsession with mealtimes unnerved me in the early days. Even now I cannot believe I was incapable of simply saying, 'Sorry, we won't be having lunch with you today, we've decided to spend the day in Paris.' If I did try to demur, the feeling of guilt and remorse was unimaginable, almost beyond belief, the curt reply invariably shattering the remotest hope of escape: 'Well, we've bought this wonderful *gigot* especially. It'll be ruined if we don't eat it today.'

This manipulative technique was applied prolifically during the long hot summer months we spent together in Corsica. At first I didn't notice, or even care that much, as I explored and fell head over heels in love with this enchanting island. At last I was going to read for myself this bewitching fairy tale, bring the map to life, see the mountains, smell the air, swim in the sea.

I remember my first sighting of Calvi's citadel, rising above the sea, as I admired the bobbing yachts and fishing barques lined up in the harbour below. The sparkling sea was churned into a frothing white mousse as our ferry crawled heavily towards its target. The backdrop of undulating, craggy mountains, the distant huddles of homes and churches clasping the mountainsides precariously, filled me with breathless awe, an indescribable urge to conquer, to unearth the wonders of this unspoilt island. Corsica has a happy thumbs-up shape that always makes me smile whenever I see this confident outline, perfectly suited to these proud, insular islanders. You can clearly see a hand with the fingers clasped tightly, the thumb raised, confirming that everything is OK. It's one of those islands that on paper appears small and easy to get around, wickedly deceiving visitors, misleading them into making careless plans, cruelly unaware of the steep, winding, dangerously neglected roads, their adventurous car journeys so easily capable of being transformed into disaster. Particularly deceptive and unforgiving is the time it takes to get from one place to the next, which is why many villagers never move farther than the neighbouring town, where they buy what they need and then happily return home. This is also why, in Corsica, once a Northerner you are always a Northerner, with no reason to visit the South. There is no significant movement between either end of the island, nor a great deal of love lost between North and South. A healthy rivalry exists in the competition for the essential tourist trade, the hazardous mountainous terrain in the centre of the island drawing a useful defensive line, keeping either end confined within its own well-defined zone. Travel is not easy, and has certainly not moved even into the twentieth century. The coastline train, the Micheline, which trundles noisily between the seaside villages and the major shopping towns, is not the most comfortable or the most speedy way of getting around the island, often slowing to a halt every now and then to let ponderous, lazy cows wander over the track. In summer, with the windows and doors wide open in an attempt to let in some welcome cooling air, the comfort is reduced considerably, often completely disappearing when the train is transformed into a human cargo wagon with perspiring bodies pressed against each other like sardines, anxiously awaiting the jolt that signals that the train has finally come to a grinding halt.

We disembarked from the ferry along with the hordes of summer visitors and tourists, searching for sun, lazy days at the beach, leisurely drinks under a shady parasol, and time to let their thoughts drift, perhaps to imagine the lives of the boat-owners displaying their wealth in the port of Calvi. They are a distinctive tribe, these visitors, parading the latest designer sunglasses, camera at the ready, smelling strongly of sun-cream. They are here to have fun, laze on the sand, snorkel, cool off in the sea and eat ice creams and lobster until it's time to board the ferry and forget. A holiday, just like any other.

We were not a part of this superficial touristy world. We were Corsican. Family. We had an island name. We belonged and, yes, this was my holiday, but I knew there was a duty to perform. I needed to be formally introduced and welcomed, incorporated into island life, spirit and soul. There was work to do. Strangely, I longed to blend into the heaving crowds of tourists pouring excitedly off the ferry and disappear, lose myself in the easy-going holiday atmosphere. Ironically I would always remain part of this tourist tribe, even when the Corsican sun had bronzed my skin to a healthy, sun-kissed glow. It seemed impossible for me to shake off my differences, my intrusive foreign traits, my golden hair and Northern features making me conspicuous, distinct, even before I opened my mouth to speak.

As I stepped off the boat, the sun's balsamic warmth massaged my face, arms and shoulders, gently welcoming me. A small man with a grin on his face, an extinguished Gitane hanging from the corner of his mouth, was waiting for us, clearly family. Gossip had spread fast: they're arriving at Calvi, Corsica Ferries, 15.45. He whistled sharply, shouting out Stéphane's name, waving frantically above the pushing and shoving, jumping up and down in front of his badly parked car, interrupting the steady flow of traffic, the laborious caravans and Italian camper vans pouring out bumper to bumper from the open mouth of our ferry. The dock officials did not appear concerned by this obstruction, waving the cars on, sweating and shrieking, urging these foreign vehicles to get out as quickly as they could, away from their port and their home. No one paid any attention to this embarrassing hindrance, oblivious to the chaos it was creating; island rules and regulations were applied or suspended on a whim, based on a mood, family arguments or favours remembered. This time the turning of a blind eye was because *Tonton*, Stéphane's uncle, a local taxi driver, was known to everyone in this small seafront town, particularly all the port officials. He kissed and embraced us both, still in no rush to move his offending taxi, laboriously heaving our bags into the boot. At last we could get away from this hot madness. Relief swept over me as we pulled out of the port and skirted the winding maze of Calvi to reach the main coastline road that would take us towards the family village and home. After a brief stop at *la pompe* to fill up with petrol and let *les cousins* who ran the station know we had arrived, with *les bises* and the casual abandoning of customers while important family greetings were exchanged, we were on our way.

This coastline drive to the family's village illustrated immediately why this island is known as L'île de Beauté. It is profoundly beautiful, a wild, savage terrain bursting with spectacular contrasts, scents and rustic charm. It has a rare unspoilt coastline, bravely defended by high-spirited and

51

determined Corsicans, warding off the high-rise developers in the sixties and to this day continuing to apply unorthodox techniques, such as the bombing and burning of undesirable or unlawful building schemes, to make absolutely certain their unique jewel continues to shine.

A savoury herbal aroma pervades the entire island, intensified by the piercing sun, wrapping itself around your nostrils. This is the unique Corsican *maquis*, used to flavour its cuisine and wine, epitomising the very heart and soul of Corsicans and their island, a haunting scent of lavender, rosemary, thyme and basil that is one of the distinctive aromatic memories of Corsica, invariably luring you back. The intensity of this scent always takes me by surprise on arrival – revitalising, mouth-wateringly appetising.

The road winds continuously and *Tonton* handles the precipitous blind bends with obvious confidence and skill, the pattern of these curves imprinted indelibly in his mind. Occasionally he is forced by the odd meandering tourist to apply his brakes sharply, cursing and swearing as he accelerates to speed dangerously past the offending vehicle. I want to close my eyes, petrified by his risk-taking, but prise them open to take in the sparkling clear blue, the sharp well-defined line of the horizon, the breathtaking beauty which I know has only partially been revealed to me. Beyond these winding roads, hidden above our heads, is another world waiting to be discovered. The island is clever. It does not give away too much at first, indeed manages to save the best for the discerning few. Many visitors only ever see a minuscule, superficial part of Corsica, and some will never get to understand the depth of its beauty, its profound inner secrets, which I now believe can only be experienced if you are *famille*. It's as if this is how the island protects itself

naturally, astutely, keeping out the bad influences, the external forces that strive for commercial wealth, the destruction
of the very landscape that holds the key to their fortune.

Eventually we reach Stéphane's father's family home,
shaky but in one piece. We are in the north of the island, in
an area called La Balagne, his parents' house situated in a
small seaside village on the railway line between the larger
towns of Ile Rousse and Calvi. It's a quaint, quiet village,
with a distinctive, run-down Micheline station just outside
the entrance to the village, its name barely legible, eroded
by the salty air. And yet there seems to be no pressure to
repaint it to help build tourism in this sleepy town. No one
seems particularly to care about such irrelevant details. A
former château, with ramparts reaching down to the sea, a
magnificent historic lookout, its towers keeping a close
protective eye on unwanted visitors, has now been
converted tastefully into profitable holiday apartments,
hinting that there may be an appetite for the development
of tourism, a clandestine desire to welcome visitors on the
part of certain wealthy, ambitious residents of the village.
Tourism is the main source of income for most of them.
They rely heavily on this brief surge of activity during the
sweltering, uncomfortable summer months, half-heartedly
embracing this aberrant activity, knowing they need the
money but exhausted by the effort of bringing pleasure to
strangers, upset by the invasion of their territory and their
peace. Corsicans have a reputation for being lazy, leaving
what can be done today until tomorrow (a typical
Mediterranean island trait), preferring to siesta, drink
pastis and play cards in the shade of a plane tree. Drive and
ambition exist only among a small minority, and these
eccentric, deviant villagers are regarded with disdain by the

53

majority; they are misunderstood, believed to be working towards the destruction of the island and its inhabitants. The wealthier they get, however, the more changes they bring, and the more control they come to exert in the village and generally in the island's small-town politics. There is a constant battle for land, the wealthy few striving to buy up potential building plots from any weak link within a family unit, from those either reduced to pitiful desperation or broken by irresistible temptation who will agree to hand over their treasured family assets. Any instance creates enough gossip to keep the village alive for a good few months.

The dry, brittle days of summer open up cracks and wounds, exposing the island's weaknesses, everyone waiting anxiously for the next change of wind as the breeze swells, pulling the sea into galloping *moutons*, and for the inevitable consequence: fire, its intense orange splendour so quickly out of control, spreading like a disease, destroying, stripping the island of green, living moisture, painting the mountains with a dark grey brush, leaving a final flourish of choking dust as a gentle reminder of its power.

On my first visit to Corsica I was greeted by the horrors of fire, which is frequently used by overambitious entrepreneurs to turn beautiful green land into charcoaled wasteland, thereby allowing it to be considered for profitable building opportunities. Admittedly many fires are also unwittingly started by unwary tourists picnicking in the dehydrated mountains, blissfully unaware of the dangers the smallest spark can unleash. I do not know who was to blame that year, but the flames swept through the mountains with a frenzy never before witnessed by the island. We had heard there was fire at Lumio, the neighbouring village, far enough away to give us time to prepare. Already we could smell the suffocating smoke, creating a hazy, eerie light as it covered the sun. I was convinced this rampage would be halted long before it reached us. My head permanently raised to the sky, I watched as the Canadair planes lunged bravely into the sea, smoothly sweeping back up into the fog to release their life-saving load. Then for the first time I saw the flames, skipping along the mountain face towards our village. Stéphane was ready, waiting determinedly with a group of male family members, inappropriately armed with buckets and garden hoses, planning how to protect the house and redirect the fire's destructive path. Where were the fire engines? Where were the professionals, with breathing gear, powerful hoses? All had been called out to the remotest corners of the island, everyone having been affected, the island's resources stretched to their limits. I watched horrified and enraged as Stéphane disappeared into the smoke. Unexpectedly the flames suddenly engulfed a lone tree, shooting into the air, the fire gaining incredible strength from so little fuel. I remember screaming, shouting out Stéphane's name, pleading for him to come back down, believing him to have been caught by this sudden outbreak. I sobbed, choked by smoke and this wave of unruly emotion, smothered by an outrageous sense of injustice that Stéphane should be taken away from me by his island, this cruel, senseless island. But he and his relations had climbed to barren, scorched land higher up, and were watching the scene from above, unscathed, yet shaken by the closeness of the danger. The reality hit home hard when we later discovered that a fireman had perished in the flames at Lumio.

Fires recur most years when we return to the island in the

summer, but never again with such intensity and destructive force. Luckily the village has always managed to remain intact, its homes, hotels and monuments unscathed.

There is a timeless charm to the village which on the one hand is reassuring and welcoming, yet on the other I frequently find irritating and frustrating. These people are just too stuck in their ways to move on, too lazy to complete projects, to tidy up the station yard or repaint the village sign. Just one glimmer of life, energy or hope would be enough to allay my frustration.

The buildings and people remain the same, but the coastline provides welcome variety, fluctuating at the mercy of storms and the raging sea, the beach bizarrely metamorphosing each year as the sand is forced closer to the road edge, prompting comments such as: 'Have you seen the beach this year? There's a horrendous drop down to the sea.' The villagers don't like it, they want it to stay the same; this uncontrollable force unnerves them and disturbs their peaceful routine. But I love to run down to the beach each year to see the wondrous new configuration. Sea and fire are the two elements the villagers fear, exposing their vulnerability, their fear of diversification, of their lives moving away from them, out of control.

The heart of the village is Le Chariot, the most popular café/restaurant, its tables and chairs and brightly coloured Kronenbourg parasols scattered freely around the majestic plane trees of the main square. Proud, uninspired Ambroise, always sickly pale, yawns heavily in front of his bustling café, shuffling his cards, an espresso to hand, determined to win the next round before the crowds start to descend from their exhausting day at the beach. Throughout the summer season the friendly, smoky smell of burning embers and spitting braziers drifts enticingly through the village as Le Chariot's infamous pizzas are baked continually from midday until the small hours. They can be eaten off large round metal platters in the square with a carafe of Corsican rosé or a refreshing chestnut Pietra beer. Many visitors take away the enormous boxes of Chariot ready meals, glowing and sore from the day's irresponsible sunbathing, unaware of the oily drip of tomato and olives from the corners of these inadequate cardboard constructions.

The villagers stand out among the visitors, a pale, unhealthy bunch owing to lack of sun. Most work unsocial hours in the restaurants and cafés; some just keep out of the aggravating heat of the day. Corsicans always complain about the sun, striving to find cool, refreshing shade, staying indoors behind tightly fastened shutters, only re-emerging from the dark once the sun starts its lazy descent and early evening activities can reinject life into the soul of the village.

They have a well-defined rural look, characterised by the *bleu de Chine* jacket – the Chinese-style fishing jacket of light blue cotton which is the uniform of the true Corsican. In order to be fully initiated into the Corsican clan I would need to take a trip to the Ile Rousse market to buy my very own *bleu de Chine*. However, the jacket needs to be faded and worn-looking, the blue washed out to dispel any signs of newness. This is done by ceremoniously dipping the jacket in the salty sea water, wringing it out and leaving it to dry in the ferocious heat of the sun, bleaching away the dye.

Next door to Le Chariot is the school yard, whose dusty, uneven surface provides the early evening venue for *boules* playing, followed by a refreshing and well-deserved pastis with Ambroise. Down from the school, the main street meanders towards the beach. At the top of the lane the village's one and only souvenir shop displays an enticing collection of highly desirable beach necessities, from the eternally fashionable espadrilles to the crocodile inflatables, classic buckets and spades and beach ping-pong sets – all broken or worn by the end of a two-week stay. This shop belongs to *la famille*, one of the ambitious, wealthy minority bringing prosperity to Corsica with his chain of souvenir shops covering the length and breadth of the island. Continue following the gentle descent of the main street, through the exotic arches of the Hôtel de la Plage, a popular venue for English visitors, and you will reach the *petite plage*, ideal for young children owing to its protected cove, often covered in dry, crumbly seaweed but always offering shade thanks to the ancient, imposing hotel walls behind it. Towards the edge of the village, just before the sweeping open beach begins, sits Le Beau Rivage, a favoured hotel, bar and restaurant, again with connections to *la famille*, the owner being godfather to Stéphane's dad. Serving the best choice of ice-cream flavours in the village, a refreshing *diabolo grenadine*, and with the most magnificent terrace overlooking the entire beach, the sea lapping enticingly underneath, Le Beau Rivage always deserves our custom, irrespective of ownership.

Finally, at the end of the village, is the beach, a long, sweeping cove of grainy, easy-to-wipe-off sand, beautiful and tranquil in the early morning but transformed into a heaving, bustling mass of towels and parasols by late afternoon.

Behind the houses, hotels, cafés and bars, craggy, snow-capped mountains stand proud, looking down stoically on the noisy bustle of village life, observing its comings and goings, the busy procession of buckets, spades and inflatable creatures to and from the beach.

These mountains fascinated and intrigued me. I desperately wanted to investigate them and reach the cooler, calmer air enticing me from above. Consequently I excitedly jumped at every occasion to reactivate my pioneering spirit, proudly climbing the enormous internal spine of mountains, triumphantly witnessing the hidden, beautifully tranquil, ice-cold mountain lakes of Nino, Capitello, Goria and Melo, braving the lower slopes of the infamous GR20, and courageously surviving a sleepless overnight stopover in a smelly shepherd's refuge. I delved deeper and deeper into the heart of the island, enjoying the immense feeling of freedom and beauty. There was a refreshing fluidity, with rippling, crashing rivers surging down the mountains from their source, desperately seeking the sea. Wild boar, donkeys, agile goats and thin, sad-looking cattle with bulging ribs roamed freely along the dangerously twisting mountain roads and grazed aimlessly around the serene hidden lakes. And yet, to my surprise, I realised that this fluidity, freedom and space had not imprinted themselves on the island's people. They remained detached, exclusive to the mountains, firmly stamped on the landscape, far removed from domestic life and the drudgery of daily living. I found the contrast startling. I wanted to embrace the power of these unique island attributes, the flowing openness of the landscape, the wild free spaces, to find a way through the rigidity of Corsican home life and the stifling control exercised by Corsicans for generations to keep the family whole. I believed there could be a better way. I would not discover it for a number of years, and until then I found the traditions of island life – the expectations, the demands – an unwelcome restriction of my free spirit. Why did I have to buy flowers every Sunday and place them at the Luiggis' family tomb? Why was everyone asking me about children, stressing the importance of starting a family? Why did they expect the women to gather in the kitchen to prepare their men's meals while the menfolk could happily play *boules* and arrive home drunkenly inept after the obligatory pre-dinner rounds of Ricard?

I found respite in the alarming beauty of nature – wild, inspiring and tempting. This managed to keep my free spirit alive, to give me hope and help me sparkle, momentarily a liberated bird let loose, flying gracefully away. The sea was my greatest temptation. For the first time in my life I experienced sea swimming in warm, oily, textured water, sparkling green-blue, crystal clear, cleansing and salty, keeping me magically afloat, bobbing cork-like in front of my conquered snowcapped mountains. Such beauty, such a profound and forceful element of nature, deserved respect and admiration. I wanted to be submerged, caressed and massaged by the relentless swaying movement of this silky sea.

One morning, as the sun was just beginning to appear, already warming the water, tempting me, calling me into its seductive embrace, I crept silently out of the house and skipped playfully down to the silent, recently combed beach, like a naughty child, checking nervously that I was not being followed. I was alone, except for a few sleepy campers who had braved the cool night air and were huddled unseen in the tight cocoon of their sleeping bags. I carried on down to the far end of the beach, leaving behind a trail of neat, clearly defined footprints, the only clues to my presence. Twitching nervously, I double-checked before I tore off my T-shirt and jumped out of my shorts, stripping frantically like an overexcited lover, peeling away the layers until the soothing warm air touched my breasts and buttocks, the fragile skin unaccustomed to open air and such brazen exposure. Laughing almost hysterically, I dived joyously into the arms of my beloved sea. In spite of my cautious planning, I was spotted performing this outrageous and shocking act upon the family's beach by a nosy, disapproving uncle on one of his regular early-morning beach checks. I was not reprimanded directly. The family approach to such behaviour is to whisper secretly, shake heads in a critical manner and pass the word to key family members. It certainly did not involve openly discussing the matter for fear of debate and the dreaded possibility that the news could spread beyond the family.

Although gradually I did begin to understand the island's people, their pride and temperament, I would remain an outsider for many years, until my life skills had matured a little more. Then I was able to loosen the island's ties, and bring my own children closer to this magnificent scenery, its fruits, herbs and odours, demonstrating to the older generations another way of communicating with the young, another way of entertaining and using food to bring people together rather than to push them away. Until then I indulged myself selfishly in this warm terrain, tolerating the obligatory dinner parties, and willingly returned each summer to rekindle the familiar urge to seek freedom and space.

Tonton Antoine and *Tata* Francette inspired me the most with their 'good life' self-sufficiency, rustic simplicity and

unfussy family dinners. I marvelled at their naive, unashamed combinations of hearty home-grown foods. A few
slices of ripe juicy tomato from the garden, sprinkled with
finely chopped shallots, gloriously coated with a green
duvet of roughly torn basil leaves, a few drops of olive oil
and a pinch of salt and pepper, were sufficient to start my
senses racing. Cured lean pork, *lonzu*, a Corsican charcuterie speciality, was often rolled and eaten with a honey-
scented, succulent melon. Freshly gathered, grainy figs
were cleverly deployed to cut through the sharpness of a
minuscule sliver of pungent, salty ewe's-milk cheese, sometimes matured Corsican-style for up to one year, then
washed and rested until reduced to a dry, crumbly mound
of mouth-blowing intensity. We dined around dimly lit
tables under vines and ivy which dropped gifts of leaves,
dust and shrivelled grapes. Mismatching plates, chipped and
worn, clashed flamboyantly with the clean, freshly pressed
tablecloth. These were chaotic, unplanned, relaxed dinners,
the colourful bowls of food squeezed on to the table and an
atmosphere I would strive to emulate at home because this
was the real thing – French living at its best.

These leisurely meals were in profound contrast to the
formal organised family dinners, arranged to placate us or
to show off, make sure we were seen and admired, on proud
display. Here there would be an atmosphere of anxiety, the
hosts fussing and fluttering nervously over the guests,
painfully attentive, straining to ensure that everyone had
enough to eat, piling food on to reluctant, polite plates,
leaving visitors uncomfortably gorged. Unfortunately this
fretful environment had the discouraging effect of smothering my new-found confidence in the kitchen. I could not
bring myself to help at all, even by peeling potatoes, feeling

intimidated, incapable of meeting the required standard, or even of being able to chop in the way in which everyone expected me to chop. Again, as an intelligent, independent, strong-willed woman, I now despair at my childish reaction, and yet I was reduced to a quivering bundle of nerves when faced with this compelling expectation to cook in a certain way.

There was no escape from the dinner parties at which Maman cooked and entertained, bringing *la famille*, uncle by uncle, cousin by cousin, to the table, to proudly show off her son and exhibit his achievements. She sorely needed to be surrounded by family, to ensure that everyone was aware of her commanding matriarchal role. She was in control, gathering her flock around her, delving, enquiring, until she knew every last intimate detail of everyone's life. Islanders crave gossip, enjoying sordid, naughty insights, the craving fulfilled only once the tidbit is squeezed gently, subtly out of the victim's hold. Without the distractions of mainland cities – no cinemas, theatre or concert halls to ease the monotony of life's routine, to help escape from reality for a couple of hours – islanders need some distractions, a few thrills to lift their drooping spirits. Investigative probing is consequently an essential lifeline, the challenge to be in the know before your neighbour, to have the edge, like a hungry journalist, striving to avoid the shame of family news being heard from an outsider.

This family was skilled at their trade, understanding the politics of the game, plying their prey with food and generous amounts of wine, loosening tongues, feigning sympathy, heads tilted caringly to one side, listening with apparent genuine concern. Everyone opened up eventually. I struggled to understand why they revealed all, why they could not see the hypocrisy of all this, and again put it down to their not knowing another way, having no other way out, needing and relying on the family for support that more often than not was financial as well as emotional.

Every summer we became embroiled in the eternal chain of invitations that needed to be fulfilled, essential dinners with each family member – no one could be missed, they all had to be visited and artificial smiles exchanged – all somehow squeezed into our brief summer break. Not surprisingly these exhausting obligations had the undesirable effect of turning me completely against family dinners, entertaining and cooking, and almost against Corsica itself. I wanted out. Freedom. My dad's bid for solitude, his decision to choose family exclusion, suddenly seemed reasonable, a sensible course of action after all.

It was the wholesome Corsican cuisine, the food itself, away from the obligatory entertaining-to-impress atmosphere, which saved me. I would have to work much harder on Stéphane, though, to gain his support and understanding in order to prevent the dramatic move towards permanent family exclusion. Of course, I loved Corsica too much to take this drastic course of action, but I spent many weepy evenings wishing I could just take the easy way out.

Tasty little ideas such as *beignets de courgettes*, produced at aperitif time, or as a delicious starter with a spicy tomato sauce; *oignons farcis*, rich, creamy stuffed onions, and *soupe corse*, both inspired winter warmers; *cughiuette*, Corsican shaped biscuits coated in sugar, ideal for children of all ages scrambling back from a day at the beach – these are a few of my favourites. My nerves and digestive system were also eternally grateful to *Tata* Francette and her jug of boiling water pressed full of fresh leaves, giving off a soothing lemony aroma – *verveine* (lemon verbena), a proven indigestion remedy, which fortunately grows profusely on the Corsican *maquis*.

I have sneaked a few recipes from my Corsican aunties. They are not particularly precise, so give plenty of scope for individual interpretation.

BEIGNETS DE COURGETTES WITH COULIS DE TOMATE

Mix together 250g of plain flour, 3 eggs, olive oil, salt and pepper. Little by little add some water to give the mixture the consistency of double cream. Leave the batter to rest for an hour.

Meanwhile, wash 8 large, ripe tomatoes and cut them into chunks. Place in a saucepan and add 2 quartered garlic cloves, 1 chopped onion, a bouquet garni, 2 tablespoons of olive oil and salt and pepper. Partially cover the pan and simmer on a gentle heat for about an hour until the water from the tomatoes has evaporated so you are left with a thick sauce. Remove the bouquet garni and push the tomato mixture through a sieve to get rid of pips and the skin to make your tomato *coulis*.

Peel and cut 4 courgettes into fine slices. Heat some oil, dip and cover the courgettes in the batter and cook until they turn golden brown (4 to 5 minutes). Remove the oil by dabbing with kitchen roll. Serve warm with the tomato *coulis*.

OIGNONS FARCIS À LA MODE CORSE

Preheat the oven to 190°C/375°F/Gas Mark 5.

For 6 people you will need 6 large onions. Peel the

onions but leave them whole and cut the top off each one. Then leaving a shell of 2–4 layers scoop out the inside of the onion. Chop the insides and soften slowly in oil and butter. Remove the chopped onion from the pan and then fry 200g of *lardons.*

Cook 3–4 potatoes in water until soft and mash into a smooth thick purée. Mix 1 egg, the fried onion and *lardons*, 120g of grated Emmental cheese, salt (not too much because of the bacon) and pepper into the mashed potato. Combine well and fill the onion shells. Cover each onion with breadcrumbs (2–3 slices should be enough). Place in a large ovenproof dish containing 1 pint of vegetable stock. Put in oven for approximately an hour and a half.

SOUPE CORSE

For 6 people, cut, peel and strip a small green cabbage, 2 pak choi (about 100g), 2 potatoes (cubed), a large onion, 3 garlic cloves and 2 tomatoes. Soak a handful of white haricot beans overnight.

Soften the onion in olive oil. Add the green cabbage and the pak choi to the onion and sauté for a few more minutes. Add the cubed potato, tomatoes and white haricot beans to the vegetables and cover with water. Bring to the boil and simmer for 30 minutes. If you can find a thick rind of smoked bacon or cured ham, throw this into the pot at this point (remove at the end of cooking). If fresh basil is available, add to the soup after 20 minutes, together with 100g of small pasta or noodles, 2 crushed garlic cloves and a tablespoon of olive oil. Cook until the pasta is al dente and then season.

AGNEAU À LA STRETTA

In a large casserole dish sauté a selection of lamb pieces (shoulder, chops, leg) – about 1kg for 4–6 people. As soon as they are golden, add salt and pepper. Dilute 3 tablespoons of tomato purée in 500ml of red wine and 250ml of water and pour over the lamb. Add 12 garlic cloves, peeled and chopped finely into tiny cubes. Let it simmer on the hob for 35 minutes, stirring once and adding more water if it starts to dry out. There should be a little juice remaining at the end of cooking time but boy is it concentrated! Serve with pasta 'farfalle', sprinkled with grated Emmental, Comté or dried Edam.

PRESERVED FIGS

Make your own preserved figs and keep a taste of Corsica in a jar all year round. Place 1kg of whole figs into a heavy-based pan, cover with 650g of caster sugar and add enough water to almost cover the figs and sugar. Place on a low heat. Once the mixture starts to bubble, leave for a minute and then pour into a sterilised jar.

Unfortunately for me, the Corsicans have a sweet tooth. They like nothing better than competing to bake the sweetest, richest, largest *torte*, a traditional Corsican cake, donated by every auntie and cousin at annual family gatherings. The mere mention of its name can bring on a breathless panic attack before I even receive the first slice. My fear of the *torte* developed at my very first big family party. Everyone was there, giggling, balancing tottering plates on unsteady knees, chasing lost wine glasses under benches, behind trees. There were just a few nibbles – bowls of salted peanuts, pistachios, mini-slices of spicy, peppery *saucisson*, with just a drop of *Tata*'s home-made *vin de pêche*, syrupy, fruity and sweet. Bowls of warm *beignets de courgettes* came out of the kitchen to begin their procession around hungry, expectant guests, followed by more charcuterie, cubed melon on sticks, ham and cheese *Chariot* pizza squares, lamb *brochettes*, spicy rice. Just a few nibbles, they said. Dripping tomatoes, overflowing with olive oil, stained our crisp white shirts; olives, black, green, stoned, were mixed with chillies, spices, hot peppers. Pretty sundae *coupes* decorated with three ice-cream *boules* of dark, grainy chocolate indicated the apparent end of the food gala. I am deceived and satiated, full to the brim. I cannot swallow another morsel. This is the fateful moment when the *tortes* make their grand entrance. Not just one but three round decorated cakes, proudly presented and cut, handed out individually by their owners, everyone treated to three separate pieces to contrast and compare. A *torte* winner is declared as our empty glasses are recharged with chilled champagne. One slice is more than sufficient of this excellent party cake, which should be relished with plenty of fresh, nose-tickling champagne.

TORTE

Try making your own celebratory *torte*. Gather together your clan and have your own competition. Don't forget the champagne – plenty will be needed. This is the Corbara family version.

Preheat the oven to 190°C/375°F/Gas Mark 5.

You will need 12 eggs, 12 tablespoons of plain flour and 12 tablespoons of caster sugar which will make a cake large enough for 12–18 people.

Separate the whites and yolks of the eggs and beat the

yolks together with the sugar until they become almost white.

Gently add the flour. Beat the egg whites until stiff and gradually incorporate into the mixture.

Pour into a well-buttered 30cm cake tin and bake for 1 hour.

Remove from the tin and allow to cool. Then cover in melted dark chocolate (at least 50% cocoa). For decoration, whisk 2 egg whites with 125g of sugar and pipe the meringue mixture through a piping bag to form a thin, white decorative swirly design on top of the smooth chocolate.

To cut the cake you need to first cut a 12cm diameter circle in the centre of the cake and then cut slices starting from the outside of this circle. Once they have been eaten you can then cut the centre circle.

Every summer we return to the island, to family, to familiar routine. Every year I rebel just a little more. I cannot face the kitchen full of prattling, gossiping women and find myself drawn to the male aperitif circle. No one complains but the glares sharpen. I can feel the horrified, stupefied eyes stabbing into the nape of my neck. It is a traditional Mediterranean island, with women sitting on one side of the room and men on the other. Women will cook, look after the babies, wash and clean while the men go out to work, bring food back to the house, fish and hunt. The men enjoy more freedom, being allowed to play *boules*, meet friends in the café and travel as their work requires, leaving the women to find solace in each other's company and their children. My English background and a university education that encour-aged independent, free-thinking women, imbuing them with the confidence to improve the world, seek challenges, question and provoke change, would always work against me, making me believe that my aim of total integration could never be achieved.

I would be saddened by tales of my own family members, trapped between the dual demands of educating their children and the monotonous drudgery of maintaining the home – brave, bright, well-read women, some of them talented musicians, reduced to a lonely, uninspiring existence, feigning contentment but unable to hide completely behind their sad round eyes the bitter injustice of not being allowed to develop their talents and fulfil their own creativity; strong, handsome adults reduced to weak, simpering infants, forced down certain paths to please and placate, unleashing tragic repercussions that were never really intended. No one ever wants to cause pain – they only ever want the best for their own, to feel pride in their offspring, and continue the line, the reassuring thread of evolution.

The inability of Corsican families to recognise the right moment to let their offspring go, unintentionally creating tensions and anguish within the family structure, would also astound me. They just could not see the damage they were causing, all so easily avoidable if they would just let go. I think sometimes the children themselves were guilty of not forcing the issue, finding it too easy to stay within the safety of the family, not encouraged to become independent and fight their own corner.

Stéphane would often find it difficult to speak out. He wanted peace, and, of course, it was easy for him, as a male, to escape and lapse into convenient macho mode. There's no doubt his character changes as the ferry heaves its laborious load into Calvi – his tone and his vocabulary toughen; he becomes Corsican. This is his territory and he exudes confidence and pride, taking control and expecting me to fit in. He speaks French, instantly leaving behind my Stéphane, the man only I knew, the inner man that belonged to me. He would only ever speak French to me at home if he was intensely angry, and so hearing him speak only in French to me in Corsica made me feel incredibly uneasy. I let him be here – he was home, this was his island, and I did not want to disappoint him or deny him the privilege of absorbing the scents and flavours of his homeland. In some ways I liked this brave, assertive man, but I missed our previous intimacy, unable as we were to communicate in our language, to sit together hand in hand, under Corsican rules, with the men on one side and the women on the other. I let him be but I was still astonished by his change in behaviour – declaring, for example, that a certain dish lacked salt or pepper, waiting for Maman to oblige and leave the table to fetch the required article; the ease with which he would let his mother take over, iron his clothes, polish his shoes, all tasks he would unquestioningly carry out himself at home.

I sometimes blame myself for not demanding more support from Stéphane, breaking the mould early on, not leaving things to fester, leading everyone to believe I agreed with their well-intentioned attitudes, letting them think I could fit in. But I was young and shy, unprepared. I was no longer confident, unhappy about cooking, incapable of entertaining, and so I feigned a lack of interest, declaring total incompetence, which utterly bewildered this food-loving, meal-obsessed family. I avoided the kitchen, running in late from the beach, windswept, doused in sand, diving into the protected enclave of the shower, safe from the chattering commotion of chopping, whisking women. I'm sure

71

they knew I was hiding, but no one could understand why I would not help out. I simply aggravated them and unknowingly developed a reputation as a vain Englishwoman, carefully prolonging the application of make-up, powdering, preening, grooming until the kitchen fell silent and movement towards the table had begun.

I was becoming more and more misunderstood. My intolerance of sugar, another potential time bomb waiting to explode, could not be hidden for long. As this obscure affliction was slowly unveiled, I decided to assert myself, prise back some control in order to protect my increasingly delicate tummy. I would have to forgo some of my former politeness. I began to gently decline the proudly presented creamy, sugar-loaded desserts, shiny glazed fruit *tartes*, rich chocolate gâteaux, generously offered gift boxes packed tight with a multitude of sickly chocolate assortments. '*Non merci*' became my automatic, predictable reply when sugar arrived at the table. This upset and bewildered *la famille*. I could see it in their critical eyes. They did not understand how I could possibly resist, could not be tempted by these carefully chosen delights. How rude, how arrogant, how English. Abstaining, rather than making myself ill, reinforced my difference, making me stand out even further. And *la famille* was increasingly worried, sensing danger, the stranger on the attack, waiting to take control and undermine their domineering hold. The sugar dilemma was turning into a battle. Systematically the sugar bowl would be passed to me, *la famille* silently pleading with me to take a lump and put it in my coffee, like people possessed, seeking victory, trying to catch me out, clinging on to the faint hope that this was all a silly façade, a childish game, playing with emotions. 'I don't take sugar in my coffee.

Merci.' They cringed, seething and silent. I would remain misunderstood.

There is no doubt that Corsican home-cooked classics influenced the direction of my cuisine, guiding me towards nourishing family favourites that, to this day, I prefer to prepare. I would have a long way to go before I started to relax again and rebuild my confidence to a level where I could actually receive and entertain guests in Corsica. Nevertheless, I immediately put into practice the appealing elements of Corsican entertaining, the informal *Tata* Francette style, which perfectly suits my home, friends and English family. Maybe for me there will always be a residue of fear in the kitchen, which is why I steer clear of sophisticated recipes, leaving these challenges in Stéphane's increasingly expert hands. Corsica taught me how to enjoy casual, impromptu gatherings, mismatching the cutlery, glasses and table linen, calling for help, bringing disruptive, gleefully messy children to table. Stews, soups and pasta – these would become my speciality, what I do best, far from the critical eye of my Corsican clan.

FOUR
Le Plateau de Fromage

CHANGE WAS ON its way. Our comfortable, predictable life was about to be turned upside down as events rolled ahead of us and we scrambled to catch up and make sense of our new world.

The dreaded news that their only son would be leaving France hurt Stéphane's parents profoundly, another frightening indication that their control was floundering. We would suddenly be far out of reach, across the protective Channel, in a foreign land. The French are not brave travellers. They possess an enviably vast and varied country of which they are incredibly proud, and so tend to holiday within the known world of their culture, visiting family and friends – a safe option with all the variety they need, from skiing in the Alps to sun and sea along the sophisticated Riviera. Our news was consequently pretty catastrophic as they could not possibly envisage braving the rough, hazardous North Sea to venture on to unfamiliar territory. They were losing their son. I tried to imagine what it must be like to lose an only son, to understand their feelings of loss and try to be more forgiving, but I was eager to return home, selfish and withdrawn.

At this time Stéphane seemed attracted to England in an untypical French way, reminding me of my romantic urge to seek adventure, speak a foreign language, and be enticed by the unknown and all things exotic. And yet he felt the burden of his parents' anxiety and so could not allow himself to loosen up completely, to become childishly enthusiastic about his adventure.

'You can always come home if things don't work out,' suggested Stéphane's father before we left, leaving us with a sour taste, introducing a niggling feeling that maybe we were wrong, that this was not a sensible course of action. I sympathised with Stéphane, for he had never experienced optimistic, supportive energy within the family. His parents have certainly always been there for him, loving their son deeply and proudly, never depriving him of anything material, any real opportunities, but they have never shared a sense of unbridled optimism with him. I will never forget the day we announced our intention to marry. They were astonished, sensibly reasoning with us, gently enquiring whether I was pregnant, rationally trying to come to terms with our impulsive decision. It took a long time before the champagne was popped and timid, hesitant congratulations were offered, but there was never any elation, no spontaneous release of heartfelt happiness. I have always longed for them both to be able to show a little exuberance and joy in response to the decisions we have made and the successes we have achieved. At this particular time I felt Stéphane's burden deeply, and was determined to help lift some of this negative weight and share with him the contagious tingle of optimism.

Once again, I was ready to return home. Silly English habits, family and friends, were beginning to be missed deeply. The pain was sharper now, more defined, churning around in my stomach. I yearned to be settled and comforted. It was a good move, coming at the right time, and essential to settle the bothersome issue of Stéphane's national service. By working for a French company abroad, Stéphane would be observing *La Coopération*, a sneaky way for an educated, privileged elite to avoid spending a year in the army.

We moved back to Nottingham, sharing my parents' house until we found our feet, with both of us in work and settled in a home of our own. My secure cocoon had not gone away – it was waiting to welcome me back into its warm, reassuring arms, sheltering me until I was ready to be released again. Dad loved having us around – for the first time he was able to get to know his French son-in-law, and he was intrigued, watching Stéphane's Gallic table manners out of half-closed, almost shocked eyes. There were horrified middle-class gasps as croissants, biscuits and bread were all treated to the early-morning coffee dunking custom. It took me a long time to lose my embarrassment, instilled by years of training that dipping food into cups was bad-mannered and simply not allowed. I still cannot bring myself to enjoy this very French habit. Roughly broken baguette was messily placed directly on the table, blatantly ignoring the neat side plate, close to hand, ready to dip into a sauce or simply to be used as a replacement for the knife, casually pushing food around the plate and then on to a fork. Stéphane still gazes bemused at side plates and butter knives. 'It all takes up so much room on the table,' he groans whenever somebody has set a classic English table, hoping to impress. Bread, particularly light, crispy baguette, was for savouring every last drop of sauce or vinaigrette, a mealtime tool essential for enjoying every flavour, for using fingers and relishing the moment. For the French eating is not a formal business, with straight backs and elbows kept well clear of the table; it is relaxed and unceremonious. Gradually my parents abandoned their middle-class reserve and really began to enjoy their food, even looking forward to mealtimes.

It would not be long before the routine of our professional lives took hold of us, draining us of energy, removing our spontaneity, blending us into the grey, homogeneous world of offices, trains, telephones and exhaustion. During the day we were detached from each other's worlds, with unconnected friends and colleagues, only allowed to briefly wallow in each other's company during short, dark evenings and frantic, pressured weekends. Eventually we would come to question this existence.

Food was no longer featuring in our lives – it was there, a necessity, an essential recharging of the batteries, but the magical role of bringing people together, to laugh and relish each other's company, was fading, fast becoming a distant memory. Life was just too frenetic, and there was a sad lack of temptations to help slow us down. Where were the bountiful, exotic, sensual markets to lure and enchant? Why could we not spark any interest in friends in gathering around a table? The pub seemed to be a more popular draw.

Dining — lingering over a succession of courses — was considered a time-consuming effort by our high-flying executive friends. These were the busy, go-getting late eighties, and time was money. Careers were vital, and now we were being drawn into the very world that had so horrified us at the Ecole de Commerce. There was a culinary emptiness that we were aware of but seemed powerless to change. We were being swept into the monotonous, hectic routine of high-achieving business, ready meals and snacking on the hoof, an indigestion-inducing merry-go-round of solitary nourishment.

Quick visits to Stéphane's parents in Paris momentarily revitalised our tired, uninspired taste buds. The contrast was staggering. Three simple meals dominated the day, the highlight of our stay, a soothing respite from an unhealthy whirlwind world. These were not heavy celebratory meals but rather consisted of quick, tasty combinations, often using whatever was available in the fridge or left over from the night before. A surprisingly moreish entrée of cucumber, coarse sea salt, lemon juice, vinegar and cream was one of my favourites. The French are big meat eaters, and so the entrée would predictably be followed by some type of meat. This would often be cold slices of garlic-stuffed *gigot* from the night before, or succulent roast veal, a particular favourite of Maman's, possibly rekindling childhood memories of her veal-farming days. I also loved picking up the ready-roasted chicken from the *boucherie*, its crisp, blackened skin and the mouth-wateringly savoury scent of tarragon promising a quick and tempting ready meal. The warm, moist white meat would be accompanied by a smooth home-made mayonnaise.

These transitory visits did not leave time for stifling

reunions or overly-organised dinners. There were just the four of us gathered around a table to savour the simple French flavours; uncomplicated meals and then a flight back home.

Unfortunately it often takes shock and sometimes tragedy to rouse dormant lives into action, to bully dull, grey individuals back into battle. And we were no exception. We heard that Dad had been taken into hospital for tests and we reacted with calm – there was no need to be alarmed, appeared to be no imminent cause for concern. Dad was fit, active, a non-smoker, a healthy eater, a moderate drinker. He was indestructible, my rock, my influential guiding star. Nothing could happen to him. My childlike conviction that my parents would always be there to cuddle and protect me now seemed even stronger. Dads are immortal, unbreakable, and so whatever they found it would be repaired, pieced back together like a broken toy, and life would return to longed-for normality.

Unfortunately this was not going to be the fairy-tale story I yearned for, was not going to be as straightforward as I hoped. We would just have to wish a little harder for a happy ending. Dad was diagnosed with cancer and needed an operation immediately. We were all shell-shocked on hearing the whispered diagnosis, numbed into inaction, disbelief. Naively I did not grasp the seriousness of this illness. My dream family world was protected, surely it could not be destroyed – death, pain and melodrama belonged in the lives of others, in emotion-packed novels, tear-jerking films, not in our lives. We were immune.

I would remain optimistic, secretly pleading in night-time prayers for a miracle cure. My plaintive demands for a reprieve, for a saviour to rescue us from this undeserved nightmare were joyously answered. The operation was a success – he was clear of cancer, set free to pursue his life, given a second chance. With so many years now ahead of him I knew he would not miss any opportunity to claim his right to fulfilment, happiness and the wonders of life.

We had all been violently shaken, our emotions and nerves shredded. Physically drained too, we were in need of healing, a warming embrace to make us whole again. Corsica beckoned, inviting my now painfully thin convalescent dad to rebuild his strength in the emollient salty waters, the therapeutic mountain air, and to reactivate his appetite with the wholesome, fresh, natural goodness of my beloved Corsican cuisine. I knew this would be the perfect tonic to boost his sense of pride and well-being, surrounding him with the island's aura of peace. I was desperately excited, longing to show off my spectacular island, share my enthusiasm and watch him become Dad again – strong, confident, full of humour, mischief and the joys of life.

My Corsican family performed admirably. Everyone participated in the drive to assist Dad, demonstrating unlimited support and sympathy, understanding and kindness, filling me with an overwhelming sense of pride and honour at being part of this Corsican clan. Soups, stews and pasta came into their own, particularly the soups, as his appetite remained understandably fragile. Rich, ripe tomatoes were plucked from the garden; gifts of aubergines and courgettes were left at the doorstep, welcome fuel for the soup-producing frenzy taking place around the clock in the industrious kitchen. A sense of purpose, of a worthy cause, rallied the family into positive cooperation, providing a focus to direct their kind-hearted energy.

Succulent, sweet, dripping melons quenched his thirst and slid down without effort, saving his precious strength. Bountiful baskets of fragrant, luscious fruit – oranges, peaches, plums and figs – satisfied his craving for sweetness and juicy, refreshing lightness. Meals were not long, paced gently to accommodate motherly care of the patient; there were no overwhelming rich recipes, simply an abundance of the healing herbal fruits of the *maquis*.

We shared my sea, diving, prowling for hours in the underwater stillness, observing the silent, flickering business of millions of glittering, fluorescent fish. We floated, supported by the salty water which kept us effortlessly on the surface, preserving our strength. Warmed through by the early evening sun, calm and relaxed, stretched like greasy seals on the grainy sand, we breathed more deeply, soaking up the medicinal, palliative air.

He was still very tender, sore and bony. It would take more than a few weeks of Corsican charm to bring him back to his former glory, but I felt so happy that he had seen and experienced my enchanting jewel. He now understood its beauty.

Back home, still warmed and inspired by my Corsican trip, I was busy in the kitchen preparing tricky stuffed aubergines. I lined them up like beautifully crafted boats and rearranged them carefully until they were ready to put into the oven. The phone rang. It was Dad, his crackly voice instantly delivering shocking news. There were no unnecessary preliminaries, just the cruel, blunt news. He had just been told by the doctor that the cancer was back. Secondary cancer was developing insidiously around his liver and now there was nothing they could do.

I abandoned the ridiculously unimportant aubergine boats

and fled to be with him, tears pouring uncontrollably down my face. In a close, tight huddle we sobbed, weeping as we had never wept before, hysterically, loudly. I shuddered as I wept, shaking the pain out of my body until I could cry no more, red and sore, inconsolable, not wanting to let go in case he disappeared, drifted away without my permission.

I did not believe he was going to die, did not allow myself to even consider this as a possibility, even during the frank discussions about burial as against cremation, about wills and long-term care. We joked, teased each other, made light-hearted banter over these intangible considerations that I simply was not going to take seriously. Dad was a determined warrior – he would fight this thing to the bitter end and prove everyone wrong.

He did fight, forcing himself to get up, walk, smile and laugh. His childish humour stayed with him for a surprisingly long time until the potent morphine swept through his pale, rotting body, wondrously extinguishing his pain but destroying his spirit, turning out the light. He was no longer able to recognise the faces around him, peering hazily through watery eyes, smiling inanely, drunkenly, drifting in and out of consciousness.

It was bitterly cold, snow blocking the roads, drifting dangerously, bringing the crazy movement of cars and people to a grinding halt. An icy, deathly quiet descended over the house. Stéphane was stuck somewhere in the snow, unable to get home. I pleaded unreasonably with him to get back quickly. I did not want to be alone. I sensed the end was near. Intuition, some inexplicable spiritual connection – whatever it was, I knew. Dad passed away in his bed at home, still fighting, demanding just one last breath, belligerently questioning the injustice of his fate. He was so young, had so much to give. Life was so cruel and bitterly unfair.

Grieving is a long, agonising process which jumps haphazardly between feelings of anger, injustice, blame and depression, engulfing you in a deep sadness, making life a questionable ordeal. Why am I doing this? If I can't share this with Dad, what's the point? Memories, photos, haunting strains of music would so easily rouse my repressed emotions into another flood of tears and rage. Unreasonable behaviour dominated our lives, such as the nonsensical banning of aubergines from the kitchen, their shiny purple-black skin and bitter aftertaste a constant reminder of my loss. When would my senses return to normal? When would I ever feel human, sane, ready to live again?

Once the initial turmoil of loss began to cool, the depth of our churned emotions served to bring Stéphane and me closer together, and we determined to bring about a change in our lives. We needed each other more than ever before, realising the extent to which we had allowed a distance to grow between us, becoming strangers, wandering in and out of each other's lives, nodding, agreeing politely, but not listening. I knew that Stéphane was missing the culinary riches of his country, the social contentment of mealtimes, and I felt panic, a desperate fear that I might be losing him. I could not go back to France – I needed to be close to Mum, my family, my home, perhaps believing that if I left it would be like running away from my memories and heartache, running away from Dad. I wanted to stay, face my hurt and find a way to remember him, rekindle the happy, life-loving and giving parent I missed so painfully. It was clear I would also need to find a way to keep Stéphane in England.

I cannot recall how the idea emerged, but we started to talk, letting our imaginations fly, stretching the boundaries of possibility, dreaming wild dreams, sipping wine, understanding each other, rediscovering our love, our passions, our desire to be together. The best ideas often revolve around something you feel strongly about, something you understand. It did not take long before we were reminiscing about Toulouse, Corsica, our lazy weekends in Paris, remembering the food, the special dinners, the overly rich dinners, the inspirational markets, the culinary disasters. As excited as over-zealous teenagers, giggly, spilling out a French shopping list of longed-for delicacies, we had hit on our idea. Suddenly our faces lit up, and the world started to make sense. There would be cheese, lots of cheese – goat's, blue, soft, hard, the pungent selection box of a French *fromagerie*; spicy, peppery *saucisson*; mind-blowingly strong Amora Dijon mustard; bottles of Ricard, aniseed heaven; Poulain *chocolat chaud*; tins of *foie gras de canard*; large glass jars of *cassoulet* (wedding memories!); *pain aux raisins* with just the right amount of *crème pâtissière*; crisp, light baguettes; *confit de canard*; *petit beurre* biscuits, great for soaking in tea; wine; fruit syrups – *menthe, grenadine* and *citron* with which to make your very own *diabolo* . . .

French Living was born in 1994, bursting with French specialities capturing the essence, the scents and sounds, of Toulouse, Paris and Corsica; this was our haven, of unashamed pleasure and selfish gastronomic indulgence. We opened its doors to a cautious, astonished public, aware that they were sampling something unique but not quite getting the atmosphere or the concept; it was not like any shop they knew or had experienced before. To start with, there was this gentleman who remembered their names, had a welcoming smile, was appreciative and passionate, talking eloquently and fervently about cheese, its history, versatility and astounding culinary potential, freely handing out friendly advice, recommendations and practical tips, sharing confidences, family crises, dinner party dilemmas. He was always there, laughing, joking and animated. This was how French Living began; this was how it built a regular and loyal following of customers who would fall in love with the French Living charm.

We were not complacent in believing we could create credibility and trust purely by providing an exceptional atmosphere and unrivalled conviviality. Stéphane and I had a lot of learning to do. Years of relishing French family dinners had not been sufficient to equip us with the wealth of knowledge we would require to become credible cheese and wine merchants. This is not something that is passed on in the genes, and we were determined to become French gastronomic professionals. Our research began with cheese. Cheeses were my salty, calcium-rich *bonbons*, my irresistible temptation, a fascinating transformation of pure white liquid into solid, nourishing food, and I delved into their magical kingdom like a child rushing to dip its sticky fingers in the tall jars of multi-coloured crystallised sweets sitting high on the shelves of old-fashioned candy stores.

An enthusiastic *affineur* in northern France opened up the cheese textbook and invited us in to the world of traditional cheese-making, where everyone clings hard to their own beloved methods, determined to resist the modern movement towards total elimination of *lait cru*, battling against the obsession with ridding the world of bugs and mould for ever to leave behind a tasteless, insipid range of pasteurised, factory-produced cheese. We visited numerous exhibitions,

85

gathering brochures, sampling, questioning, slowly piecing together the world of French gastronomy. It was during a particularly tiring food salon in Paris that we approached a cheese stand and introduced ourselves to a tall, distinctive, narrow-featured young man, with a bizarre accent that I struggled to recognise. Stéphane confidently cited the names of all the cheeses he was searching for – Chaumes, Port Salut, St Agur, Bougon – to be abruptly, almost rudely, interrupted by the unforgettable phrase *'Monsieur, c'est du pasteurisé!'*.

Bewildered, we listened to what he had to say. He defined succinctly, this time gently, the distinction between mass-produced industrial pasteurised cheeses, created for the uniform, high-volume supermarkets, and the traditional small-scale *fermier* or *artisanal* cheeses made with unpasteurised milk using the methods and traditions of previous generations. This was Dimitri, our Belgian cheese connoisseur, a passionate, enthusiastic cheese-loving man who influenced us enormously and made sure French Living would contribute to the protection and promotion of real, hand-made *fermier* cheese. This would become a mission, a crusade to educate and preach about France's cheese marvels.

'You must realise that this requires true devotion and loving care,' Dimitri explained, 'because you are dealing with living, changing products that cannot just be displayed in a fridge to sell themselves. They demand expert care if they are to be allowed to reach maturity, must be turned, wrapped and cut at just the right moment to make sure your customers discover for themselves the superiority of farmhouse cheese. You are going to have to understand and explain the maturing process,' he continued. 'For example,

LE PLATEAU DE FROMAGE

soft, bloomy, rinded cheeses like Brie always ripen from the outside towards the inside, which is why a young Brie has that unwelcome chalky line through its middle. Instantly recognising a ripe Brie is essential, because once you cut into the cheese the ripening process will be slowed down, even stopped completely.'

Dimitri started to scare me, his tone urgent, concerned, making me doubt my abilities and question just what we were letting ourselves in for.

'It is imperative,' he barked. 'You must recognise all the signs, cut at just the right moment if you are genuinely determined to sell a perfect, unique farmhouse Brie de Meaux.'

I looked across anxiously at Stéphane, who I realised was trying not to laugh. Please, Stéphane, control yourself. We must not offend this man. He is the key to our cheese success.

'Look at the rind, dissect it,' Dimitri continued. 'Look closely – can you see? This is a young Brie. It's white, firm, its character has not yet evolved. A ripe, ready-to-cut Brie is distinctive and easily recognisable because its pure, solid white complexion will have disappeared and a personality will be starting to shine through as in an ageing face. It will be softened with wrinkles and charm. Yellowy creases and lines will develop over the cheese as its thickness reduces and it becomes soft and characteristically more pungent.'

His discourse gathered pace as he sensed our keenness, the fact that we were desperately hanging on his every word.

'In contrast, a blue cheese such as Roquefort ripens from the inside towards the outside, which is why a young blue cheese can be easily spotted by the lack of blue mouldy lines on the outside. Ideally, the blue should be evenly spread throughout the cheese.'

He checked to see that we understood, whether we wanted more information.

'You will need a balanced range of cheeses from all the different families,' he continued.

Families? What are the families? Dimitri did not despair; he continued to be patient and thoughtful faced with such ignorance. I thought I had gathered a reasonably healthy amount of knowledge having tasted many cheeses on my travels, and yet only now did I realise the incredible breadth and depth of this wondrous French industry.

Dimitri began to wade fastidiously through the family groupings, the key to balance and proportion in a successful *plateau de fromage*.

First, there are fresh cheeses, made from cow's, ewe's and goat's milk, never mature; these cheeses are often soft and white, without any rind, sometimes salty with a variable fat content, between 0 and 75 per cent, depending on whether the milk is whole, skimmed or enriched with cream. *Fromage blanc* belongs in this category, something I adored in Paris with a sweet chestnut purée mixed in to take away the bitterness of the cheese. Cottage cheese and industrially produced cheeses such as Boursin are classed as fresh cheeses. The farmhouse fresh cheeses of interest to us are the distinctive garlicky, herby *cervelle de canut* from Lyon and *le brocciu corse*. Very often these fresh cheeses are served as a dessert, as I had experienced during my au pair days, mixed with sugar, honey, fruit *compotes* or jam, as well as being used widely in cooking and patisserie, for sauces, stuffings and garnishes for *tartes* and canapés.

Les croûtes fleuries, or bloomy-rind cheeses, are the next key family. Here you are talking about soft cheeses with a delicate white duvet rind which tend to be made from cow's milk. The rind develops over two to four weeks, and the inside of the cheese should be soft and rich without becoming runny. Cheese classics such as Camembert, Brie and Chaource belong to this family. It was during Dimitri's description of these cheeses that I jumped in with my incredulous question.

'Are you saying a Brie or a Camembert should never run and ooze all over the plate?'

His emphatic and defiant reply quashed a long-held conviction that soft cheeses such as these are tastiest and best enjoyed when they start to escape. Apparently, once a cheese starts to run it has become too warm and is damaged, and its flavours will consequently not be at their peak. How would we ever explain this to our unsuspecting English customers, who had always innocently requested our runniest, most oozingly soft Brie?

As these cheeses ripen, turned frequently, the rind becomes golden, stained with reddish or brown spots. If they are left to mature for too long the flavour can easily become too sharp and piquant, so beware.

Next are the *croûtes lavées*, or washed-rind cheeses. These are made in a similar way to the bloomy-rind cheeses, also mainly from cow's milk; the principal difference lies in a brushing and washing process that takes place during maturation, encouraging the development of a very specific personality. A smooth, distinctive orange rind appears with a powerful flavour and a not very discreet aroma – these cheeses smell! Very often the flavour is not as strong as the odour would suggest; nonetheless this is the family of pungent, highly flavoured, undiluted cheeses, the 'smells of old socks' varieties, treasures such as Munster, Maroilles, Pont l'Evêque, Epoisses, Livarot, Vacherin and Langres, which all belong in this idiosyncratic family.

Dimitri moved on promptly to the *pâtes persillés* or blue cheeses, made from cow's or ewe's milk. These are soft with a mouldy interior, smooth white or slightly yellow with veins of blue running decoratively throughout, and again possess a powerful, pungent flavour. French blues include Bleu d'Auvergne, Bleu des Causses, Bleu de Gex and la Fourme d'Ambert. Roquefort, a ewe's-milk cheese, its manufacture a carefully preserved mystery, hidden in the secret corridors of the Combalou rocks, remains, according to Stéphane, the king of cheeses.

Les pâtes pressées, pressed cheeses, have a notably different appearance to all those previously mentioned. They are firmer, but remain supple. The rind is hard but the flavour is gentle, although they are capable of building to a fruity, almost piquant strength as they age. Included in this family are cheeses such as Morbier, St Nectaire, Cantal, Les Tommes, Reblochon and Les Pyrénéens.

Les pâtes cuites, the cooked cheeses, require the most work as they are both pressed and cooked. Cheeses such as Comté, Emmental and Beaufort belong here, and owing to their monumental size they continue to be mainly artisanal, typically mountain cheeses.

Finally Dimitri moved on to my favourite category of cheeses, *les fromages de chèvre*, so varied and dainty, a multitude of shapes and forms, some wrapped like the Provence *banon*, parcelled in greeny-brown chestnut leaves, some coated in soot, others showered with herbs, some plunged and soaked in jars of olive oil. Displaying all the variety and fun of a sweet shop, these enchantingly feminine goat's cheeses would always hold an entrancing allure, working their magic, making me smile, sometimes even giggle, in anticipation of their beguiling appeal.

Dimitri was guiding our search for the authentic, unpasteurised, traditional farmhouse cheeses, overflowing with scent, flavour and variety. He helpfully invited us to visit his warehouse, which housed the cheeses until they were ready to move on to new homes. *Affineurs* such as Dimitri had the challenging task of sourcing long-established, traditional farmhouse cheeses from producers throughout France and bringing them to their high-tech, top-of-the-range warehouses, where they would be lovingly cared for, washed and turned until they reached a perfect state of maturity, ready to be sold and delivered to *fromageries* and shops such as French Living. I recall asking Dimitri where the cheeses came from. He began to tell the amusing tale of one of their mountain farmers who produced cheeses in an isolated village. He would come down from the mountainside only when weather conditions were favourable, sitting on the back of a donkey with the cheese in large sacks strapped on precariously. He would meet up with the *affineur* at the bottom of his mountain, and there the business of selling cheese would begin. Apparently this mountain village is so isolated they have no need of cash because there is simply nothing to spend the money on, and so the cheese-making peasant was making this hazardous and tiring journey to exchange his wares for cigarettes – Gauloises, Gitanes; strong, distinctive French tobacco – which he packed tightly into his well-used, cheese-smelling sacks, ready to make the muddy uphill trudge back home in the dim early evening haze, a lit cigarette drooping from the corner of his mouth.

We wandered around the vast array of shelves bearing mounds of all shapes and sizes, taking in the fascinating metamorphosis happening right before our eyes. We carefully noted how to cut, wrap and care for our prized parcels, becoming increasingly protective and possessive, like doting parents wanting to nurture them fondly and be seen to do them justice, give them a fair chance to grow and develop into strong, perfect individuals.

Round cheeses such as Camembert, Munster, St Nectaire and Brie should be halved and then cut like a cake; blue cheeses require a more delicate touch and so a *fil*, a cheese wire, is recommended to slice through the cheese without reducing it to a crumbly pile. The hefty chunks of hard mountain cheese require a sharp double-handled knife, an impressive implement that always manages to raise customers' eyebrows whenever I proudly and deftly wave it in front of my impressed audience.

We discovered how to compile a well-balanced, perfectly proportioned cheeseboard, choosing at least four but no more than five different cheeses to provide a variety of textures and flavours to suit every taste: a soft bloomy-rind cheese such as Camembert or Brie, a hard cheese such as Beaufort, Comté or Cantal, a blue cheese, maybe Roquefort or Bleu d'Auvergne, and then possibly a goat's cheese, a firm, crumbly, bluey, mouldy Crottin de Chavignol or a fresh, creamy Pelardon disc.

Le plateau de fromage is an integral part of the French table; meals are selected and balanced to make sure that everyone will have enough appetite left to enjoy the cheese. In contrast to its English counterpart, the French cheeseboard is far from being the focus of an exclusive male moment, dominated by large proud chunks of masculinity to be savoured with a glass of port and a cigar. Men, women and children all participate in the interlude before dessert, selecting tiny slivers from all the textures on display, delicately choosing a neat arrangement of cheese to place on some freshly baked bread, prolonging the savoury flavours of the meal before the contrasting sweet finale makes its dramatic entrance.

Stéphane became equally absorbed, passionately engrossed in understanding and finding the ideal complementary wine for each cheese, simplifying his task by adhering to the timeless rule that a wine made in the same region as a cheese will probably be its perfect partner.

For example, the pungent, powerful Munster from the Alsace is subtly enhanced by a syrupy Gewürztraminer; a dry, crumbly Crottin de Chavignol from Sancerre will partner the dry acidity of a white Sancerre wine extremely well; a fresh, herby, garlicky Cervelle de Canut from Lyon perfectly accompanies a chilled, light-bodied and fruity Beaujolais; and let's not forget the spectacular combination of creamy, rich Mont d'Or and the dry, pricey *vin jaune* from the insular, mountainous Jura region.

Cheese should not always be relegated to the cheeseboard. The French also put their generous array of cheese flavours and textures to good use in a wonderful parade of cheese-based dishes. Here are just a few of my favourites:

TARTIFLETTE

This is a cheesy, creamy speciality bake from the Savoie region of France which uses the orange-rinded cheese produced in this area, Reblochon.

Preheat the oven to 220°C/425°F/Gas Mark 7.

Peel and parboil 1.2kg of potatoes. Slice roughly. Peel an

onion, slice and gently sauté until soft and golden. Blanch 400g of *lardons* by immersing them in cold water, bring them to the boil, then remove and refresh immediately under cold water.

These quantities are enough for 6 people so you will need 6 individual oval earthenware dishes (about 20x12cm). You will also need 200ml of single cream and 200ml of white wine.

In each dish layer the potatoes, onion, *lardons*, some cream and a little white wine, salt and pepper. Be careful with the seasoning, remembering that the *lardons* and cheese are already a little salty. Top with strips of Reblochon cheese without removing the rind (500g will be enough). Cook in the oven for about 20 minutes until golden and bubbly.

LA FONDUE SAVOYARDE

Fondue moves in and out of fashion in England but food trends do not exist in France – the fondue is simply considered a friendly, delicious way of celebrating the flavours of tasty, well-made cheese. So, ignore your trendy instincts and dig out your fondue set.

Choose a combination of cheeses such as Comté, Beaufort and Emmental (1kg in total for 6 people) and select a white Savoie wine or one from the Jura.

Remove the rind from the cheeses and cut them into thin, regular-sized strips. Avoid grating the cheese as it will melt too quickly and congeal. Peel some garlic and rub the inside of the fondue dish.

Pour 500ml of white wine into the dish and place it on a gentle heat. Add the cheese progressively and let it melt, stirring regularly.

Simmer for 3 minutes. Just before serving the fondue add a half a tablespoon of kirsch and check the seasoning, perhaps adding a few gratings of nutmeg. Serve with bread cut into equal shapes and sizes – slightly stale is best. There you have fondue, one of the most sensual and warming winter dinners ever.

In much the same way as fondue, a Raclette party makes excellent group entertainment. You will need a Raclette set with grill and individual cheese trays to slide under the heat until the cheese is bubbly and warm. Raclette, a flavoursome mountain cheese, is perfect for this melting treatment; no other cheese responds to heat in the same way, so it is impossible for me to suggest an alternative if you have difficulty finding Raclette.

Pour the melted Raclette over baked potatoes or boiled new potatoes and garnish with a selection of hams and *saucisson*, such as Bayonne ham, Paris cooked ham and Rosette salami from Lyon.

TOURTES AU CANTAL

These little Cantal pies are delicious as a starter or as a light lunch with a green salad and vinaigrette.

Preheat the oven to 220°C/425°F/Gas Mark 7.

For the filling for 4 people, make a béchamel sauce by melting 20g butter in a pan. Add 20g of plain flour, stir well and let it cook for a minute or two. Add 250ml of milk, stirring until taken up by the flour. Let it simmer for 3 minutes. Season with salt and pepper. Let the sauce cool. Add 100g diced Cantal and 100g diced ham. Roll out 500g puff pastry (you could make it but bought pastry is just as good) and cut into circles of about 15–20cm in diameter.

Put the pastry on a baking tray and pile the filling on to half the pastry circles, leaving the other half as lids. Moisten the edges of the circles holding the filling with egg yolk. Cover each with the remaining circles and press down well to seal. Paint the lids with more egg yolk and bake in the oven until puffed and golden, approximately 20–25 minutes.

LE FIADONE

This is a classic Corsican cake made from a typical fresh Corsican ewe's cheese, *le brocciu*. You can replace the *brocciu* with cottage cheese if you want.

Preheat the oven to 190°C/375°F/Gas Mark 5.

Break 7 eggs, separating the whites from the yolks. Finely grate the zest of 2 lemons. Pour the egg yolks into a dish and add 160g of caster sugar, beating the mixture until frothy and pale yellow. Progressively add 1kg of *brocciu* and then the lemon zest. Mix until homogeneous. Beat the egg whites until firm and add a pinch of salt. Incorporate the firm egg whites into the *brocciu* mixture, lifting gently without mixing too hard. Oil a deep (20cm) tart dish and pour in the mixture. Bake the cake in the oven for approximately 30 minutes. Let it cool before serving.

Our learning adventures also led us to the romantic pottery of Gien, founded in 1821 and still situated on the beautiful Loire river. We were in search of *faïence*, a more informal, brightly decorated tableware, more durable than porcelain, and so able to cope with more adventurous designs requiring deeper, intense colours. Here we watched the skilled workers deftly, painstakingly painting by hand the classic Gien designs, many of which were used to decorate the tables of the *grandes familles d'Europe*. I was struck by the thoughtful layout of the factory, with the artists' tables positioned around a central window overlooking an internal enclosed garden oasis with fountains, bird tables and exotic flower beds to inspire the painters and help focus their minds on the creative task at hand. Gien designs feature in the work of the Comité Colbert, which brings together those companies best representing *l'art de vivre* in France. We selected the designs that for us encompassed French family dining – bright, luminous, playful pictures that are a joy to use every day. Gien *should* be used daily, not just on special occasions; their designs can be mixed, creating surprising combinations, helping to recreate a Corsican table. I had those fun, warm dinners in my mind, images of fruit, vegetables and fish, of colourful bowls and chipped plates, inspiring my choices. This was such fun, bringing back so many memories, making food alive again – and more importantly bringing Stéphane and me back together as we excitedly discussed our day's findings. Gien is unusual, extremely French, and a delightfully lustrous addition to our shop's shelves.

Our experience, confidence and happiness grew daily within our French oasis. We were surrounded by the food we loved, rekindling images and soft memories with every blink of the eye: pictures of Dad dancing at our wedding reflected in the jars of cassoulet; Christmas celebrations reawakened by the tins and jars of *foie gras*; memories of Normandy shining brightly in the bottles of Calvados. I felt safe, whole again, secure in our future as a couple, in which we would work together to create an island of hope.

It was hard work and long hours, as Stéphane ran the shop

alone and I continued the old office routine to keep our heads above water, joining him after working hours and at weekends. We lived, breathed and loved French Living, nurturing its potential with every minute, hour and day, changing the window display, wrapping and folding, designing our popular Christmas baskets down in the damp cold cellar. We were in love again, with each other and with our lives.

Stéphane was a natural with the customers and the products, enthusiastically recounting stories and humorous anecdotes, using Dimitri's precious knowledge to sell and entrance every visitor who walked through our doors. '*Bonjour*, Madame Richards, and how is your husband today? Did he enjoy the Brie you bought last week?'

Customers were taken aback by such consideration; this was not just a shop, it was personal, intimate and passionate. Visitors imagined themselves on holiday, even breaking into embarrassingly crude, staccato French, and Stéphane played the role required of him, flattering, encouraging, luring them deeper into his own private world. The romance of one islander communicating with another further strengthened the bond with everyone who called in; they were our guests, our friends. Corsica fascinated and intrigued them, and the more Stéphane talked about his hidden gem, the more I sensed he missed it, needed to be closer to those scents, that magical, healing *maquis*. I could feel him searching for his mountains through the tone of voice he used, nostalgically reliving his homeland secrets with strangers, urging them to visit, promoting and contributing to the island's economy, eradicating some of his guilt.

One summer in Corsica we set about sourcing possible

products to recapture the essence of the island, these being the only gap on our shelves, which were devoid of its colour, flavour and sun. French Living was increasingly becoming an essential, life-saving capsule of memories and souvenirs for Stéphane and me, reactivated through flavours, textures, shapes and words. I was uncertain about Corsica itself; my memories were so confused and mixed. I would sometimes feel emotional, balmy affection, remembering the last visit with Dad and the admirable tenderness of *la famille*, but then, without any warning, a familiar tightness would squeeze my body, numbing my limbs into inaction. I did not know if I could cope with a constant reminder of my private battles, inadequacies and personal challenges within the confines of my safe, free world.

Commercial necessity dictated that a range of Corsican liqueurs produced in Calenzana, just next door to Calvi, should be brought in for the Christmas trade. *Liqueur de figue, châtaigne, myrte and mûre sauvage* hit the shelves and proved to be an incredible success, enticing our audience into the savage, wild terrain of the Corsican *maquis*. Some were even inspired to visit the island, returning with their holiday snaps, excitedly recounting their experiences while I nodded and smiled wryly, insisting they return the following year.

The shop started to evolve as we placed a couple of stools and tables in the centre, giving the visitors a place to sit and absorb, reflect and decide. One regular customer, a doddery, jovial character called Bob, would often call in to sit and chat with Stéphane, egging him on with his childlike humour. 'The French have pinched our words, haven't they, Stéphane? What do they call it, *le week-end*, and then what about *le sandwich*?' This would be followed by an infectious guffaw.

Bob was good fun. He liked France but was now too old and frail to be able to travel long distances, and so a quick bus trip into town was for him like an adventurous holiday abroad. He was grateful to us for letting him just hover in the warmth of the shop, making a few wisecracks now and again. His obvious, childlike love of France reminded me of Dad and our holidays of discovery and culinary adventure. It seemed so strange to be surrounded by all the things Dad had loved, the food and atmosphere he had introduced into my life so many years ago, now embodied here in our tiny shop. Many of Bob's mannerisms brought back memories. His attempt to speak French, gesturing awkwardly, using pantomime charades to mime his request, almost forgetting he could speak English and be understood, rekindled nostalgic recollections of our cosy camping adventures. Dad would have been so proud of French Living and would definitely have become our best customer. It was sometimes as though I could see him standing there, longing to stay, maybe sip coffee and watch the world go by, just as he loved to do at a welcoming *café terrasse*.

To the absolute joy of Bob, and eventually many more customers, we installed an espresso machine at the back of the shop, transforming the atmosphere again. The smell of coffee, threading its aroma around the sugary, savoury fragrance of recently baked croissants, *pain au chocolat, pain aux raisins* and crisp, willowy baguettes, standing to attention in their tall woven basket, enticed customers into the shop. They would all stay longer, particularly Bob, the excuse of a hot drink preventing them from leaving, hovering, rocking from one foot to another, dreading the inevitable moment when a miserable cold drizzle would slap their faces, brutally jolting the reality back into their unprepared bones. We proudly gave our coffee the names used in French bars and cafés: *grand crème, petit crème, express, double express*, giving ourselves more and more work in translating their names and describing them, reassuring our customers that *grand crème* is a version of cappuccino or latte. The English are so educated in the Italian terminology for coffee that they panic at the sight of new, unrecognisable foreign names. Our smooth, 100 per cent arabica coffee calms anxious faces, changing fraught individuals into more approachable, softer people. I love to see the transformation, the surprised, contented smiles.

Our shop-cum-café began to draw in more and more custom when we introduced snacks. French filled baguettes allowed customers to sample our cheeses, pâté, *saucisson* and hams. We did things the hard way. Despite the incredible temptation to give in to the whims of English taste and squeeze the baguettes full to bursting point of cucumber, onion and tomato, reducing any residual flavour to a bland mishmash, we remained steadfastly loyal to French culture and heritage. There would be no mayonnaise, no onion, no compromise of our authentic beliefs in order to make a quick buck.

A French *sandwich* is a last-minute option, an unavoidable necessity, reserved for a train journey or a lunchtime appointment that just can't be missed; it is certainly not a planned daily routine. These snacks therefore always tend to remain simple, an unadulterated form of nourishment, intended to provide flavour and highlight the chosen *sandwich* ingredient, not as a substitute for a real meal: *saucisson* and gherkins on lightly buttered baguette; a *Paris beurre* (a plain cooked ham – *jambon de Paris* – baguette with butter, its catchy nickname often shouted out by the brasserie

101

waiters in Paris); thin slices of Comté cheese covered with slivers of ripe juicy tomatoes and a drizzle of mustard vinaigrette; Raclette cheese accompanied by its close friend and partner, *rosette de Lyon*, spicy, peppery *saucisson*; a ripe Brie sprinkled with a few mixed leaves and a hint of dressing – each ingredient celebrated and allowed to shine within its casing of bread. This simplicity took a little getting used to, not appealing to all but still attracting a keen following of converts, of those ready to sample something new. Once they were drawn in there was no going back. The café expanded, moving on to the more sophisticated offerings of *salades composées*, *assiettes* of cheese and charcuterie, the intimate space filling up as people patiently stood waiting for a free stool, any available surface on which to place their cup or plate.

Our devotion, enthusiasm and hard work still seemed to be bringing in little financial return. I reluctantly continued outside work, but I was increasingly drawn and tired, having to divide my loyalty and energy in two. We needed to build this business more quickly, before the drive and commitment ran out.

Stéphane had the inspirational idea of bringing in fresh ideas, energy and sorely needed help by calling upon the *école* in Toulouse to send us eager, dynamic students to carry out their foreign work placement with us. This started the chain of young, lively individuals sharing our home and shop, our hopes and aspirations, living together, working to promote the pleasures of their homeland.

Agnès was our first student, and one I will never forget. A calm, hard worker, quietly spoken, she was full of enterprise and new ideas. Agnès was an intuitive, sensitive soul who for the first time helped us to blend the social and emotional values of our business with commercial realities. Together we decided to invite a party of local children from a poor inner-city school. It was a particularly deprived, impoverished area with few opportunities or glimmers of hope for the kids. They were not likely ever to have travelled or been taken on holiday; many had never even ventured out of Nottingham. So this trip to French Living was designed to be an adventure, an opportunity to cross the Channel, hear a foreign language, taste different foods, listen to the culture and lifestyle of another world.

With cynical, wary eyes, holding their noses, the children were shepherded into our tiny French world, older than their years, reluctant to show their natural inquisitiveness, reserved and determined to hate anything foreign. I looked across at Stéphane concerned, unsure how to break through this defensiveness. We each decided tentatively to approach the most troublesome and frightened, those who refused to even wander and look. I walked up to a scowling, dirty little boy with his arms folded tightly across his chest and asked whether he wanted to look at the computer. We stared at the lists of strange names, scrolling down and across, flashing up prices and stock figures, until he started to ask what the words meant. 'What's this one mean? *Es-car-gots?*'

I explained the wonders of eating snails, demonstrating the gadgets, waving a fragile shell caught within the tight clasp of a snail tong.

'That's disgusting,' he blurted, and walked away.

'Here, take this. A souvenir from France,' I pleaded, anxious to give him something to remember, a reminder of this glimpse into another world.

I handed him a shell, a beautiful, delicate snail shell. He took it, bemused and clearly unused to acts of kindness, at first unsure whether he should accept. Eventually he reached out and grabbed it, stuffing it into his pocket, fearing I would change my mind. Briefly, only for a matter of seconds, he made eye contact. Even today I am convinced those eyes were saying thank you.

Agnès was the creative genius behind this initiative, having invited along our local newspaper to witness the event and avail themselves of a worthy community story. It provided very welcome publicity, announcing our existence to a wider unsuspecting public, helping to give our business an essential boost.

Agnès stayed for only six months, the duration of her work placement, and I recall vividly the day she left. She walked down the path, her enormous bag wound around her shoulders by its strap, bearing her down, turning to wave goodbye with a tear slowly dripping down her cheek and no free hand to wipe it away. Neither Stéphane nor I could speak for days without choking, gulping back the tears, filled astonishingly with an emptiness that overwhelmed us, taking us completely by surprise. We were thoroughly taken aback by our emotions, having expected to feel relief and happiness at having our privacy and house returned, but instead we deeply missed this wonderful addition to our life and began excitedly to plan her replacement.

Numerous characters came and went, always sharing our home and all bringing their own individuality, creativity and passions. They also contributed to reactivating our interest in mealtimes. Surrounded by appetising temptations at work and appreciative, food-loving company at home, we moved back into the kitchen, our students often beating us to the stove and preparing their favourite regional specialities.

Agnès was from Bordeaux, but she was remembered not

so much for her regional specialities but more for the endless platefuls of *pain perdu* she would produce from our tiny, drafty kitchen. Leftover baguettes, of which there were many in the early days, would be recycled into this delicious, simple delight of stale bread, dipped into a mixture of beaten egg, milk and caster sugar and then fried gently in butter until crisp and brown, with another sprinkling of sugar added before serving. Agnès made sure our bread did not go to waste.

Véronique from Lyon, with her happy, smiling personality, loved to spend time in the kitchen. She would prepare beautifully presented salads, even on her day off. We would return home, tired and hungry, to find carefully dressed plates of fresh, nutritious salads waiting for us in the fridge, ready to enjoy immediately. One day she introduced us both to the Lyon speciality called *foie gras de pauvre*, or poor man's foie gras. This is a chicken liver terrine with wild mushrooms possessing the rich, smooth texture of *foie gras*, designed to try to trick the unsuspecting into thinking they are eating an expensive *bloc de foie gras*; this terrine is a cheap and clever way of reproducing the luxurious flavours of duck's liver.

Lucien, our laid-back, cool Parisian student, whose family were originally from Martinique, brought an exotic island charm that filled the house with fun, Caribbean music and rice. Lucien loved his rice and was particularly fond of producing an excellent *riz créole*. Cooking rice *à la créole* in plenty of salted boiling water then reheating it in the oven in a gratin dish lightly smeared with butter, often mixed with cheese, is a very popular way of cooking rice in France, and one that Stéphane and I grew to love when Lucien was sharing our home.

RIZ CRÉOLE AU BASILIC

Try this variation of the Lucien favourite, particularly excellent served with fish.

Preheat the oven to 190°C/375°F/Gas Mark 5.

Bring to the boil a large pan of lightly salted water. Add the juice of half a lemon. Throw 225g of long-grain white rice into the water and boil uncovered until cooked.

While the rice is cooking, crush 1 clove of garlic with a little salt and olive oil. Add several fresh, ripped basil leaves, crush again, and then mix in 1 chopped tomato and about 55g of grated Comté cheese. Season with pepper.

Drain the rice and refresh briefly under cold running water. Drain again. Reserve until about 15 minutes before you are ready to serve.

Grease a gratin dish with some butter. Put the rice in the dish and place in the oven until piping hot. After you have removed it from the oven, spread the basil and tomato mixture on top of the rice, gently stir and serve immediately, decorating with fresh basil leaves.

Once again I was encouraged to cook, pestered by our students, hungry for knowledge of another culture, to introduce them to English cuisine. I was quick to jump in, becoming proudly patriotic and determined to salvage the poor culinary reputation of *les rosbifs*, regarded as unimaginative and dull, based on fish and chips and not much more. I dazzled and surprised with my warming casseroles such as Lancashire hotpot and cottage and shepherd's pies, explaining the difference between the two as we sat together devouring my ever popular stews, food again bringing us together, encouraging communication.

Similarities between French and English home cooking

were recognised as our classic shepherd's pie appeared at the table.

'This is like our *hachis Parmentier*,' exclaimed Véronique, and she went on to describe this classic French dish to which many French homes resort to use up the meat left over from the roast the day before. Although spiced with garlic and more seasoning than our classic dish, it does have comparable origins.

Even with English dishes the magic had not disappeared – apple crumbles, vanilla-rich custard, moist, raisin-filled bread-and-butter puddings more than satisfied the Gallic sweet tooth, everyone, including myself, mesmerised by my creative achievements.

Cooking and eating became a pleasure once again, even with a tough, tiring work routine that showed no signs of easing. Stéphane rediscovered some lost inspiration thanks to a vast, enticing fridge of French Living cheese; at least we now could present a varied, full-flavoured *plateau de fromage* and he could envisage an authentic mealtime, recapturing the smells of home, creating dinners over which to linger, dinners for dreaming and dinners for planning.

Shopping remained difficult, both of us disliking the strain of supermarkets, the uninspiring aisles of indispensables. We became more determined to look out for markets – covered, farmers', small-town markets, anything that might relieve our routine, take away the sterility and bland uniformity that had so brutally quenched our appetite. It was more arduous than in France, but at least we could maintain the passion, the devotion to wholesome, tasty ingredients, thanks to our own private *épicerie*.

We had come through a corridor of sadness, emptiness and

culinary darkness to reach a shining opening, drawing us through, bringing us back in touch with ourselves. We entertained at work, cosily perched on stools, leaning lazily on our elbows, listening to customers confide, admit their fears and own up to kitchen blunders and party disasters, and tried to encourage their successes and aspirations. I found myself calming their nerves, confidently preaching about the food I loved and had learnt so much about, unconsciously letting go and sharing my knowledge and beliefs.

We were no longer alone, opening our arms to new experiences, new faces, building a business, securing our future in an unusual blend of commercial enterprise and nostalgia. We brought people together through food, gave them a brief glimpse of another world of relaxing nutrition and healthy discussion, allowing them to take the time to sip coffee, sit for five minutes and sample a mouth-watering, tempting delicacy, temporarily renouncing the familiar scenario of breathless racing between meetings and snacking. I felt a growing sense of pride and personal achievement in this unique creation, this colourful oasis, which provided an educational journey, promoting healthy self-indulgence and tasty ideas for the home. And yet sometimes I would look at it all and feel frightened by my self-gratification, my longing to stay near my family, my bizarre re-creation of part of Stéphane's world, designed to keep him close to me. At such times those nightmare feelings of death and loss resurfaced and I came out in goose bumps, petrified that Stéphane would slip away.

We had artificially recreated Stéphane's homeland – the smells, the scents, even the memories of home. In a way I was almost taunting him, saying this was all he could have – take it, there's nothing else. I had stripped him of his language, denying him his mountains, his sea. I would flit from shame, guilt and remorse back to contented fulfilment, not knowing quite where I wanted to be. It did not help having customers query our decision to live in England.

'What made you live here? Corsica sounds gorgeous. Why on earth did you move to Nottingham?'

I had an incredible urge to yell hysterically like a demented mother fearing for the safety of her children: 'Just be quiet, we're fine, it's OK, just leave us alone!'

But a stupid giggle, a nod or a wry smile was all I allowed to escape, hoping they would be distracted by a brightly coloured bowl or the cheese of the week, not wanting to share these intimate feelings, my personal dilemmas, my guilt and shaky disquiet. There was no quick and easy answer. I still had a lot of soul-searching to do before I would become more at ease with my decisions and this selfish creation. Meanwhile I wanted to relish the positive aura washing over us all, the healthy move back to cooking, entertaining and laughing around a tempting table.

Thankfully we were now moving away from the culinary wasteland of fast food and heading back towards a celebration of youth, fresh ideas and energy – entertaining freely at home with renewed vigour and inspiration, setting the table, taking the cheese out of the fridge, organising the fruit bowl . . . I suppose it's a little like riding a bike – once you have mastered the technique it can never be forgotten. We had not forgotten, just lost our way. We were now on a new journey, stronger, fitter and happier than before.

FIVE

Les Légumes

SPRING WAS ON its way, a green wash of colour lifting my
spirits, drawing me out of winter's poignant, gloomy associations, always more intense after months of sharp, icy,
snow-filled days. Living in the countryside, I have always
found my moods affected by nature's miraculous metamorphosis, as colours are subtly modified and new growth
materialises magically without any human interference – an
eternal cycle that helps us cope with the fresh challenges we
face in the year ahead.

Life was certainly hectic as I flitted between the demands
of an office-based managerial job and the all-consuming
nurturing of our own business. We appeared settled,
content with the path our life was taking. We had a business
to be proud of and the help of inspirational, energetic individuals who willingly shared our ambitions. Sometimes they

looked on with disbelief, finding it hard to accept our odd concept of transposing a portion of French culture to England, protecting its exclusivity, no succumbing to temptation to broaden the appeal with a taste of Italy or Spain. Eventually they understood, smiling ruefully as they began to see the wider picture and figure out the business logic as well as the emotional connection, realising too that this was also a ploy to maintain the sanity of my husband.

And yet there were rumblings, a brooding ambiguity, gaps that needed filling. We wanted more. There was no question that I would ever go back to the office routine, the darkness years of plodding, merging into dull insignificance. I could no longer live my life that way. I thrived on perpetual change, cheeky risk-taking, the tingling excitement of launching a new idea and nervously awaiting for it to be declared a success. This was my way of keeping my spirits alive, activating my senses to prove that I existed. I could fulfil dreams and aspirations, make a difference to other people's lives, open their eyes, trigger their senses. I did not want to stand still and let things be. As the first buds appeared, with a smell of rebirth in the air, a warm glow diffusing over us as the March sun cut through the early-morning chill, I could sense we were ready for more change.

Stéphane was anxious about the shop's seemingly slow rate of growth. The bank was putting pressure on us, and we knew that at any moment they could pull the plug and destroy our creation. Business was good, but we wanted to rid ourselves of the burden of the bank, of their short-sighted inability to see the potential of our unique enterprise. Unwittingly, our prudent bank was to stimulate an impulsive expansion.

Beneath the shop was a huge damp cellar, which we had taken over from the unit next door, whose owners had declared they did not want it. We did not particularly need all this room but it came in handy for keeping stock and making up our gift baskets on a long, rickety trestle table, not having to think too much about where to store things. There was masses of space in which to spread things out haphazardly. I had often joked about how fantastic it would be to hold a massive party down there, the high ceilings creating a feeling of spaciousness that would make you forget it was a windowless cellar. It seemed a highly improbable possibility, transforming this cellar into a venue for parties or anything else for that matter, with the bank twitching nervously; they would certainly not facilitate more commitment, and besides, Stéphane did not want to extend his involvement with them any further. This wasted, mouldy space would have to remain a frustratingly unexploited opportunity.

One evening, after the last customer had begrudgingly left, I joined Stéphane in the shop to help rearrange the displays, wrap the cheese and talk about the day's takings. I drove directly there, leaving behind a painfully political day at the office. As soon as I saw him I knew there was something wrong. He was not his usual calm and collected self. He could not wait for me to get through the door, not able to stand still, fidgeting excitedly, grabbing both my arms and urging me to follow him down the treacherously steep stairs to our vast, badly lit, musty-smelling cellar.

'I've sorted it. It's all decided and agreed. We're going to open a restaurant,' he blurted out, animated as I had never seen him before, not even during the thrilling shop-opening days.

I stopped trying to calm him and let him drag me around to the far side of the cellar. Here there was a rectangular space clearly divided from the main area that we used as a dumping ground for our empty delivery cartons, piling them high until we could organise a collection. 'Look. This will be the kitchen. Can't you see, there's plenty of room – ovens here, sinks and dishwasher over this side ...'

I let him go on, thrilled to see him showing such optimistic energy and drive, having become so used to lifting his spirits, raising his hopes when things did not go our way. Stéphane could be annoyingly pessimistic. I suppose he had inherited this trait from his parents, who would always anxiously highlight the potential problems and inevitable complications inherent in our new ideas before reluctantly congratulating us and encouraging the move forward. So this surge of enthusiasm was gripping.

Flushed with an excitement that was contagious, Stéphane rambled on and on about the number of covers, the position of the bar area, the toilets, the fire exits; this had clearly all been mulled over for some time. He finally hit me with the astounding news that he had also resolved the funding; he had found the money. Now I did cut him short. 'Hang on a minute. Did you just say you've got the money to renovate all this? Have you seen the amount of work that needs doing? It's dripping wet, there's damp everywhere. It will cost an absolute fortune.' I was starting to feel upset and disappointed that he had gone ahead and arranged a deal without me. 'Who is giving us the money?' I demanded, trying to control my disbelief.

'It's family, no banks. We'll be all right. No ties, no catches, just family,' he replied nervously.

I did not know whether to be happy or sad, my staunchly

independent streak blazing to the fore, unreasonably pushing me to reject this offer, to proudly deny any help. Support from a financial institution somehow felt acceptable, but family was different. The outrage I had increasingly harboured about insecure family members clutching the purse strings of their parents, never moving on to achieve independence, suddenly became too much. I burst into senseless tears. Stéphane was taken aback, nervously restraining the urge to laugh, initially believing my outpouring of emotion was due to pure, overwhelming joy. He promptly sensed that there was something wrong, as I had never reacted in such a pathetic, unrestrained manner when faced with exciting, challenging news. I was always so controlled and quietly enthusiastic about any new challenges, any brave next steps. He turned towards me, his voice full of gentle concern. 'What's the matter? Why are you so upset? I don't understand. I thought you'd be pleased.'

He continued to explain, desperately trying to reassure me as my inexplicable sobbing began to subside. While the deal was with family it was apparently to be a professional, tightly structured business arrangement. Everything would be transparent, coherent and precise, with no ambiguity – everyone would gain. This was an opportunity I could not turn down. Let the family help, so we could move on.

Once the work got under way – clearing out the rubbish, brushing down the damp walls, exposing gorgeous red bricks – I could not contain my eagerness to see it all completed. Already, at this early stage, it was starting to look more and more like a Toulouse cellar restaurant, and it thrilled us both to think we were recreating a part of our beloved pink-bricked city. It was a dusty, noisy, apprehensive time, piecing together the components of our expanding business. Unknown to both of us, an even more glorious change was about to fill our lives at this time.

I cannot recall planning or talking about starting a family with Stéphane. Admittedly he was distracted by the upheavals at work and did not have much time to worry about my maternal stirrings and the biological clock incessantly ticking, resounding loudly inside my head. Classic anxieties were beginning to chase each other around my mind: maybe I could never have children, maybe my body would not allow me the unique privilege of giving birth, of creating our own family. I decided I needed to try now. I naively thought it would take at least a year before anything happened, just enough time to get the restaurant up and running, to be more financially secure.

Stéphane had boldly brought about his own change, designing his unique dining experience, putting the emphasis back on informality, bringing freshness back into fashion, and taking pride in making sure that every detail, every dish, had been exhaustively considered. Now I had decided to bring about another pivotal change in our lives.

I was genuinely shocked when I saw the blue line appear, repeating the test twice before I convinced myself that I was not infertile – I could have babies, and I was expecting one now. So soon, so supernaturally clever – we were not ready. We had no money, no time. I felt panic, and for the first time out of control. What had I done?

I do not think I accepted there was a baby coming until very late on in my pregnancy. There were no clothes ready, no pram or feeding things, the nursery was still a sterile, uncosy office. I was totally overwhelmed by it all. I remember wandering into Mothercare, my legs heavy, like

someone in a trance, my eyes open yet blinded by the fluorescent brightness. The reflective whiteness of clean cotton
sheets, towelling nappies and intriguing sterilisation units
brought distinct memories of hospital. I picked up a packet
of minuscule plain cotton vests and peered at the sizes; a
complicated calculation involving the weight and the length
of the baby seemed to be required. I remember feeling hot,
panicky and breathless, pushing the foreign article clumsily
back with the others, making the pile tumble and slide, and
fleeing. I walked fast out of that alien place, swearing never
to return. I did not know what to buy, what the baby would
need. It was not there, I could not see it or feel it, and
consequently I could not relate to anything to do with it,
not even contemplate its needs. I recall a fretful, restless
nightmare I had one unsettled night, tossing and turning,
trying to escape from this turbulent, troubled dream. The
baby had just been born and I was standing over it, watching this tiny, vulnerable creature, pink and naked, with so
many soft creases and folds, looking up at me. I suddenly
realised there was nothing in the house to dress this baby in.
I had no bottles, no milk, nothing. Frantically I sent
Stéphane out in the middle of the night to buy something
quickly and, at that moment, with the dream door slamming, I woke abruptly, with a cold, unnerving feeling that it
was all real.

Mum came to my rescue, sensing my unease and my need
to come to terms with this pregnancy slowly. Her calm and
wise words were just what I needed.

Christmas was approaching, and we had received an ambitious, bigger-than-average order for 250 gift baskets.
Surrounded by bales of straw for the basket filling, I
proceeded to methodically stuff the tightly woven oval

baskets with a delectable assortment of French Christmas delights, wrapping flamboyantly with cellophane, the final flourish made with a silky gold ribbon. Mum would tease me about giving birth there and then on the mountains of crunchy straw bedding. 'Don't worry, Louise, it has been done before!'

I had straw sticking ridiculously out of my hair like a well-pecked scarecrow, and sticky, dusty hands. I yawned with relief as the final basket was wrapped. It was as though the baby knew that now was the right time to disturb our peace. The gift baskets completed, the shop closed for the weekend – it had a perfect sense of timing!

Our beautiful baby girl and the first authentic local French restaurant were born in Nottingham at about the same time, and we were reeling, dazed by our creative flair. Luckily for us Nina slept like an angel, the dream baby, offering me eight hours sleep and the energy to keep our retail heaven thriving, as well as the drive to launch a new dining venture. I rashly decided to abandon my outside job and focus on baby and business, bringing Nina into the shop with me, rocking her gently in her adaptable car seat with one spare foot while I deftly cut sizeable wedges of St Nectaire for my fascinated customers. Nina quickly became an intriguing part of French Living, customers coming in just to monitor her progress, amazed at how easy it was to combine baby and business. I would change the window display with Nina strapped tightly to my waist like an African field worker slaving in the heat of the sun. Under the spotlights in the window I juggled jars of cassoulet and bizarrely shaped Provençal shopping baskets, carefully repositioning them, creating a story to entice passers-by, the baby watching out of her serious newborn eyes. With

the restaurant just launched and my 'proper' job magnani-
mously abandoned we were severely strapped for cash, but
for the first time ever we were both blissfully, unashamedly
happy. Dad, Mum and baby, contentedly working together
to make French Living dreams come true.

Our restaurant was a sublime, unconscious blend of the
simplicity of Louis XIII, the atmospheric, red-bricked
charm of Chez Fazoul, and the excellent value for money of
most of the restaurants, brasseries and bars we had
frequented in Toulouse and Paris. There were three-course
menus, all with a choice of starter, main course and dessert,
available lunchtime and evening. This was a French concept
of dining out, using authentic ingredients brought over
from the restaurant wholesalers in Paris, expertly crafted
by real French chefs, and it was to become a restaurant that
won the hearts of the people of Nottingham. No trends, no
gimmicks – just good food at impossibly reasonable prices.
Where was the catch? There was no trick, no sneaky ruses;
this was French, a hundred per cent authentic, with no
caving in to English whims and peculiarities – it was not
going to be a sham. This was a place where you could be
guaranteed to sample divinely sumptuous French classics,
those regional specialities, some plain, many simple, that
have become lost in the rapid move towards more eccentric, extravagant and exotic concoctions. The brave, honest
omelette is one of those forgotten delights. Such an ingenious, fluffy creation, so suited to lunchtime, and a simple,
timeless invention that many restaurants are just too embarrassed to offer. They fear ridicule and derision, all because
of the pure simplicity of a beautiful, elegant egg. French
Living decided to place the omelette in pride of lunchtime

place. It formed part of a menu option that included *dessert du jour*, and deservedly reinforced its status as a lunchtime mainstay.

If you have become engrossed in the flamboyant trends of today's cuisine, perhaps a gentle reminder of how to recreate French simplicity will not go amiss.

LES OMELETTES
I usually make my omelettes with butter, sometimes with goose fat. The quality of the eggs you use is critical – obviously they must be fresh, and at room temperature.

In terms of quantities, play it by ear and discover what works for you and your eggs, but to give you an idea, plan on using 2 eggs per person.

For an *omelette au naturel*, I lightly beat the eggs and add a dessertspoon of either milk or water, salt and pepper. For an omelette for 4 people I melt 100g of either goose fat or butter on a high heat. In two minutes the butter stops frothing and should turn a golden nut colour. At that moment I throw in the eggs and for about 30 seconds let the middle of the omelette cook without touching it. You can then lift the edges with a wooden spatula, tilting the pan to let the liquid move in and fill the gaps. Continue this operation for about 2 minutes, fold the omelette in half and you should have a moist, runny result.

OMELETTE AUX POMMES DE TERRE, CROÛTONS FRITS ET JAMBON
For 4 people, heat a blend of 1 tablespoon of olive oil and 1 tablespoon of vegetable oil in a frying pan. Sauté 200g of cubed potatoes for 5 minutes. Make some garlic

119

croûtons by cutting 3–4 thick slices of stale baguette, rubbing them with a clove of garlic and then cutting them into cubes. Add the bread cubes to the potatoes in the frying pan and let them cook until golden. Just before this is fully cooked, add 2 large, finely chopped slices of Bayonne ham (or Parma ham if you have difficulty finding French cured ham). Put the potatoes, croûtons and ham to one side in a dish and lightly salt. Break 8 eggs into a bowl, add salt and pepper and 1 teaspoon of crème fraîche and beat together with a fork. Do not beat too hard because you will break the body of the egg and it will become too liquid and mousse-like. The less the egg is beaten, the lighter and more flavoursome the omelette. Heat some butter in a frying pan and pour in the eggs. As described above, move the edges towards the centre. Just before you fill the centre with more liquid egg, add the croûtons, potatoes and ham. Fold in half and serve moist and runny.

Running a restaurant involved interminable hours, from morning to the early hours of the next. Stéphane worked as a commis chef for the first few months until we were confident the idea would work. He had no formal training, just a passionate belief in the food he wanted to offer and a determination to keep the menu simple to avoid unnecessary mistakes. He avidly observed and copied every chopping and whisking manoeuvre undertaken by our hired French professional. He asked direct, astute questions, and learnt at astonishing speed. I greatly admired Stéphane for his courageous decision to immerse himself in the sweaty, pressured world of the professional kitchen. He not only learnt a great deal about proficient food preparation, able to reproduce dishes at a slick, consistent pace, but now understood very well the pressures a young chef can experience. Having coped with such a position at first hand, Stéphane turned into the most discerning, perceptive manager anyone could wish to work for. And the proof of this talent lies in an amazingly low turnover of staff. Our chefs often stay for up to three years, something that is unheard of in this frenetic industry. Unfortunately this idyllic chef management scenario did not materialise immediately. We had to negotiate a painful learning curve, attempting to make sense of the alien realm of the professional kitchen, making recruitment errors that would rock our confidence and throw into question the wisdom of our decision to open a restaurant.

Stéphane had decided he was just not cut out to work such long nights; he was having to put in more hours than the chef owing to his unfamiliarity with the professional kitchen. His arms were scarred with the telltale burns of inexperience, his whites soiled, and it was apparent that his talents would be better utilised out on the open stage, dealing with our growing, idiosyncratic collection of customers. He was pale, looking decidedly undernourished; it was time for Stéphane to come out of the heat of the kitchen and let in young, trained and energetic talents.

Stéphane's move away from culinary duties meant a change of staff and routine. We underwent a complete upheaval in the kitchen as new faces appeared, introducing a phase of turmoil in our ingenious plan. A seemingly harmless, well-qualified young Frenchman stepped under the brash kitchen spotlights and immediately began furiously wielding lethal-looking knives, hurling abuse at any sign of weakness or timidity, seething and sweating, only to revert abruptly to civil normality on completion of his harrowing evening's service. We tolerated this unpredictable, manic character for a few weeks before deciding that he was unlikely to calm down – this was how he had been taught, and this was how he behaved in a kitchen. We were both bewildered by his childish, outrageous method of coping under stress – a sad plea for attention, a desire to be the supreme ruler, claiming total kitchen jurisdiction. I could no longer step into my kitchen without confronting a piercing angry glare combined with a perverse query as to why I was there. I would shrink pitifully under his intractable gaze, backing away humbly, crawling shamefully out of the door, relenting and returning his space to him. He had claimed his territory and all we could do was sit outside, shocked and confused. Was this the way of all chefs? Many well-intentioned advisers had warned us about the fiery nature of this breed of kitchen professional, claiming it was a regrettable aspect of the cooking scene, but something we would just have to accept.

'He's a thug,' Stéphane exclaimed one day, storming out of the kitchen, exasperated at having to deal with another unreasonable rage. This was certainly not part of our dream. We had made a triumphant escape from office monotony, politics and incomprehensible authority. Our workplace was about generating goodwill and amity among customers and staff alike, creating a haven of delicious food and smiling faces. It all seemed to be slipping away from us, like soap through foamy, slippery fingers, impossible to restrain, always flying out of control. We bowed to this man's temperament because this was a new experience for us both; we were unaware of kitchen etiquette, had no training in cuisine management or the handling of hot-headed chefs. What would happen if he left? Finding another French chef at such short notice was inconceivable.

Corsican rage, when ignited and stoked, would burn savagely until the danger to livelihood and sacred beliefs was over, and I knew it would not be long before trouble would start to trickle and then flow like a Corsican spring dancing down a rugged mountainside.

'He's gone. I've sacked him,' Stéphane suddenly announced to me. 'We're safe, free from the madman.' He was proud, strong, and for the first time back in control.

'You've done what?' I was horrified, dumbstruck, anticipating action but not this impetuous dismissal. 'And what do we do now about the party of twelve booked in for tomorrow evening?' I shouted, enraged at his haste, the fact that he had allowed his Corsican temper to take over, leaving a messy aftermath, a chain of consequences for me to resolve.

These were worrying days and sleepless nights, our stomachs churning, our nerves tightened to breaking point. I sensed that this precipitate action would lead to further disturbance as an uneasy disquiet spread through our empty cellar. The cold and damp seemed to seep through the bricks, bringing with them a whisper of caution, making me shiver.

That morning no chefs appeared, everyone declaring that it was too hazardous working for an impetuous Corsican who was ready to throw them out at a moment's notice, seemingly oblivious to our reasons for getting rid of their colleague. I felt sympathy for these poor souls, who unquestioningly accepted the constant rages of their superior, blind to his cruelty, but were curiously unable to cope with Stéphane's one-off display of fury. I felt sorry because they would now miss the opportunity to discover another way, a civilised approach to teamwork based on mutual respect.

Much scrambling, rummaging and shouting ensued and continued for a long time until a combination of expensive agency chefs and Stéphane, who was reluctantly forced back under the kitchen spotlights, saw us through the next few days and weeks until recruitment was completed.

One thing was certain – this anxious period sharpened our personnel skills and guaranteed a succession of staff that would blend perfectly into our small family structure. We always knew there must be another way and that we would eventually be able to find talent without temper, culinary skills fused with cool serenity. This became our clear mission whenever new faces were required, and eventually became the most straightforward task we ever had to perform, turning those regrettable naive mistakes into a distant, hazy memory.

Stéphane's professional stint as commis chef and emergency cook left him exhausted but mightily empowered in the knowledge that if ever people let us down or threatened our beliefs again we could now cope. It proved to be a tough yet worthwhile trial, as later his professional experience would start to filter into our home kitchen, introducing a higher level of culinary knowledge and skills to transform our domestic environment. Daily cooking chores were facilitated by clever tips and insider advice, as was the ability to entertain vast numbers of guests with ease and proficiency, unfazed by what used to be considered a daunting task.

Stéphane's spirits lifted once he finally escaped from the strain of kitchen duties, and a healthier, stronger man reappeared. The hours were still long but not as lonely, physically demanding or strenuous. He could socialise, chat and joke with the interesting selection of characters that came through the door. Fascinating and hugely entertaining, Stéphane was once again in his element, using his wicked sense of humour to defuse potential flashpoints, his shrewd business head to manage any crafty customers looking for a free dinner, and a profound knowledge of all aspects of food and wine to dazzle perplexed diners accustomed to dozy, unenthusiastic student waiters. French Living's reputation was starting to spread fast, word of mouth a spectacularly powerful device that would serve us well in the months ahead.

One quiet evening we received news that Stéphane's grandma was ill and unlikely to survive the next few weeks, so we prepared to travel down to see her, probably for the last time, and at least give her the chance to see our baby. This was Maman's mum, who lived in the family farmhouse in Tulle, a nondescript town of approximately 50,000 inhabitants far from any major city of interest, between Limoges, renowned for its porcelain, and Cahors of wine-growing fame. *Mémé* shared their working veal farm with her second daughter, Marcelle, and her husband Jean. As soon as the Saturday restaurant service drew to a close, we began our expedition to the Corrèze area of France to pay our respects to a frail, dying old woman.

Once the labyrinth of grey, winding streets and the plain shopfronts of Tulle *centre ville* are left behind, and the road starts to spiral into the open, lush countryside, tiny hamlets of one or two rambling farm buildings appear, dotted haphazardly among the verdant valleys, many aptly named after the one house making up the village: La Maison Rouge, Ste Fortunade and then Les Tords, its sign hidden by the overgrown hedge. No one needs to see the sign, however; they all know this is Les Tords, home to the Buisson family.

As we pulled up in front of the ramshackle, almost derelict house, I spotted *Mémé* Buisson, a floppy straw sunhat on her head, perched on a stool in front of the open kitchen door, surrounded by masses of leaves which she was picking then throwing into a worn, dirty sack. She was preparing *tilleul*, a lime-flavoured tisane, similar to my favourite, soothing *verveine*. She looked happy enough, not the picture of ill health I had prepared myself for – perhaps a little thinner, drawn and pale, but not bedridden, still wanting to be useful. She was clearly overjoyed to see us, her face lighting up, but unexpectedly the cheerful smile faded, as though she had suddenly remembered she was not going to be happy today. Her mouth lapsed into a pinched, hard line, and tears began to roll silently.

'How are you, *Mémé*? You look busy,' said Stéphane. He knew his grandma well, particularly her sneaky attention-seeking foibles. She seemed to withdraw into herself like a hibernating creature, shrinking from life and denying herself the pleasure of high spirits or the serene contentment that comes from a solid faith. 'I don't understand why you are so miserable, *Mémé*,' Stéphane continued. 'Look around you. There are lots of people, you know, who would love to live surrounded by such beauty. Just look at that pear tree, it's magnificent. You don't realise how lucky you are.' He was determined to pull her out of her self-centred sorrow.

'That stupid tree has not produced any fruit for the last two years,' was the curt reply, reducing Stéphane and me to fits of giggles while *Mémé* looked on, totally bewildered by our incomprehensible reaction.

The house had not changed since the last time I had visited, the one main room acting as kitchen, dining and living space. A huge table with benches running alongside it dominated the room, with one comfy chair reserved for *Mémé*, presiding at the head of the table. There was a massive walk-in fireplace with a cushioned seat on either side, the ideal place for the telephone and a pile of old newspapers, well-thumbed gossip magazines and the indispensable TV guide, *Télé7Jours*. An enormous television on a wheeled stand would blast out loudly at 11.30 precisely so *Mémé* could sit and watch her favourite daytime soap series, *Tonton* Jean having left the house in the early hours to tend to his livestock. As we sat around the table with bowls of coffee and croissants, he would join us with a plate of well-matured cheese, coarse country pâté, gherkins, home-made bread and a tumbler of wine. He would then pull his beret over his eyes, put his head on his arms as we used to do as young children at nursery, and snatch a deserved forty winks before starting the next round of chores.

The house was musty, smoke-stained, with greasy yellow walls that had not seen a lick of paint for a very long time, their only decoration a threatening hunting gun hanging above the utility door. Flies buzzed all year round and a lingering smell of cow dung seemed to hang in the air despite the delectable cooking smells seeping out of the simmering *cocottes*. The bedrooms and cold, draughty bathroom extended to one side of the house, with the apple-filled, cobwebby *grenier* also doubling up as a bedroom when guests came to stay. *Tonton* and *Tata* always gave up their bed for the comfort of rare visitors. This was a poor farming household, and life was not luxurious – it was hard, cruel and monotonously routine, the animals perpetually requiring attention even on the harshest of days, when tiredness and sore, painful limbs yearn for a deep, snug cushion, or a lazy soak in a hot bath. These were indulgent comforts that Marcelle had never known, having cared for her mother for most of her married life, tied to the farm with rare trips away, but somehow managing to retain the happiest face among the entire *famille Buisson*. I had great admiration for this modest, kind-hearted woman, who knew how to laugh and share excitement for a world she would never experience. She never tired of listening to our adventures and latest schemes, retaining a wicked sense of humour.

Outside the house there were numerous sprawling outbuildings and one enormous barn, a beautiful structure, the sort that would be snapped up in England and swiftly converted into an expensive, desirable country residence. This barn was still in operation, containing rusty, hazardous farm equipment and machinery, possibly abandoned; sacks of livestock feed stacked precariously high; a growing woodpile, anticipating a tough, bleak winter; a disorganised storeroom leading to an entire corner full of hutches piled securely one on top of the other, with gorgeous grey and black fluffy rabbits poking their twitching noses through the resistant chicken wire. I can recall thinking how adorable and rural it was to keep a selection of rabbits, even though the children had all now left home. This was what a farm should be like, with animals to be stroked and cuddled scattered indiscriminately around the outbuildings and land. I was genuinely shocked by my naive romantic notions, so unrealistic and middle class. I had momentarily lost touch with the austere, brutal realities of this community, the level of wretched poverty these people endured, and was unkindly chastised by Stéphane. 'They're for eating, you soppy creature! You really didn't think they could afford to keep these animals for pleasure, just to stroke now and again?'

He then went on to tell me the horrifying story of one of the dogs *Tonton* had bought to help work the cattle in the fields. They usually had two working dogs at any one time, to encircle the unsuspecting cattle and guide them proficiently back into the cow sheds. Unfortunately this particular dog had problems adapting to the work required. It would run away, lie around lazily, and refuse to jump into action when called. The dog was inefficient, a recalcitrant worker who was creating difficulties for *Tonton* in the fields. Consequently he was shot. They could not afford to keep him as a pet, he needed to pay his way, and no one else in the area would want an animal that could not work. This was a world where cruel actions were thrust upon these struggling farmers by bitter financial necessity, an economic environment where emotions and sentimentality were buried, firmly controlled for the protection of the family. The French are not as sloppy about animals and pets as we are in England. Admittedly this extreme farm environment is not typical, and such brutality is not universal throughout France. In towns and cities pets are enjoyed and well looked after, but the French do somehow manage to retain a cold detachment from animals and remain a nation of carnivores where a meal without meat is considered by many as a meal without a heart. Vegetarianism is not as popular as it is in England, and this has a great deal to do with the relationships the French develop with animals, the clear distinction they make whereby pets are pets and the rest are raised for food. Live chickens, geese and ducks can still be seen and bought at markets. We have become increasingly isolated from the origins of our foodstuffs in England with such markets being banned and many of our children unable to tell you how a sausage is made; it's just there in its clean cellophane wrapping, ready to pop under the grill. The French remain close to their food, understanding the realities of its production, striving hard to maintain quality and high standards, distinguishing effortlessly between fresh and last season's dull produce. Consequently they are prepared to pay more for expertly produced, flavoursome raw ingredients. In England, thankfully, we are also moving the same way with the development of the organic movement, but in comparison with France this remains a minuscule market, and the majority of our population continue to be seduced by the low prices of mass-produced food of doubtful and worrying quality.

The Buisson family not only raised animals for eating, they also tended an abundantly rich vegetable and fruit garden, a relatively small fenced-off square area at the side of the house, next door to the utility entrance, uninspiring to look at, with at first sight nothing much appearing to grow there, but this small area of land fed this family throughout the year. They were almost totally self-sufficient, proudly growing nearly everything they ate, making their own wine and bread, making what for others would be a customary trip to the local supermarket a rare adventure indeed. There were garden peas, wild spinach, potatoes, cabbage, parsnips and carrots, strawberries, gooseberries and raspberries, nurtured in soil fertilised by the manure of the cattle, gathered, processed and preserved, then stored away in the *grenier* to see them through the infertile winter months.

Beyond the garden you could freely cross the open fields

and drop down into dense woodland. This was where *Tonton* and his son would secretly sneak off to, furtively glancing behind them to make sure they were not being followed, for they were out gathering mushrooms, a clandestine operation. These two knew where all the different varieties of fungus grew and certainly did not want anyone else to find out and get there before them. Both carried large knotted canes to reveal the hiding places, gently rearranging the leaves, covering their tracks so that no one could tell where they had been. Mushrooms certainly have an aura of mystery, somehow seeming to belong to the realms of fairies and sorcery, with a scary potency, capable of inducing wild hallucinations, even death. I had always been fascinated by the names given to mushrooms, all evoking this curious magic – *trompettes de la mort, pied de mouton, rose des prés* – and in English names such as Herald of Winter or Destroying Angel.

The forage always took place on damp days, after a night of rain and a morning of bright sunshine, when the grassland was steaming, creating a ghostly aura, everyone aware that after a good spell of rain there would be a rich, plentiful supply. The king of mushrooms, the fungus held in highest esteem by the French, is the *cèpe*, known in English as the cep or Penny Bun, which grows most readily in oak and beech woods. The woodland at the back of the farmhouse was a notoriously bountiful spot for *cèpes*, and *Tonton* instinctively knew when the mushrooms would spring up, perfecting his timing, ensuring a gathering of full-sized *cèpes*, mature but not past their sell-by date.

They would stomp back into the kitchen escorted by their mud and sticky, damp leaves, shaking their precious cargo over the table to be weighed and sorted. Once they were washed and chopped, Marcelle would instantly whisk together an *omelette aux cèpes* as a congratulatory snack. Made with goose fat, this is the simplest and most delectable way I know to taste this treasured delicacy. The others would be washed thoroughly, some preserved in sterile glass jars, the others ready to be cooked for the evening's meal.

Here are two more ways of savouring the full flavours of the prized *cèpe*, should you ever discover a secret picking ground.

CÈPES RÔTIS AU FOUR

I think this is the simplest, most authentic way of preserving the aroma and chewy flesh of the *cèpe* mushroom.

Preheat the oven to 220°C/425°F/Gas Mark 7.

You will need 1.5kg of firm cèpes mushrooms for 4 people. Separate the tails from the heads of the mushrooms. Keep the heads whole or cut them into four if they are just too big (the ideal size should be about 8–10cm diameter). Cut the tails lengthways into two or three pieces, depending on their size. Brush the base of an ovenproof dish and the mushrooms copiously with some olive oil. Place the heads, hats facing upwards, and the tails into the dish. Lightly salt. Put in the oven and after 15 minutes take them out and, with a fork, turn the mushrooms over to let them become golden on the other side. Lightly salt again and sprinkle with some finely chopped parsley. Leave in the oven for another 10 minutes. Sprinkle with pepper and then serve.

DAUBE DE CÈPES

Just like a cassoulet, the more often this dish is reheated the better it becomes.

For 6 people you will need 2kg of firm cèpes mushrooms. Separate the tails from the heads. Cut each head into 8 or 10 pieces, no bigger than half a sugar lump. Chop the tails very finely to approximately the size of a grain of sweet corn. Peel 3 tomatoes, remove the pips and cut into pieces. Put them to one side. Put a blend of olive oil and vegetable oil into a frying pan, warm the oil without letting it smoke, and throw in the chopped *cèpes*, allowing them to turn golden for approximately 1 minute. Remove the *cèpes* and in the same oil sauté 2 finely chopped shallots, 2 finely chopped onions and 2 roughly chopped cloves of garlic for 3 minutes on a gentle heat. Add the tomatoes, a *bouquet garni*, 3 glasses of sweet white wine and 750ml of chicken stock. Add salt and pepper, mix well and leave on a gentle heat for 15 minutes. Pour the tomato and onion mixture and the *cèpes* into a large cast-iron casserole dish. Leave to cook on a gentle heat for 3 hours. From time to time stir with a wooden spoon. Take out the bouquet garni and serve directly from the dish.

Our flying visit to the Corrèze allowed for only one evening meal with the entire family. We gathered snugly together side by side on the benches, knee to knee, elbow to elbow, and conversation flowed, ranging from mushroom-picking escapades and the new bed bought for *Mémé* to our life of restaurants, shops and babies back home. Every meal would always begin with soup, *la soupe*, an indispensable element of dinner for Jean, and this night was no different. He could not come to table and be satisfied without a hearty portion of soup to start. They would often be clear bouillon-style soups mixed with minuscule noodles or transparent pearl barley jewels – never a thick broth, more like a thirst-quenching, warming drink. Just before the last spoonful he would carry out the ritual of *faire chabrol*, pouring a drop or two of red wine into the bowl, slurping loudly to finish every last droplet of liquid. Soup was followed by home-made rustic terrines accompanied by a slice of powdery country-style loaf, expertly cut by Jean, drawing his *laguiole* knife from the belt of his trousers, later to be used to cut the flesh of his chicken. I had never tasted such firm, white, succulent flesh as that from this fowl, the most free-range chicken ever, slaughtered, plucked and roasted that after-noon in anticipation of our final meal. That evening we tucked into wholesome, classic country French cuisine that even the most reputable restaurants could not imitate, unable to obtain freshness such as this. *Petits pois aux lardons* had never tasted so exquisite as this freshly picked garden variety, with an intense, rich, lingering pea flavour, stronger than that of the mushiest of fairground peas. Wine was drunk out of tumblers which doubled up for water and then for the coffee to finish. Basic, rustic simplicity, so similar to and yet so removed from island life in Corsica, sharing the wholesome, garden-grown riches but without the stark, cold severity of everyday living. It was a calm rural beauty far removed from the material values of our modern world, its different ethics and beliefs briefly opening my eyes to the shallowness of our existence. Marcelle was not embarrassed by the run-down, crumbling house she lived in; she felt no need to apologise for the chaos that greeted us. Everything worked: the ovens were hot, the lights illuminated every-one's faces, dinner could be served. She welcomed us in with wide, embracing arms to share momentarily a few memories and moments of joy, a woman who could instinctively distinguish the important issues from the utterly irrelevant.

Mémé sat proudly at the head of the table, tucking in greedily to this highlight of the day. With hardly any distractions apart from the television to fill her hours, delicious feasts with guests were a gratifying means of entertainment. She was flagrantly enjoying herself, slurping, burping, lavishly licking her fingers and lips, demonstrating a healthy appetite.

Unsurprisingly, *Mémé* lived for another five long years after this anxious, fleeting visit, but this did prove to be the last time we saw this clever, stubborn old lady in action, unable to satisfactorily convince her of just how lucky she was to have experienced such glorious, healthy food and magnificent rural splendour.

It was always a pleasure coming home after tiring albeit brief excursions such as this one. They filled me with renewed energy and ideas, inspired culinary schemes, imparted secrets to share with my fascinated audience. I would look at *petits pois* with refreshing clarity, challenged to reproduce a tasty vegetable delicacy, thinking more carefully about the accompanying vegetables and garnishes, now convinced of their startling, appetising powers. I could more easily turn a blind eye to the peeling paintwork, the kitchen tiles that were in need of a firm, thorough scrub, focusing on my friends, my baby and husband, relishing their health and carefree company.

Lucien, our most recent Ecole de Commerce placement student, was due to leave us and move on. I was always sad and withdrawn as the next departure loomed, sorry to lose invaluable help in the shop and a friendly, supportive presence in the evenings when Stéphane was still working in the restaurant. Our situation had changed since Lucien had arrived, with a young, increasingly active baby transforming the sort of help required. I had mulled over in my mind for some time the possibility of forgoing student help for more practical assistance with Nina. This baby was growing fast, already crawling, toddling, touching, and starting to make it more difficult to focus on customers and our expanding business. Thrown back to my memories of the only sort of baby help I knew, I triumphantly declared we should find an au pair. Not only would I be free to manage the shop more professionally without being distracted by an urgent nappy change, but Nina would also hear more spoken French, helping the development of longed-for bilingual skills. This was something we both felt very strongly about – ensuring that our children would be able to speak both languages and so benefit from contact with their grandparents and extended French family. I had always insisted that this responsibility should not rest on my shoulders. I really did not believe it was my job to speak French to the children because of the inevitable danger of their picking up my silly mistakes and quaint, sometimes appealing, accent. With Stéphane frequently working long hours in the restaurant, Nina not surprisingly heard more English than French. I would read stories to her in French, particularly if she picked out a French book herself, and she would hear me speaking French to our students and family, but I was adamant in refusing to use any language but my own on a day-to-day basis. Stéphane's parents rarely came over to visit and so could not be relied on to promote their language and culture to their grandchild. True, they had forced themselves across the treacherous Channel on to unfamiliar territory at the announcement of a new member of the family, keen to set eyes on the long-awaited offspring. The power of a vulnerable young life to spur the old and frightened into activity and help them rediscover a little of their former vitality still leaves me feeling amazed and at the same time very sad.

This visit was brief, but Stéphane was delighted. For the first time he could proudly show off his treasured baby and perhaps more importantly reassure his parents by sharing with them his thriving business. They were clearly uneasy in this alien environment, with its foreign culture and no means of communication. Rather than boldly seeking adventure they would withdraw into the protected confines of the house, transforming it into their familiar, controlled domain. I would return home from work to find the kitchen cupboards rearranged, plates ordered and stacked in the cupboard by the fridge rather than in my favourite place by the oven, Corsican charcuterie hanging from the ceiling, that evening's dinner already bubbling in a pan. Rather ungratefully I seethed at the sight of my territory being invaded. I felt offended by this overbearing, controlling behaviour – well intentioned, I know, but threatening all the same. I was upset, because for once it was my turn to be the confident hostess and receive them as guests, to proudly demonstrate my worth as a mother, wife and cook. Thinking back, I realise that they had no reason to believe I could cope, given that I had only ever exhibited laziness, incompetence and lack of interest. To my enraged way of thinking this still did not justify their blatant encroachment on my home, which offended me. Once again Stéphane could not appreciate or sympathise with my unreasonable feelings, saying nothing, clearly enjoying the attention and relishing the savoury scents and flavours permeating every corner of our home. I said nothing. Now and again I attempted to reposition my belongings in their rightful location, only to have them promptly relocated again as soon as my back was turned. I declared defeat and decided to wait until they had returned to Paris before re-establishing my home again.

One day I was flicking through the latest edition of *The Lady* magazine when my eyes were drawn to a simple little advertisement from an eighteen-year-old French girl eager to au pair in England. I excitedly asked Stéphane to give her a call. She was currently staying in Paris. We had no trips planned and knew we would not be able to meet, to check her manner, her sparkle, look closely into giveaway eyes. Our intuitive questioning and listening techniques would have to be put into action once again. This genuinely did not concern me, as I had been selected in much the same way for my position in Paris all those years ago. So far we had fallen brilliantly on our feet with all the students we had chosen to work in our business and share our home. It's difficult to explain, but it's as if each and every one was destined to meet us, to bring their individual characteristics, knowledge and gifts. I never worried about getting it wrong, misjudging their characters, always using a few telephone conversations to test the ground, listen to their voices, edge towards some sort of connection. Stéphane had become extremely proficient at this sort of telephone interview technique, listening closely to language, tone and manner, cracking a few jokes to test for a sense of humour, probing for family history, looking for a happy stability, until satisfied they would fit in and cope with our life at work and at home. I recall Stéphane's conversation with Celia because he seemed so much more serious and intense than usual, and I quickly realised this was because he was recruiting someone to look after his child, his precious, cherished offspring. He came off the telephone smiling, decided and assured, pleased with his choice.

'So. What did she say? What does she sound like? Does she want the job?' I gabbled excitedly, always animated at the prospect of a new character moving into our world.

'She sounds superb. A little anxious about the exact nature of the job – she seems to want a few details.'

We did not really know what the job would involve but somehow managed to reassure our next French guest and persuade her to come and stay with us in England.

I recall vividly my first sighting of Celia as she came through the arrivals gate at East Midlands airport. In fact we could not miss her, wearing as she was a luminous red coat, hauling heavy, overfilled bags, including a dainty yet brash scarlet handbag, tottering precariously on high, stylish heels. She looked as though she had stepped out of the pages of a Parisian fashion magazine, oozing style but confusingly displaying a sharp rebellious streak. This girl was charismatic, demanding attention, yet her eyes, almost sullen and doleful, revealed a wariness that prevented her from succumbing completely to our warm welcoming embrace. She smiled uncomfortably, clearly unsure about her new companions, stepping back from my outstretched arms, resisting my natural tendency to reach out and cuddle, to protect and reassure. She visibly relaxed once settled in the car next to the calm, sleeping baby, cosily curled in the padded car seat. She did not take her eyes off Nina all the way back home, amazed at her tranquillity, soothed by this introduction to her young charge. Noticeably unwinding, she said, 'I think everything's going to be all right.'

Stéphane was always determined to put our new arrivals at ease, considering himself their equal rather than an older counterpart who demanded a respectful '*vous*' – his opening announcement to all new guests was that they should use '*tu*'. '*On se tutoie, eh?*' he proclaimed now.

'*Comme vous voulez,*' spluttered Celia, smiling at her clumsy reply. And even after all these years, after the friendship and intimacy we have shared, Celia is unable to *tutoie* us. This social nicety (*vous* versus *tu*) is a French oddity that even now I have difficulty deciphering, swallowing my words conveniently to avoid the social embarrassment of getting this crucial piece of language etiquette shamefully wrong.

On the drive back home we probed Celia for more information about her family, what they did and where they all lived. She was vague, not particularly forthcoming, and it was only years later that the full extent of her troubled feelings about her parents, particularly her mother, were completely apparent to us. She spoke fondly about an auntie who lived in Troyes, a pretty town right in the champagne-producing heartland of France, describing her impressive chateau, where Celia appeared to spend a lot of time, playing with her cousins, and later using it as a base to be close to the attractions of Paris. Cold, detached and very matter-of-fact, she disclosed that her parents were divorced, and ever since this upsetting event she had hidden herself away in this secure, rambling chateau, losing herself in the sprawling estate, away from the emotional turmoil surrounding her parents. Her father remained in the family home in the South, living in a secluded rural hamlet near the wine-producing, *foie gras*-rich area of Cahors, not far from Toulouse, but she was not as forthcoming about the whereabouts of her mother, and I felt it was not my place to ask any more questions. She would talk when she felt ready. I immediately sensed that Celia was probably using this au pair experience as more than just an educational trip – maybe she was escaping again, trying to run away from some unhappy memory, or possibly it was just determination to discover her independence and prove her capabilities. I did not know enough about her past or her family to be able to confirm my intuitive observations, but I did strangely warm to her slightly quirky, unpredictable nature, to her touch of rebellion, and particularly to her offbeat and daring dress sense. I could not help but admire her courage in maintaining a style that was just so un-French, because I knew how much dismay this would have generated within her family, such original, head-turning flair inevitably causing embarrassment. In England there was nothing particularly strange about Celia's choice of colours and designs, but in France she probably stood out like a spiky-haired, nose-ringed punk. This all sounds rather para-doxical, Paris being the capital of the fashion world, leading the way in stylish haute couture, and yet in everyday life French women follow a strict, extremely conventional dress code. I remember the students at the Ecole de Commerce, all identically clothed in immaculate, well-pressed jeans and pure cotton shirts with stiff collars, with lambswool or cashmere jumpers always draped casually around the shoulders in a cool, uniform manner. Even at the tender age of eighteen Celia had developed a style that was all her own, drawn to silky, ostentatious fabrics and eccentric accessories of any nature, fusing feathers, beads and sparkly paraphernalia to shape her creations. She was thrilled to discover my creaky, little-used sewing machine, only rarely brought out for essential repairs or to whip up a new pair of curtains. Now this machine could be heard trundling away in the early hours of the morning, speeding up the final design to be triumphantly paraded by an over-joyed Celia. Fashion, creating and designing were in her genes and proved to be extremely valuable assets in her role as an au pair. Her imaginative moulding, cutting and gluing, her artistic recycling of household tubs and cartons, kept Nina distracted for hours.

Once back home, we heaved Celia's bulky luggage into our humble townhouse. We had prepared dinner earlier – perhaps a little too well organised of us, but we were eager to settle our new visitor as quickly as possible and create a welcoming atmosphere to calm her nerves and put her at ease. Neither of us was prepared for her surprise announcement as we gathered around the table for dinner. Stéphane proudly produced a hefty cast-iron casserole, which bubbled and steamed, filling the room with the aroma of its heady wine sauce, proclaiming my favourite *coq au vin*.

'Oh, I'm so sorry, I forgot to tell you – I'm vegetarian,' Celia confessed nervously, anxiously wanting to put things right. 'Don't worry – I'll make myself an omelette.'

Vegetarian! A French vegetarian! This was unheard of. She must eat some form of meat; all French eat meat. Stéphane was utterly amazed by this admission, having only reluc-tantly given in to adapting the French Living restaurant menus for our increasing number of vegetarian customers. He could be incredibly belligerent at times, and this was potentially one of those occasions. Please, Stéphane, just give the poor girl a break, I pleaded inwardly, not wanting to frighten her away. I had decided I liked her fiery, head-strong spirit and resolute rejection of conventions and traditions. I could see my own obstinate, individualistic behaviour mirrored in her, and I had an overwhelming desire to protect and defend her, to share my own insecurities and doubts with her. We would have to work extremely hard on Stéphane to help him overcome his narrow-minded classification of the French, his tendency to brand them all as faithful carnivores with no time for any other form of diet, but even he could not stop himself grinning at this amusingly different French girl. Celia was most definitely unique, very special, and I loved her all the more for her defiant energy. I suppose it was the fact that I could relate to her need to escape, her reasons for seeking sanctuary with us, seeing myself reflected in her protest against French family ways, the orthodox, routine traditions, and particularly the culinary habits. Maybe this is why we were to become long-lasting friends, understanding each other, identifying with the other's past experiences, from the very start.

I found life with a vegetarian extremely easy. I had tasted and been delighted at first hand by the delicious vegetable recipes frequently used in French family homes, always amazed at how rarely these dishes appear on restaurant menus. Following their holiday visits, many of our customers often moaned about the lack of vegetables accompanying their main course in French restaurants, and it is true that in France they do not tend to garnish with a wide choice of vegetables. However, they are experts at creating sumptuous dishes with just one or two ingredients, lovingly blending them to produce a single flavoursome vegetable dish. Vegetables are certainly not an afterthought to them. The French would be deeply ashamed if they were ever to serve up quantities of soggy, unseasoned boiled vegetables just to meet others' expectations.

Stéphane did eventually come round to this new life with *les légumes*, after I had gently reminded him of the variety of delicious, healthy recipes available. Together we discovered a focus on a category of ingredients that are very often ignored, considered insipid, just an accessory. We both began to thoroughly enjoy the challenge of cooking exclusively with vegetables, having to think more carefully about what we would prepare, keenly scanning market stalls for ripe, in-season vegetables. We rediscovered the pleasures of simple dishes such as *gratin de chou-fleur* with a green salad and crunchy, crumbly baguette, and the au pair dishes I had relished in Paris – seasoned spinach with egg and artichokes dipped in vinaigrette dressing, one of Celia's favourites, and something that led to an animated dinner conversation as I confessed to my embarrassing artichoke inauguration in Paris. We did not particularly miss meat and avoided making the mistake of creating separate dishes, one vegetarian, another meat-based, which would inevitably lead to resentment at the extra work involved. If we fancied something meaty we simply grilled or pan-fried our desired cut and served it with the main dish of vegetables.

Here are two of Celia's special favourites.

RATATOUILLE

This is such an easy, flexible dish, which can be made in advance and is even better when eaten a few days later. It can be varied by adding a fried or poached egg, even an *omelette aux fines herbes*, mixing with pasta, even baking as a lasagne, and is delicious eaten hot or cold. It is also easy to get it wrong and turn it into an overcooked mush. I like this recipe because I adore celery, but feel free to experiment with your own choice of vegetables – this is the beauty of a ratatouille. Just remember to cook each vegetable separately before you mix them together in one pan.

For 6 people, wash and cut, without peeling, 300g of aubergines into cubes approximately 2cm wide. Sauté for about 10 minutes in sunflower oil. When they begin to change colour, place them in a sieve layered with kitchen paper. Cut 4 stalks of tender celery into small batons. Poach them for 5–6 minutes in boiling salted water. Drain and put to one side. Put 4 fresh tomatoes in the same boiling water for 3 minutes and then peel them, remove the pips and cut into pieces. In a casserole dish heat some olive oil and on a gentle heat sauté 1 chopped onion and 4 chopped shallots for about 3 minutes, stirring well with a wooden spoon. Add the aubergines and tomatoes, a bouquet garni, and the celery. Add a little sugar to soften the acidity of the tomatoes – something I always do when cooking with tomatoes – salt, pepper and a tiny amount of cayenne pepper, and leave to cook on a gentle heat for 45 minutes or according to taste. Keep testing from time to time until you are happy with the crunchiness of the vegetables.

GRATIN DAUPHINOIS

This is usually eaten as an accompaniment to meat, but we decided to devour this rich, garlicky potato heaven in individual earthenware dishes with a mixed salad,

sometimes with grilled peppers and aubergines. I
particularly love this version.

Preheat the oven to 180°C/350°F/Gas Mark 4.

For 6 people, peel, wash and slice 600g of *terre rosa* or
roseval potatoes into thin round discs. Rinse them in cold
water and dry thoroughly in a tea towel. At the bottom of
an earthenware dish spread a layer of crème fraîche (you
will need 300ml in total for this dish) and then a layer of
potatoes; on each layer place a crushed garlic clove. Add
salt and pepper and a tad of nutmeg. Repeat the operation
until all the potatoes have been used. Finish with a layer of
crème fraîche, keeping a little to one side for later. Put the
dish in the oven in a bath of water (a *bain-marie*) for
approximately 50 minutes. Remove from the oven, pour
away the cream that has turned into butter and spread the
remaining crème fraîche on top of the potatoes. Mix it in
well with a wooden spoon. Put the dish back in the oven,
still in the *bain-marie*, for 15 more minutes. Wait for this to
become golden without letting it turn hard.

Celia was an animal lover, a sentimental protector of all
God's creatures. I found this difficult to believe after she
recounted her upbringing on a self-sufficient farm, her
parents having decided in the late sixties to leave behind the
bustling chaos of city life to seek a sort of hippie freedom,
raising animals in the middle of nowhere, surviving on love
and peace in this physically challenging and cruel environment. It all sounded like life in the Corrèze, except Celia's
parents had chosen this path, opted to abandon the privil-
eges and luxuries of urban living. Celia consequently grew
up surrounded by rabbits, ducks and geese, fed and
watered, fattened ready for the pot. Some were preserved

for home consumption, the rest taken to market and sold. She described happily playing with these comical creatures, stroking and caressing them, knowing full well what was going to happen to her friends. She told me she had no problem with the killing; she often used to sit watching her mother wring the animals' necks, hang them, pluck and prepare the flesh, resigned to their destiny. She even admitted to having loved the flavour of a moist, succulent piece of *magret de canard* before she completely rejected the presence of meat on her plate. So how on earth did this abandoning of all meat produce begin? She did not really understand exactly why, but remembered feeling bitter anger and an intense longing for her parents' attention, for their love, support and security. Maybe by giving up meat she was hoping for some sort of recognition, a concerned response, for someone to sit up and take notice of her, for an end to all the squabbling. Maybe she was also unconsciously hitting out at the decisions made by her parents – the move to the middle of nowhere, the subsequent divorce, sending her away to boarding school. Who knows? Celia and I would often sit and discuss all these possibilities. She was able to cry as she let her feelings resurface, releasing some of her obstinate anger, something she had never previously been able to do at home in France. It was easy here, far away from her memories, from the realities of home, in another language and with a new family. Progressively she came to trust our love and support, steadily blending in as an integral member of our household, developing an endearing bond with Nina. I recall being greatly amused by Nina's early vocabulary as animal names and descriptions started to flow eloquently, and animal songs and rhymes echoed throughout the house. One of her first words, and the most

147

popular, was *chat*, chanted incessantly, and loudly shrieked whenever a cat wandered past. As every cat in the neighbourhood became wise to the fact that there was a feline worshipper in the vicinity, both Nina and Celia would be followed by queues of cats of all shapes and sizes – neglected, shabby moggies, sleek, jet-black crooners, feisty gingers, soft, fluffy white kittens – coming from all directions, purring, awaiting their share of smothering caresses.

We eventually established a routine whereby Celia and Nina would accompany me to the shop every morning, hauling pushchair, goody bags of fruit, light syrup drinks and nappy-changing essentials, making sure there was a clean, fresh-bottomed, smiling little person ready to face the world as we opened up for business. We shared breakfast in the restaurant before embarking on the day's batch of baguettes and classic *viennoiserie*. I considered myself the luckiest mother ever, being able to bring my child and childminder to work, allowing me treasured moments – Nina on my knee sharing a favourite rhyming book, giggling, the two of us raising our heads as the next customer opened the squeaky door, smiling, welcoming them in. Celia equally felt privileged because she was given the opportunity to run the shop alongside me; we handed Nina back and forth, depending on who fancied pushing the pushchair around the nearest commercial centre, or whether a favourite customer demanded particular attention. Celia was always smiling, her unique look unchanged, tottering behind the pushchair in her high, painful heels while I looked on with admiration in my practical flat boots. Our informal style delighted everyone – a specially made gingham curtain would be theatrically swept in front of a cupboard stacked full of children's books, puzzles, pots of pens and crayons and piles of experimental artwork as a customer entered; a musical soft toy would accidentally be activated when a casually thrown book landed on its head, startling unsuspecting customers, who believed there was a cat trapped in the cupboard.

Nina progressed at an astounding rate, learning to count by stacking the pâté tins, sorting the empty snail shells and numbering all the wine bottles, cautiously wise for her years, never touching anything she shouldn't. Our routine was working; we were all settled and benefiting from each other's company. Even the chefs in the restaurant rose to the challenge, and loved to impress Celia with her favourite vegetables, ravishingly cooked. She would smile appreciatively, sitting downstairs in the restaurant, sharing lunch with her young charge, relishing a version of France that listened, accepted and tolerated. I saw her grow in confidence, lifting her head even higher in the most outrageous, colourful outfits.

Our chefs would try to woo Celia with these simple vegetable dishes.

LES TOMATES PROVENÇALES

Cut 4 large ripe tomatoes in half. In a pan heat a little olive oil and press the tomatoes down firmly in the hot oil for about 15 minutes on each side until golden. Add salt and pepper and leave them for another 15 minutes on a gentle heat. Remove and place on a serving dish. Sprinkle with a finely chopped mixture of 1 clove of garlic, 2 tablespoons of *herbes de Provence* and 2–3 branches of fresh parsley and then drizzle with olive oil. Place herb side down in the pan and warm through again gently.

149

ENDIVES AU FOUR

Preheat the oven to 190°C/375°F/Gas Mark 5.

Bring a large saucepan of water to the boil and season with salt. For 4 people, add 12 small heads of chicory, washed and trimmed, and the juice of half a lemon. Bring back to boiling point and blanch the chicory for 4 minutes, then drain and leave to cool. Grease a gratin dish with some butter. Gently squeeze the chicory to extract as much moisture as possible. Pack tightly in one layer in the dish and season. Sprinkle over a pinch of sugar, sage and nutmeg. Dot with some butter and cover with foil. Bake in the oven for 15 minutes.

In a bowl mix 45g of grated Comté cheese with 3 tablespoons of crème fraîche and season with pepper. Take the dish out of the oven and turn the heat up to 200°C/400°F/Gas Mark 6. Spread the cream and cheese mixture over the chicory. Dot with a little more butter and bake without the foil for a further 10–15 minutes until the gratin is golden and sizzling.

I also prepare this dish for Stéphane, in which case I wrap each head of blanched chicory with a slice of cured ham, like Bayonne or Parma.

GRATIN D'AUBERGINES

For 6 people, wash, dry and cut the ends off 2kg of aubergines. Slice them lengthways into pieces approximately 1cm thick. Sauté in hot vegetable oil until golden on both sides. Drain and salt, and leave overnight if possible.

Preheat the oven to 180°C/350°F/Gas Mark 4.

In a casserole dish reduce 1kg of peeled, deseeded tomatoes with 5 crushed cloves of garlic, salt, pepper and

a little olive oil until you obtain a thick sauce. In an
ovenproof dish layer the aubergines, tomato mixture and
150g of grated Comté, making sure the cheese forms the
final layer. Cook for 1 1/2 hours. This gratin is excellent hot
or cold.

I felt different with Celia around, more confident and
adventurous, perhaps even a little wilful and daring. I don't
know why but I wanted Stéphane's parents to come to
England again so that I could show them the new me. It was
a childish, selfish need, but I genuinely did want them to
approve of and begin to like me, maybe even accept me and
my heritage and culture. I felt like a conspirator planning an
insidious campaign of devious action, plotting events to
manipulate their emotions, guide them down my chosen
path. Celia and I became co-conspirators, giving each other
knowing looks. This amused Celia enormously, but she was
the only one who really understood, who completely shared
my French anxieties and dilemmas. My devious scheme
involved christening Nina and using this ceremony as a
cunning excuse to get Stéphane's parents back over to
England, allowing me to try a little harder with our relationship. At the same time we could enjoy a rare family celebratory party. Now we had our very own restaurant we had
the perfect setting for such an occasion. Dauntless, self-
assured with my supportive ally near by, I felt more in
control and ready to handle my French in-laws.

Celia was a superb party organiser, helping me sustain the
French spirit of this sort of celebration. *Dragées*, pretty, light
pink icing-coated almonds, are essential accessories for
weddings, christenings and any other major celebration in
life, and Celia wanted lots of them so she could hand-make

our own voile parcels of these cute, pastel-coloured sweets. Oblivious to the fact that these seemingly innocent sugary treats were subject to a grading system in France – for those in the know, almonds that are thickly coated in icing sugar are considered of poor quality, and those thinly coated of a superior standard – I was destined to make a monumental *dragée* error. We spent hours cutting out delicate, rustling netting, fiddling patiently, mixing pale pink and white with minuscule silver balls, wrapped firmly in a voile bundle and tied securely with a double ribbon of pink and white. We were delighted with our efforts, lining them up on the table to check we had made just the right amount. Name tags were written and positioned against each gift, one for every guest attending the ceremony and party. Perfect.

Stéphane's parents accepted their invitation, and I instantly felt a sickening anguish, a tightening in my stomach – I so desperately wanted this to work. My scheme principally involved organising a perfectly executed feast and party after the church ceremony, intricately planned, no details overlooked, combining French food and music with English guests. I was hoping this time to demonstrate my new-found skills as French gastronomic expert and mother, making Stéphane's parents feel relaxed enough to leave us both in control and allow us the pleasure of over-seeing the entire event without their interference. All aspects of the expertly managed menu would be taken out of their hands: the professionally selected wine, sensitively positioned flowers, gifts, *dragées*, music – nothing would be missed. Getting my family members and friends together would also perhaps encourage mutual understanding, iron out our differences and allow us to develop a little more tolerance of other customs and ways of living.

My plans did not get off to the smooth start I would have liked as Celia greeted Stéphane's parents at the door, smiling knowingly, cheekily. I instantly recognised those familiar wary eyes, the look I had received in Corsica: suspicious in the face of someone foreign, unsure of her intentions, thrown by her unexpected replies to polite, insignificant questions. I suppose they could have coped admirably with this high-spirited, eccentric-looking young girl if she had been one of our students, just here to work in the shop, but Celia was an au pair, here to look after their precious only granddaughter. They seemed painfully ill at ease in trying to accept this relationship, particularly when Nina bounced innocently on to Celia's knee, squealing for her to play their favourite game rather than showering her expectant grandparents with warm affection. Jealousy, hurt and misunderstanding reigned almost immediately. My plan was crumbling before it had even got under way. I knew Celia would be upset if interrogated about private matters she did not want to share. Celia was our au pair, chosen by us, our decision was a good one. Before anyone had time to open their mouths I jumped to her defence. 'Celia's a great au pair and she loves your grandchild. Now shall we leave it at that for today? Dinner's ready. Let's eat.'

Stéphane had prepared a stunningly beautiful platter of *tomates farcies*, primly arranged with their cute hats like plump public schoolchildren, neatly divided into two sections, those with meat and those without. I joined Celia in a meat-free option, trying to dispel the earlier strain and introduce a little light-hearted banter. Stéphane is the specialist in this sort of chit-chat, and so we pleadingly stared across the table, willing him to lighten the atmosphere, soften the tone.

'What do you think of my smart *tomates*?' he enthused. 'You can have them with or without meat – either way they're easy to make. Thanks to Celia I've been discovering loads of great vegetarian ideas.'

Unwittingly he had offered grounds for another bout of anxious questioning. 'You mean you don't eat meat?' his parents said incredulously to Celia, unleashing an outpouring of dogmatic intolerance. Vegetarianism was an unhealthy, unnecessary, whimsical fad that Celia would inevitably grow out of, and was certainly not something to be encouraged.

I breathed deeply and slowly and began to clear the table, looking forward to the next day with its new beginnings.

Stéphane had dealt with the menu planning. For this big party we had decided to allow for a little luxury and indulgence, offering *foie gras de canard* to start followed by *gigot d'agneau* accompanied by a *gratin d'aubergines* with crisp roast potatoes smothered in goose fat and coated in coarse sea salt. There would be an exceptional *plateau de fromage*, including a rich selection of my favourite goat shapes and flavours, an impressive Pyrenean cow's-milk mountain cheese and Stéphane's king of cheeses, salty, blue Roquefort.

We treated ourselves to the other great French celebratory classic – a superb mountain of choux buns stuffed with *crème pâtissière*, cleverly stuck together with a cloying caramel glue drizzled down the sides of the bun pyramid. This is the magnificent *croquembouche* or *pièce montée*, highly impressive and divinely delicious – even I could happily manage a mouth-watering choux all to myself.

My aunts and uncles, cousins, sister and brother and their children noisily clambered down to the restaurant to enjoy the glorious feast. French classic love songs intermingled with nostalgic 1970s hits almost turned the atmosphere into that of a carnival as the children leapt exuberantly around the room, showing off in front of the glowing, merry adults. I was overcome with dizzy emotion, watching this noisy party in the very place where I had sat and fantasised about parties, dinners and large family gatherings. I never imagined we could so quickly and successfully transform this peeling, damp chamber into such a vibrant, warm haven.

I watched transfixed by the ebullient mood, suddenly struck by the bizarre realisation that this was the converse of my wedding day. Here were Stéphane's parents, the sole French representatives, surrounded by alien faces, floundering in a language they could not decipher, forced to communicate flamboyantly with facial gestures, grimaces, arm movements and mimes. They visibly relaxed. Maybe it was the champagne, but for the first time they looked as though they were enjoying themselves, letting down the barriers, not worrying about what others might think, far away from any potential family gossips.

Celia and I glanced at each other across the chattering tables and grinned, sensing victory – well, at least partial success, a step closer to my goal of harmony, understanding and tolerance.

A final glass of champagne was poured as Celia circulated among the tables with a beautiful round basket stuffed with our *dragée* voile parcels, making sure everyone received their lovingly made gift. Stéphane's mother did not hesitate to try one, crunching into it with frowning concentration and then discreetly whispering in Stéphane's distracted ear. 'Have you sent any *dragées* to family in France?'

Stéphane explained that we intended only to distribute the *dragées* to family attending the ceremony but that we had informed everyone of the christening with a little card.

Later we received a surprising collection of polite notes from family in France, thanking us for the stunning *dragée* parcels we had sent. I glared at Stéphane, bemused and then ferociously angry. His mother had taken it upon herself to deliver *dragée* parcels to French family members as if sent by Stéphane and me, without our consent or knowledge. I fumed for days, the harmony, peace and goodwill dissipated in minutes, my desire to understand and accept this inconsiderate behaviour lost in a turmoil of rage and despair. Eventually I calmed down and accepted that change would not happen here in England on the basis of brief shallow visits; it would have to take place in France, in Corsica, in front of the entire family. I was not just dealing with parents but an entire family structure of interconnected behaviour, impossible to untangle so that the individual components could be handled separately. I was disappointed, and over the next few days I became sullen and despondent, annoyed with myself for having naively believed that a spell could be cast over my French family to make everything miraculously all right. But at least the party had been a huge success. I had failed with the *dragée* episode, but what a brilliant atmosphere and superb menu, what perfectly executed food!

Shortly after the excitement of our party, Celia announced she would be leaving us to start a new course of studies back home in France. I was pleased that she had finally decided what she wanted to do, was planning her life and would be starting to train for a career. I never expected to keep Celia for long – she was young, and it would only be a matter of time before she found her feet and moved on. But I was intrigued, hungry to know more, greedily plying her for more information.

'So, what will you do? What's the course?' I pestered her.

I was surprised, because Celia appeared strangely unforthcoming. She did not seem to want to share her decision with me. I knew she had spent a couple of evenings in tears after a number of heated, impassioned telephone conversations with her mum, and there had been an increase in the number of letters received from France, but apart from these clues I had nothing else to help me figure out her sullen mood. I left her for a few days and waited until she was ready.

'I'm going to study English with Spanish and biology,' whispered Celia one evening.

'Well, that's great, but what about fashion, your love of textiles? What about your creative side? What happened to those ideas?' I asked, genuinely concerned.

Apparently she had been strongly advised to give fashion a miss as it was a field with very few prospects, perhaps best left as a hobby. As she was relying on Mum to pay for the course she really had no choice but to take her advice.

It was at times like these that the urge to protect and defend grew unbearably strong. Why could she not rebel now? This was the time to make her opinions known. Celia had learnt how to do this only on the outside, externally proclaiming who she was. Inside she wept silently and obeyed. She desperately wanted to start moving her life forward but simply could not get excited about going back to France to study something her heart was not in. There was no sensible advice I could give without sounding arrogant and disrespectful, but with a touch of flippancy I giggled and said, 'Whatever you do, Celia, don't start eating meat!'

We hugged each other for a long time, tears falling slowly

and poignantly down our distraught faces. There was nothing more to say. Celia was a soulmate, someone with whom I could share intimate feelings. She understood what it meant to be quashed, swallowed and trampled on, to wander away from the recommended path but be forced back again and again. For the first time I had an ally, a support to lift my spirits and give me hope, inspire me to make changes. I was still waiting for Stéphane to become my valiant knight, to stand alongside me and conquer my enemies, but I was resigning myself to the improbability of this only child suddenly being capable of radically changing the only relationship with his parents he had ever known. With Celia deciding to leave, a momentary twinge of panic overcame me, but strangely I knew she would return. I would not be alone. My ally could never truly abandon me. This departure was not like the others because Celia was now family, she belonged and had bonded with us all. While the other students had become friends they always disappeared, maybe writing one or two letters but then always gently floating away like twigs thrown from a bridge, bobbing and diving, still in view but after a cursory blink of the eye gone, out of focus then out of sight.

Life continued without Celia. I found an au pair replacement relatively easily – a pretty young Manchester girl who had studied French and wanted to improve her language skills by taking a year out before university. She was caring, hard-working and pleasant company, but lacked the spirit of my precious French friend.

My life seemed to have fallen into a pattern. As in the past, after any major traumas or changes I would reflect, withdraw and then exuberantly come to life again, rejuvenated and eager to move on, frightened to let the days wind down into a monotonous, dangerously stagnant tempo. This was one of those moments. I could feel the change in the air, as if someone were whispering soothing words of advice, some sort of supernatural guidance.

I jumped for joy when I discovered I was pregnant again. And this time I knew it would be a boy. I felt so desperately ill, tired and uncomfortable that it just had to be a boy. Celia was overjoyed by my news, her latest letter bubbling with excitement. By the time I reached the last paragraph I understood why there was such joy in every word she wrote. Celia was proposing to come back and au pair for my new baby and complete her final year of studies by correspondence. I think I must have hopped around the room like a demented rabbit for a very long time, twirling Nina round and round until we collapsed dazed, kissing and laughing until it hurt. Celia was coming back. *Vive les légumes.*

The first announcement Celia made on her return concerned a slight change to her diet. 'You'll be pleased to hear I now eat fish,' she declared, 'but don't worry, Louise, I still refuse to eat meat.'

And so we celebrated Celia's return with lots of protein-rich fish – parcels of cod steak wrapped *en papillote*, in foil, on a bed of fennel, with salt, pepper, some lemon juice and a dash of olive oil, baked in the oven for ten to twelve minutes. Served with plain boiled potatoes and sprinkled with fresh parsley, with maybe some *haricots verts* or broccoli, this was our quick ready meal.

Our anticipated baby boy, Pierre, was brought home to a proud papa, a bemused sister and an over-enthusiastic au pair. Our job-swapping experiment had worked extremely well in the past and now did so again as I doted peacefully on my newborn parcel in the comfort of home while Celia confidently managed both shop and customers. I relished the opportunity to play housewife and mother, baking and cooking, for once given the luxury of time to prepare meals for the workers. They would come home to the smells of garlic, cheesy *gratins*, my popular stews and soups, bubbling and simmering, filling the house with savoury scents. I loved preparing fish classics such as the *brandade de morue*, a French home favourite and again reminiscent of the English home classic fisherman's pie. The main difference lies in the seasoning – the French are experts at subtly embellishing a dish through the simple addition of herbs, spices and basic salt and pepper. *Brandade* is made by blending potatoes and salted cod; the mixture is then spiced with crushed garlic, nutmeg and olive oil and milk is stirred in until the whole is *onctueux* and homogeneous.

A year of fish and vegetables ensued, *en papillote* used often as a quick means of nourishment as our days became longer and harder with a demanding business and two young children. But it worked – the old routine was re-established.

It was not long, however, before Celia was on the move again, and this time I was relieved to hear that she had finally found the courage to follow her heart and talents. She was on her way to learning more about her treasured world of textiles, to immerse herself completely in fabrics, design and creativity, finally moving in the most appropriate direction for her future happiness. There were no tears this time. Our friendship was solid, true and long-lasting; we had grown in strength and confidence together, striving to find our places in this baffling French family circus, moving closer to understanding how to both enjoy and take control of the events in each other's lives. This time everyone was happy with her decision. I could let her go, confident that she could still find a way back.

She did not let me down. Every summer Celia would come to England and look after our house and business while we spent a few long, hot, leisurely months in Corsica. She will never go away – a sister to the children, a friend to Stéphane and me, an ally, a special French eccentric who continues to charm us all.

Our time with Celia influenced my dietary habits considerably, helping me discover just how flexible and adaptable food can be. We are guilty of introducing restrictions and intolerances into our diet, and the French are no different. They really do bewilder me at times. On the one hand I have experienced an open, experimental approach to eating, watching them accept the broadest range of ingredients – protein-rich snails, pig's trotters, frog's legs, cockerel's crests – and then almost abruptly, and with no logical explanation, they are capable of switching to a virulent intolerance to alternative ways of eating. Their hushed, derogatory whispering of the word vegetarian seems crazy, almost incomprehensible, because the French are among the best equipped to cope with a vegetable-rich diet. They have the most amazing selection of vegetables available all year round and imaginative methods for converting them into proud, stand-alone dishes. Watching and learning from friends, family and strangers is the greatest way of enriching a tired, routine world, as well as opening eyes to alternative ways with food. Students, au pair and the habits of old rural France inspired me to rethink my recipes, to look again at dishes I thought I knew, helping me to search for more freshness, seasonality and flavouring.

Certainly, I still regularly revive Celia's memory with colourful ratatouille combinations, delectable aubergines and a wide range of *gratin* creations, varying the seasoning, adding fresh herbs, playing with the formulas and relishing the unique flavours of Celia's *légumes*.

SIX

Les Soirées Découvertes

WE WERE ON a journey of discovery, and at times it was hard for us to appreciate exactly how far we had come since the days of our instinctive purchases in the Toulouse markets. We had discovered fine food combinations; we had sampled, tasted and digested, harvesting a bounty of culinary secrets, some traditional, others uncovered accidentally. Sometimes things could seem almost too obvious, and we would naively assume a prior familiarity where none existed.

'You know,' Stéphane said one day, 'it amazes me but there are lots of my customers who have never tried pungent Munster with a syrupy Gewürztraminer, or even a classic *foie gras* and Sauternes combination!'

Their compatibility seemed so transparent, so self-evident, that he was almost reluctant to advise people, not wishing to appear pompous and pedantic. Everyone recognises the superb combination of a well-made, mature Stilton with cloying sweet port, but this is possibly the one and only perfect food match almost anyone can quote. Stéphane became increasingly determined to let our food marriage guidance skills out into the open for the benefit of our attentive audience.

One evening we sat leisurely unwinding, our thoughts stirred by a rich, warming wine, nostalgically casting our minds back, reminding me of the night we had created French Living. I could almost predict that something extraordinary would happen. We were discussing partnerships, ideal matches, all those food harmonies that had left their mark, lingering still on our alert taste buds.

'I remember Monsieur in Paris encouraging me to try dried figs and walnuts,' I said. 'You know, I wasn't sure, but they go really well together.'

Stéphane joined in. 'Actually, if you're looking to really bring out the full potential of figs, I don't think you can beat reducing them down into a sweet, sticky jam to soften the blow of a powerful, salty cheese.'

Memories of flavours and scents continued to surface as we reminisced – rich Normandy Calvados with a tart, acidic apple; moist, smooth *foie gras* with a mouthful of succulent sweet wine; dark, bitter, cocoa-rich chocolate with a sturdy, oak-flavoured red wine.

There had to be something we could do to give our loyal, enthusiastic customers a chance to discover such melodious compatibility, to unveil for them this world of food surprises, awaken even further their burgeoning appetites. Stéphane suddenly recalled a regular customer, a local parish vicar from a neighbouring Nottinghamshire village, who had talked to him about organising a cheese and wine tasting evening to help raise money for the local church. Stéphane had muttered something about being rather busy, reluctant to accept such an English idea, such a quaint fund-raising concept. Cheese and wine tastings? So boring, so predictable, and not particularly French, sitting around, supping wine and picking at cheese. In France cheese is thoroughly integrated into a meal and not to be taken out of context, allowing the salty, tangy flavours to be a continu-ation of the savoury courses, easing the diner towards a sweet conclusion. If an excuse were needed to open a few bottles of wine then a gastronomic feast would be the answer – certainly not a cheese and wine party.

Stéphane pondered as he silently busied himself in the kitchen, chopping fiercely, lost in his thoughts. Now accus-tomed to his rituals and moods, his mannerisms and irrit-ability before he hits upon a new big idea, I prepared myself for his next great scheme.

'OK, we'll do a cheese and wine tasting for this vicar, but let's introduce a new angle, get everyone to activate their senses and really taste the cheese and wine,' he proclaimed later.

And so the idea for our very first outside cheese and wine tasting was launched. French Living would go on the road with a concept of tasting that would revolutionise the classic cheese and wine party. I don't think the vicar and his wife really had any idea of what lay ahead, believing this would be a civilised gathering in the draughty village hall for a few warming tipples and a couple of wedges of fine French cheese.

We decided to turn up at the hall early, anticipating the sort of sterile welcome we would receive – bright fluorescent strip lights harshly whitening the room, making us squint; easy-to-stack, inhospitable metallic furniture, reminding me of uncomfortable hours sitting in school exams. This was our venue for a night of French fun and discovery. We certainly had a lot to do before we would be ready to let in our unsuspecting audience. Our priority was to create a mood, soften the brash, cold atmosphere, and so we resorted to our quick and easy remedy. We plugged in the sound system, flooding the room with the strains of Brassens, Souchon, Montand and the outrageous Gainsbourg. Stéphane's mood instantly lightened whenever music was playing, and he burst into a powerful rendition of 'La Bohème', the ultra-cool Charles Aznavour classic, as he threw our old gingham cloths over the drab square tables. I rummaged nervously through the CDs, removing all those likely to shock, including 'un zest de citron' by Gainsbourg and his bohemian daughter – their infamous erotic panting might just distract the vicar and his friends from the serious business of tasting cheese. Highly amused by my prudish, uptight behaviour, Stéphane began to bellow out the rudest, most scandalous French songs he knew. Right on cue Mr Vicar opened the door to find out how we were getting on, whether we could find everything, politely advising us to turn down the music as the neighbours had a tendency to complain. I just hoped his French was rusty, even non-existent, because my embarrassment was plain to see. I reverted to my conforming, conservative childhood while Stéphane looked on, rebellious and nonchalant. I whispered a defensive excuse for my embarrassing husband. 'He's French, you know. A strange lot!'

The vicar had called me at the shop one day and talked about the sort of evening he had in mind. He envisaged creating a French café atmosphere, half-jokingly suggesting that maybe we should consider dressing Stéphane in beret and striped shirt, and push the French clichés to the maximum. I had mumbled something under my breath about not worrying, he could leave it all to us, we knew what we were doing. The vicar's preposterous suggestion was deliberately forgotten and certainly not passed on to my husband; I knew full well the sort of reaction it would have received. Clichés were not what French Living was about. Our reputation had been solidly established on pure, authentic honesty; we had always remained true to our origins and the spirit of Stéphane's homeland. As most French people do not go around wearing berets, striped shirts and onions around their neck, we were not going to begin brandishing this sort of sham nonsense for the delight of the vicar and his friends. Anyway, we had other French-style surprises in store for the evening's entertainment.

The lights were extinguished and replaced with gentle, flickering tea lights scattered on each table and a selection of mellow, soothing table lamps brought in from home. We put up posters of artistically positioned cheese, fields of deep lilac Provence lavender, elegant Parisian landmarks – an eclectic mix of French imagery to distract everyone from the stark reality of these four dreary walls.

Platters of cheese were carefully prepared and positioned precisely on the brasserie-style tables. Little flags proclaiming the names of each cheese drew the eye, and the platters were surrounded by sparkling, empty glasses. Wine bottles, uncorked, ready for action, waiting patiently to be poured, were lined up in military fashion along a typical village hall trestle table, usually reserved for the annual PTA raffle and village-get-together tombola prizes. Stéphane had also brought in a huge, cumbersome map of France, displaying the various wine regions, which he clumsily attached with Blu-Tack to a board in front of the brightly coloured, flag-strewn tables.

We were ready. I sneaked one last cheeky grin at Stéphane as we politely shook our guests' hands and waited for everyone to settle.

Stéphane launched into his welcoming speech, beginning an instructive and knowledgeable talk about wine, its regions and grape varieties. He then abruptly stopped and, as if he had just come up with the idea, declared that we would be adding a little spice and an element of rivalry to the evening's proceedings – there would be a competition, a sort of cheese and wine quiz. 'I want to see if your taste buds are working, if they're alive tonight,' he announced. 'You all thought you had come along for a quiet, relaxing evening with a glass of wine and a nibble of cheese. Well, I'm sorry, but you are going to have to work, concentrate and taste.'

People looked at each other, thinking that there had been a mistake or perhaps this was a French joke, laughing nervously under their breath, searching for clues. They looked petrified, like guilty schoolchildren who had not done their homework for the fifth consecutive weekend, whispering something about not knowing one cheese from another, happy to drink wine but certainly not able to distinguish one bottle from the next.

'Don't worry, this is just a game. An initiation into the world of perfect partners,' Stéphane reassured them, sensing their discomfort, not wanting to spoil their fun night out. On the contrary, we intended to make this an evening to remember.

We explained our cheese and wine puzzle. Each table had a selection of five cheeses, clearly named. Stéphane would talk a little about the wine they were about to taste and then a drop would be poured into everyone's glass. The idea was to make sure every guest tasted a mouthful of each cheese with every wine. Five different wines were to be tasted alongside five different cheeses, with the aim of working out the perfect cheese and wine partners. Which cheese and wine created a harmonious marriage of flavours? A prize of one of French Living's luxury champagne gift baskets sat regally on an elaborately decorated podium, glistening under a dramatic spotlight, successfully encouraging our intimidated and timorous crowd into determined slurping and concentrated savouring. We were entranced as the gentility of this village gathering was transformed into almost aggressive competitive fervour. It all made fascinating viewing. We gradually increased the volume of Yves Montand, allowing his crooning to be heard above the raised tones of excitable babble filling this temporarily French hall. Red, glowing faces were swaying to the mellow tempo of the music; even the vicar could not resist a swift waltz with his reluctant wife, weaving in and out of the tables, as the congregation stared and drunkenly giggled, bemused and intrigued by such unpredictable behaviour.

Most had drunk much more than they had intended in their resolute quest for victory. They listened entranced, however, like wide-eyed, expectant children, as the marriage partners were finally unveiled and the identity of the evening's cheese and wine hero declared.

On the cheeseboard we had arranged a pungent Munster, a fruity hard Comté, a creamy Bleu d'Auvergne, a sooty-lined Morbier and a nutty young goat's cheese, Selles sur

Cher. Five carefully selected wines stood alongside the cheese – an Alsace Gewürztraminer, a dry white Sauvignon Blanc, Cheverny, a light, fruity Gamay, Coteaux de Lyonnais, a Corbières, and a light red Sancerre.

There was only one competitor out of the entire fifty people present who had managed to replicate our recommended answer. This did not particularly surprise us as taste will always remain personal. There really is no right and wrong when dealing with food, but an exercise such as this can help refine our analysis of flavours, make the senses begin to operate harmoniously together and lead us to reconsider stilted preconceptions. Once the dazed and slightly tipsy party had absorbed the identities of the winning partners, they could not resist the urge to return to their platters and try again.

PERFECT PARTNERS

1. Munster partners Gewürztraminer, an easy combination thrown in to build confidence, particularly as Stéphane had mentioned in his opening speech how wine and cheese made in the same region tend to complement each other extremely well.
2. Comté cheese is delicious savoured with a dry white wine such as a Sauvignon Blanc. The acidity of a fresh white wine such as Cheverny cuts perfectly through the fruity greasiness of Comté cheese.
3. Bleu d'Auvergne, a smooth, creamy blue cheese, needs a light, fruity red wine that will not overpower or detract from the intense flavours of a blue cheese: Coteaux de Lyonnais.
4. Morbier is a semi-pressed cheese, fruity and full-

flavoured, and is superbly accompanied by a fruit-packed regional red such as Corbières.

5. Nutty, creamy and distinctive, Selles sur Cher is beautifully delicate, and when young, as this one was, it is best enjoyed with a wine from a nearby region to help bring out its character and charm – a red Sancerre.

We turned up the volume of the music. No one understood the lyrics, but it was enough to persuade the vicar, determined to savour this French cabaret soirée, to encourage his wife to dance again. Tasting continued until every last drop was poured and the last sliver of cheese had been scraped off the plates, the twirling and smooching to Aznavour's romantic favourites continuing until very late. Stéphane and I whispered our goodnights in the vicar's ear and contentedly crawled away from the merry, satiated party.

I had never experienced a cheese and wine do quite like it and given the notes of thanks and congratulations received by the vicar I don't think they had ever enjoyed a fundraising evening quite like this one, despite the painfully sore heads most appeared to suffer the next day.

The warmer, soothing days of summer were fast approaching, reminding me of our next trip to Corsica. This year the trip would unfortunately have to be cut short – a cursory dip in the salty sea and then back home to our tireless kitchens to cope with painful staffing shortages and awkward holiday rotations, the downside to owning and running your own business. Stéphane was in dark, moody Corsican mode, his brooding reminding me of his dear Corrèzean grandmother. He resented these commitments, which denied him the customary pleasure of a lazy month

COME TO THE TABLE

under the Corsican sun, but it just was not going to happen this year.

We prepared for our break anyway. They seemed to follow a predictable pattern every year – a relentless car journey through France, phoning a few family members and friends to invite ourselves over for a brief period of recuperation before reaching the coast and boarding our familiar yellow ferry over to our awaiting island. The children were high, screeching and leaping under my nose, doubling the time needed to pack a few bags as I struggled to avoid embarrassing packing mistakes, leaving behind essentials and causing catastrophe before the holiday has even begun.

Stéphane moaned incessantly, like an irritating dripping tap requiring attention when you don't have enough time or skill to get it fixed. I eventually snapped, losing my control alarmingly quickly, screeching almost violently to make myself heard and release the pent-up anger. 'Stop, the lot of you, and listen. I'm disappointed too. We're all annoyed about this holiday but let's try and make the most of it, brief though it may be. Why not try to bring back something of value, make it worthwhile?'

Stéphane looked at me amazed, silenced. He walked away, picking up the abandoned T-shirts he had thrown to the floor in childish rage, and then turned, calm and finally collected. 'Do you know, you're absolutely right. That's exactly what I intend to do.'

My angry outburst had a profound effect on Stéphane. After a few evenings of note-taking, telephone calls and computer-tapping, he had come up with a new proposal for the restaurant. Corsica was to be the inspiration for our first *soirées découvertes*, or discovery evenings, giving new impetus and purpose to the forthcoming holiday and initiating a concept that would spectacularly dazzle the taste buds of all our customers. The aim was to squeeze into the boot of our car all the flavours, scents and tastes of our magical island and create an inspirational menu of partners – sparkling combinations of food and wine that everyone should have the opportunity of experiencing at least once in their lifetime.

We came up with an uncomplicated format, to include an aperitif to complement the theme, an entrée, a *plat*, a cheese selection and a dessert, each with its unique wine companion selected to enhance it, and finally 100 per cent arabica espresso – a set menu with everyone appreciating the same food together (in fact all the guests would even arrive at the same time, as if it were an amicable dinner party at home).

I suppose this was never really going to be a family holiday like the others, being so brief – a fleeting visit to smile sweetly at family while Stéphane launched himself into his new project. I built sandcastles on the beach with the children. Sometimes a cousin or aunt would join me, but mainly I spent solitary days entertaining the children while Stéphane travelled the length and breadth of his island in search of exclusive, protected wine vintages. While Corsican wines are not spectacular, and cannot compete with those from more prestigious areas, there are a few select vineyards of worth, hidden gems, proud vintages that Stéphane was determined to track down. On his return we would sometimes all run down to the beach together so we could show him our sandy works of art, already crumbling under the encroaching sea. The children were used to these disappearing creations, calling it magic. It reminded them of the wiper boards they drew on, which could be miraculously erased at a stroke. The beach was the same, ending the day cleansed, ready for the next. We sat on the cooling early-evening sand while the children stoically rebuilt their dream castles and Stéphane recounted his latest eventful trip in search of authentic, quality island wine.

On one occasion he called upon the services of an old, island family friend, who just happened to be intimate friends with one of the best Muscat growers in Corsica, M. Jean-Noël Luigi, based on the Cap Corse. Rose was an essential tool in releasing this exclusive vintage, as Corsicans have a strange possessive tendency to cling on to their prized superior-quality wines. Produced in very small quantities, often just enough to supply island demand, treasured vintages would be jealously protected and reserved for very special customers, family and friends. This is why Stéphane's mission to return home with the very best of Corsican wine was never going to be straightforward, particularly as Rose had a pivotal role and she was not renowned for being the most cooperative and obliging of ladies.

Being a true cautious Corsican who would happily travel as far as the market town of Ile Rousse and back, and maybe if really pressed to the famous Napoleonic port of Bastia, but no farther, she was not at all keen on this hot, dusty trip. Fearing the unpredictable tourists who forced the islanders to drive irately, provoking accidents, Rose had to be prised out of her cluttered house. Stéphane charmed and mellowed this wiry old lady, flattering her ego, glorifying her role, transforming her into an exalted heroine to be adored and worshipped for years to come thanks to her self-less involvement in retrieving the valuable Muscat. This seemed to work. Rose eventually climbed into the car and their journey began.

She grumbled under her breath all the way there, reserving the courteous smiles and flirtatious charm for her close friend, Jean-Noël. Stéphane was not at all sure what they were whispering and giggling about, but he swiftly lifted a few cases of Muscat Clos Nicrosi 1996 into the boot of his car, slamming it firmly shut before anyone changed their mind or this cosy friendship unexpectedly turned sour.

Stéphane had the calmer company of his father for his journey to the south of the island, to Porto Vecchio, where he hoped to lay his hands on an excellent vintage of Oriu Rouge about which he had read stunning reports. Nothing was guaranteed with this trip. This time there were no helpful contacts, and there was the unpredictable peril of venturing on to southern soil. Stéphane would simply have to rely on his wise father, the persuasive islander who could always converse in Corsican to establish a bond, reassure the supplier of our origins and guarantee that his cherished bottles were moving into safe, appreciative hands.

A young assistant welcomed the weary travellers to the vineyard, treating them rather like any other tourist, letting them sample their recent production. 'I was hoping for something a little more structured,' Stéphane suggested hesitantly.

Stéphane's father made a few sneaky comments in Corsican which made the young boy giggle, and he ran off up a narrow staircase forbidden to the general public. A good ten minutes later he came back, holding a more promising, dusty carton of bottles. 'I found this case and believe this might be what you are looking for,' he said gleefully, obviously wanting to please and independently finalise a big sale.

Just at that moment, as if he had been shiftily overlooking the entire proceedings, the owner himself stepped forward, politely shaking hands, exchanging introductions and beaming proudly over the wines they had been tasting. He was a charming yet conceited man who was clearly uncertain about the intentions of these two crafty Northerners, and before long his smiles had turned into the most frightful scowl. 'What is this case doing here?' he demanded.

The poor young boy trembled, petrified at the outburst, realising he had committed an unforgivable crime.

Stéphane's father, always ready to come to the aid of victims, took control of the potentially embarrassing situation, casually drifted into Corsican and began to move the red-faced proprietor gracefully away from the offending box. Stéphane did not even dare ask his father what he had said as they made another quick getaway with the 1990 Oriu Rouge, racing around the hazardous mountain roads, seeking the familiarity of our half of the island, far from the unpredictable rage of southern Corsican wine producers.

I sat on the beach, running sand therapeutically through my fingers, listening in amusement to my husband's tales of his intrepid wine hunt, and wondered. 'I do hope your customers will appreciate this wine. They simply have no idea what you are putting yourself through for their pleasure and culinary education.'

Stéphane smiled, contented and fulfilled. I suppose it did not matter what they thought because my islander husband was secretly relishing every minute of his journey of discovery, distracted from the brevity of our stay and focusing on a greater good. 'Why don't we all climb up to the shepherd's refuge tomorrow and collect the cheese? The children would love it!' he exclaimed suddenly, jumping up, instinctively wiping the sand off his shorts.

And so we took the children on their first climb up the Corsican mountains, Pierre cosily strapped on to Stéphane's back and Nina clutching my hand tightly. Admittedly this was not a very high or complicated climb, but it was a real expedition for our two young adventurers. They smelt the herbal scent of the *maquis* and appreciated at first hand the magnitude of the rugged mountains hitherto only seen as distant objects from the bobbing sea, on top of which we were now sitting like kings, peering down at a faraway, shimmering blue haze.

The shepherd offered a toothless grin as we approached his primitive hut. He stayed here during the temperate months and moved down the mountain, herding his sheep into fenced areas, during the brief cold spell, anxiously waiting until the warm winds would blow them back up to their solitary grazing. He seemed genuinely pleased to have his isolation interrupted by this unusual group of visitors. We all sat around a musty table and tried a variety of cheeses, some very young in Corsican terms, some more mature and powerful. This was when Stéphane had the ingenious idea of letting our customers allow their taste to guide them through the maturing process of a Corsican cheese, and how we ended up transporting back down the mountains smelly rucksacks full of incredibly ripe ewe's-milk cheese, fresh from the shepherd's fromagerie. This had been a fascinating experience, testing the cheeses with our fingers, packing them away with the smell permeating our hands even through the greaseproof wrapping. Fortunately we stumbled across an ice-cold river towards the end of our descent. Desperate to wash away the odour of this cloyingly pungent cheese, we splashed playfully, rubbing our hands furiously together, eventually stripping off to swim in this invigorating, numbing bath. On our return, this was the menu we prepared for our first *soirée découverte*.

CORSE

Cap Corse
A rich, dark Corsican aperitif classic made with red wine, herbs and spices, served with ice and lemon.

Assiette de charcuterie Corse
Selection of cold cured meats and pâtés, home-produced in Corsica, served with condiments.

Calvi – Clos Reginu 'E Prove' Rosé 1996
Salmon-coloured and very bright rosé with the right balance and a long finish; excellent with the Corsican Charcuterie.

Langouste au Cognac
Rock lobster with light brandy, cream and shellfish sauce, served with saffron rice and baked tomato with a courgette mousse.

Patrimonio – Antoine Arena Blanc 1995
A bright, lively wine made with the native Malvasia grape, to accompany the Langouste.

Fromage de brebis
Shepherds' ewe's cheeses at different stages of maturation.

Porto Vecchio – Domaine Torraccia 'Oriu' Rouge 1990
Admirable wine, powerful and harmonious with intense smoky flavours of red fruit, made with the native Niellucciu grape. Perfect with the strong Corsican cheese.

Figues rôties au Muscat Corse
Fresh figs roasted with butter and Muscat wine served hot with fresh mint leaves.

Muscat du Cap Corse Clos Nicrosi 1996
A pale green patch of ground surrounded by wilderness is where this naturally sweet wine is made. Its reputation is immense, its taste magical. It is the perfect wine partner for our figs.

Coffee
100% arabica espresso.

Everyone was oblivious to the effort and determination involved in constructing this menu. And that's the way it should be – effortless, easy and fun. A date was set for a repeat performance, and incredibly bookings were taken before we had even decided on the theme or the food and wine.

Stéphane became the master of these special menus, spending hours planning, calling his suppliers to check on availability, relentlessly pushing them to be more dynamic and creative, urging them to be part of his unique vision.

After much debate we opted for Normandy as our next theme – a superb area, packed full of memories not only for me but also for many customers whose first French holiday experience had been a trip to nearby Normandy. Stéphane grew in confidence as he reconstructed his journeys, tempting his guests with delectable descriptions.

After Normandy we introduced our intrepid explorers to the culinary traditions of Alsace, the region's comical, copious *choucroute* still making me laugh after all these years. Our evening launched everyone into the Germanic atmosphere of the Alsace. We adapted the music accordingly as we brought on the glorious *choucroute*, with sauerkraut cabbage, potato, Strasbourg sausage and cuts of smoked and salted pork served with hot Dijon mustard. Even the cheese, full-bodied and pungent Munster, was served authentically Alsatian-style on a hot potato ring instead of bread.

The Basque region was also explored, testing Stéphane's research skills to the full. I discovered him furtively flicking through a copy of a Gault Millau restaurant guide, jotting down telephone numbers on a scrap of paper. He later confessed to calling restaurants in the Pays Basque and interrogating the head chefs, probing for typical regional specialities, tricking them into exposing their secrets, prolonging the conversation until he had extracted from them exactly how to prepare their unusual dishes. This was brilliant detective work and resulted in us offering *chipirons in su tinta*, young calamari tubes stuffed with seafood and served with a sauce that incorporates the ink. Always anxious to be as authentic as possible, Stéphane was determined to serve a true Basque dish, such as this interesting yet complicated delicacy. So popular had our discovery evenings now become that they had now been extended to two evenings rather than one to accommodate the increased demand. This meant stuffing an impressive 240 *encornets* with chopped tentacles, onions and herbs. Feeling rather guilty for suggesting this fiddly dish, Stéphane stepped into the kitchen to help the chefs out with the laborious stuffing, which had the unfortunate effect of leaving his fingers smelling strongly of fish, a smell that he could not shift for a good forty-eight hours. These were some of the joys of our discovery days; rummaging, researching and getting our fingers dirty to make sure our ideas worked.

Even the chefs relished the chance to show off their talents a little more, and we listened closely to their ideas. This was how our next scheme came about. With both chefs from the Berry area of France, eager to promote the specialities of their homeland, we created a menu dedicated to them. I thought this an admirable idea until the day I poked my head into the kitchen, rummaging around for chopped walnuts, which were urgently required in the café upstairs. I have never screamed so forcefully. Stéphane and the chefs could not help but respond, running in to find me paralysed, staring horrified at a sink full of squirming eels. The *matelote d'anguilles* is the only dish I cannot eat; the sight of those slimy snakes still brings my skin out in goose bumps.

We would soon exhaust the regions of France in our search for food and wine marital bliss, which only served to send Stéphane's imagination into overdrive in his quest for divine inspiration. I love the menus he produced, his irreverent explanations of their creation, his confident style, revealing just how far we had travelled. The most rewarding comment on one menu came from a discerning gentleman who announced to Stéphane that he had tasted the Roquefort quenelles and the sweet Muscat individually and disliked them both but had then decided to give them a second chance together and proclaimed the result triumphant, a heavenly combination.

Stéphane was particularly interested in wine, developing

a keen passion for grape varieties and *le terroir*, the timeless traditions of French winemaking, just as I had become absorbed in cheese-producing customs and folklore. There were so many stories, characters and traditions involved in both processes – of committed families, passionately driven for generations by their love of the product, enthusiastically working the land. On one occasion Stéphane invited me along to a grower's vineyard and cellars in Burgundy, hoping to transfer to me some of his passion for this silky, intoxicating liquid.

Walking behind two Frenchmen in a forbidding, dusty cellar, skipping in order to keep up with their authoritative strides, I sympathised with the timid cheese and wine congregation who had paled with panic at Stéphane's tasting test. I would soon have to sip some wine and comment. I knew more about wine than ever before; my nose had certainly sharpened, and I was now capable of distinguishing between major grape varieties and confidently able to identify key aromas. However, the subtleties of the descriptive language required, particularly in French, still filled me with unreasonable consternation.

After we had wandered up and down several aisles, the men's pace slowed and we came to a halt around one of the beautifully formed oak barrels, each of which was surrounded by sawdust and sported a conveniently positioned tap through which to siphon off some of the liquid inside. Three glasses appeared and a drop of light, raspberry-coloured wine was poured and solemnly handed over. Luckily I hesitated, cautious about making the first move, and watched our host slurp loudly, gargle at the front of his mouth, as if he were enjoying a satisfying rinse with a minty mouthwash, then spit the liquid out in a tidy jet impressively aimed between two barrels, where the wine was miraculously absorbed by the awaiting sawdust. It looked so easy, just like cleaning your teeth. I took a good mouthful and swilled it around uncomfortably, trying to overcome the natural urge to swallow. I eyed up my target, took aim and spat. Fortunately the two Frenchmen had turned to continue their procession among the rows of wooden vessels and missed my embarrassment as a wonderful deep burgundy stain permanently stamped my presence on one of the barrels with a marvellously contemporary abstract design. Not only had I left a mark on the barrel but the deep red spray had also splashed on my coat, leaving an impressive scattering of stains to remind me of my visit. I unceremoniously wiped my mouth with the back of my sleeve, giggled and skipped after the serious, wine-slurping professionals.

I decided to leave wine-tasting in Stéphane's capable hands, occasionally continuing to test my knowledge at home just for fun – blind-tasting a few bottles, selecting those I liked and those I didn't, helping me become more discerning when choosing a bottle when out shopping or at a restaurant.

Stéphane had been hunting again for wines to feature on his end-of-year menu. We had decided to hold a magnificent New Year's Eve party, *le réveillon*, to finish our year in style and share with our guests a genuine French celebratory feast. We wanted this to be a party, not just a dinner, and so we reduced the numbers invited in order to allow enough space for us to push the tables back and dance, providing one of those rare opportunities to let our hair down and welcome the new year in with carefree abandon. Stéphane was uneasy at the prospect of the atmosphere falling flat, with everyone glued to their seats, unwilling to join in. Restaurants are strange places — we could not choose our guests, we just took bookings, and so had no idea what sort of age mix and personalities we would attract. Planning a party with this level of uncertainty was always going to be risky. The food and wine we could control effortlessly, but the conviviality and ability of our guests to fuse harmoniously were scarily out of our hands.

This was our *réveillon* menu.

FORMAL WEAR – BALLROOM DANCERS WELCOME!

Planteur
Exotic cocktail from the French West Indies with white rum from Martinique, vanilla pod, cane syrup and exotic fruit juices.

Foie gras aux raisins pochés au Banyuls
Foie gras of duck on toast served with grapes poached in sweet red Banyuls wine.

Jurançon Moelleux – Jean-Bernard Larrieu 1999
One of our favourite wines with *foie gras*; we keep choosing it for its abundance of fruit without the heaviness of some sweet wines, and because it comes from a *foie gras*-producing region.

Assiette de langoustines à l'Armoricaine
Fresh langoustines with *sauce Armoricaine*.

Bergerac Blanc – Luc de Conti 2000

Creamy Sémillon matured on the lees (this means the wine has been allowed to stay in barrels for between a few months to up to 18 months). It has a wonderful richness in texture and is loaded with ripe fruit and exotic notes. Perfect with langoustines.

Fricassée de faisan au Calvados

Pheasant fricassée with Calvados sauce.

OR

Filet de chevreuil Grand Veneur

Fillet of venison cooked pink with a peppered gamey redcurrant sauce.

Both dishes served with *pommes dauphines* and glazed vegetables.

Crozes Hermitage – Albert Belle 1997

Without doubt a leading grower in the *appellation*. Pure Syrah matured for twelve months in old oak barrels, this wine has aromas of warm tar and wood smoke, then a palate that explodes into a crescendo of blackcurrants, peppered plums and prunes. Delicious served with game.

Assiette de fromages

Plate of unpasteurised farmhouse French cheeses served with bread and dressed salad.

Bordeaux – Château Deville 1998
A juicy claret chosen deliberately for its approachability and easy tannins though retaining typical Bordeaux flavours. Perfect for our cheese board.

Farandole de desserts festifs
Trio of traditional Christmas hazelnut *bûche*, white chocolate *bavarois* and orange *tarte tatin* with a Cointreau sauce.

Champagne – Jules Féraud
The famous cooperative from Vincelles delivers a consistently flavoursome blend of Pinot Meunier (80%), Pinot Noir (10%) and Chardonnay (10%).

Midnight champagne top-up

The Christmas tree glistened poignantly in the corner, squeezed in on my insistence, Stéphane complaining about the lack of space and the needles dropping with alarming regularity in the unnatural heat of the restaurant. He was fiddling with the music, winding and rewinding his tailor-made cassette, checking the timing – one hour of dancing until the midnight countdown followed by another hour of dancing before the lights were dimmed, the music silenced and taxis called. 'It'll be fine. After all that wine of course they'll dance!' I reassured him as he gave me one of his very French frowns.

I poked my head into the kitchen. The usual combination of confident calm and industriousness reassured me and lifted my spirits. I was confident that the cuisine would dazzle even if our attempts to make the party go with a swing might fail.

Our guests more than performed that evening, so much so that we had difficulty encouraging them to go home. Watching this animated scene of strangers uniting, laughing and celebrating, filled me with hope; the monumental effort and long, long hours all seemed to evaporate. Weeks of ovens breaking down, light bulbs blowing, the wrong wine being delivered, coffee machines leaking – the pressure had often been intense. Winding down in front of a collection of extremely contented individuals is an indescribable perk of this tough, wearing job. One day we will tire of the strain, but for now a warm glow of friendship and goodwill fills our souls.

I began to believe in myself and my cooking again, cosily sharing the kitchen at home with Stéphane, leaning dangerously close over his bubbling, spitting concoctions, feeling my cheeks redden and glow. I watched him intently, remembering those days in Toulouse when I had been bewitched by such raw natural talent. He had developed into a more self-assured cook, creating our meals after a long day at work effortlessly, quickly, spontaneously. Even our fridge looked different. Lined up inside the door was a selection of tiny plastic tubs with lids, the kind I used for storing home-made mushy baby food. 'What do you keep in those baby pots?' I asked.

'In this one I have ready-to-use roux and then in here I've peeled and chopped some garlic and covered it in oil so you don't waste time fiddling with smelly garlic when you need it straight away,' he told me.

Roux, a blend of melted butter and flour, cooked lightly and, as Stéphane had demonstrated, kept in the fridge in solid form until needed, is the starting point for a number of French classic sauces that all originate from this base.

ROUX

First make a roux by heating a saucepan over a moderate heat.

Add 55g of unsalted butter, reduce the heat and wait until the butter has completely melted.

Add 55g of plain flour and stir vigorously with a whisk or wooden spoon. Stir constantly over a low heat for 1–2 minutes until the mixture is smooth, without letting it colour.

Put the mixture into a small plastic container and keep in the fridge. (This would make a pint of *béchamel* if you added a pint (575ml) of milk.)

By adding milk you make a *béchamel*, essential for creamy sauces and adding richness to pasta dishes such as lasagne. A great *gratin* sauce is *Mornay*, made by simply adding grated Comté cheese to the *béchamel*. Pour over cauliflower or even broccoli and pop under the grill until golden and you have an instant warming dish made in minutes. Add some *concentre du tomate* and a little greyfish butter and you then have *Nantua*, a classic fish sauce, and by adding crème fraîche you produce an even richer *onctueuse* sauce, used mainly for special occasions. Stéphane would complain if I used the roux too often, concerned about his waistline, forcing me to fall back on the simple island flavourings of olive oil, lemon and herbs. Roux and the sauces it inspires are brilliant when used sparingly, and so I continue to rely on its magic to help liven up vegetables or a solitary fish dish.

Our chef was cool, quietly spoken and extremely accommodating. Past experience had left its mark, making me hesitate before stepping into his territory. The kitchen is a chef's confined work-space and it should be respected. If ever I borrowed a knife from Chef's impressive collection, conveniently displayed on the wall, it would always be returned in exactly the same place. Work surfaces would be wiped down methodically after croissant-baking, all evidence removed, every last crumb disposed of.

I gradually stayed longer in the kitchen, not feeling unwanted, having earned respect and developed an unspoken mutual understanding. I was often rewarded with a smile, virtually unheard of in the macho kitchen environment, where coolness prevails. Animated discussion is seldom heard in this stark white environment as the instructions required are delivered concisely, without wasted vocabulary or unnecessarily elaborate language. I was worming my way in, seeking to lay my hands on valuable information. Chef was innocently unaware of my intentions but still managed to make my quest frustrating. A chef's work is an instinctive process that evolves over time, finally reaching a peak of optimum efficiency. By invading his world with my irritating questions I was asking him to think about every action and ingredient, to break his techniques down into individual steps.

I would hover at delivery time, watching Chef squeeze, smell and check his raw ingredients. It was the meat which caught my eye – the various cuts and joints separated and positioned ready for preparatory work. 'What on earth is thick skirt?' I asked, looking bemused at the tatty invoice sitting on top of the delivery. Maybe I had misread it, but this was a piece of meat that did not even look familiar.

'It's *onglet*,' was the reply, delivered with the succinctness I had now become accustomed to. I decided to give the chef a rest and look for more willing elucidation from Stéphane.

He brought out an old-fashioned 1960s-style book all about meat and butchers, with stilted photographs of chunky, pale-faced men in starched white coats proudly holding beautifully prepared joints, and an impressive diagram of a cow, highlighting the cuts, individually labelled in French with their technical names. Stéphane pointed out that, although the book might seem ridiculous, it was an essential bible for our chef when ordering meat. Apparently the French section a cow into edible joints in a very different way to English butchers. *Onglet*, for example, comes from an area adjoining that from which fillet steak is cut, and the French frequently cook it as a tender alternative to fillet or sirloin; surprisingly, I learned, the English throw this section away, along with a number of other pieces used by the French, such as *bavette*, which is minced or cubed for slow stewing. This beautifully tender and tasty morsel is even classed as offal in England, relegated to the lowest status possible, a sumptuous delicacy carelessly discarded. I felt a sense of liberation in bringing this gorgeous slab of flesh to its rightful place on our plates. We have to order it specially to make sure the abattoir keeps it whole rather than throwing it into the mincing machine. It needs to be cooked rare, as overcooking makes it tough. Scored along the length of its visible fibres to stop it from shrinking, flash-fried in the pan, red inside with pink juices flowing, it is a delectable French classic, illogically deprived of its bona fide status as 'steak' in the English butcher's shop.

ONGLET À L'ÉCHALOTE

This is a classic method of preparing *onglet* steak.

For 2 people, chop 2 shallots finely and sauté in rapeseed oil over a very gentle heat until soft.

Add 300ml of *jus de veau* (veal stock) to the softened shallots, reduce and thicken with roux. (You can buy *jus de veau* in powder form but if you can't get hold of it then beef stock would do.) Keep the sauce warm until the steaks are cooked.

Heat a frying pan and then add a mix of rapeseed oil and butter. The steaks should be prepared to half an inch of thickness, scored along the fibres and then seasoned with salt. Add them to the hot pan. Reduce the heat a little and cook for 1 minute on each side to ensure they are rare and do not become rubbery and tough.

A simple alternative is *steak au poivre vert*. Using a pestle and mortar, crush 1 tablespoon of green peppercorns and add to stock thickened with roux. Add a teaspoon of brandy and 2 teaspoons of Madeira. Whisk well before pouring over the cooked steaks.

Chef got used to having me around, quietly observing, occasionally handing over a spoon to let me taste something. A few words were sporadically exchanged – bare, courteous explanations – but mainly I learnt with my eyes and used Stéphane for clarification, to put flesh on the bones when more depth was needed. Washing salad leaves or scraping mussels helped me fit in and appear less conspicuous as I peered over my shoulder, secretly observing his techniques. I swiftly deduced that chefs are the most amazing housekeepers, meticulously tidy, manically clean and kings of recycling. I was captivated by our chef's stringent control of ingredients and avoidance of waste, and was transported back to Toulouse, my red-bricked city of liberated cuisine and carefree wandering brought back to life by this slick, dextrous professional. He did not always follow the recipe book to the letter – he would blend available ingredients to develop his own versions of the classics. These would be the daily *plat du jour*. I almost jumped for joy to discover that this was the essence of French cuisine not only at home but also in the professional kitchen – a loosening of the spirit and a focus on flavour, apt combinations and seasoning, taking a favourite dish and making it your own. Classics were the exclusive basis of main menu items, but for the daily lunchtime special there was room for creativity and modification.

I always left during the actual service, focusing on the most important aspect of kitchen activity – the *mise en place*, literally the 'putting in place'. Chef regularly reiterated how vital a thorough *mise en place* was. Without it there is no service – customers will suffer long delays and mistakes can very easily slip in. Very simply it involves getting everything ready – vegetables washed, chopped and parboiled, meat cut and tenderised, plate decorations of chopped parsley, pepper or sliced lemon all close to hand. This sounds obvious, but it is often where I go wrong whenever we are invaded by a large gathering of guests. Chef prepares potatoes, rice and vegetables by pre-cooking them, not quite to completion, leaving them under a gushing cold tap to halt the cooking process. During service he will simply have a pan of salted boiling water at the ready in which to dip the vegetables and finish the cooking, able then to serve them al dente and, most importantly, perfectly hot. This is a basic technique that everyone could benefit from to overcome the soggy, overcooked and tepid vegetable scenario that dinner parties always seem to encourage. Sauces are prepared well in advance, ready to be warmed through and served, with appropriate pans, serving dishes and platters at the ready. Another simple error we are all guilty of committing is using the incorrect-sized utensil for the job. You cannot hope to serve up enticing golden-brown morsels of meat by cramming it all into one small pan. Compressed, it will sweat water and end up pale and bland, tasty enough perhaps but lacking colour and attractively crisp dark edges.

I was starting to feel like a professional, keeping an impressive *mise en place* in my fridge to ensure a swift service for the children's dinner. They certainly did not complain, pleasantly surprised by Mum's efficiency.

I suppose that, as restaurant owners, we were both different now – absorbed in good food and special wines, engrossed in continual seasonal menu planning. One Sunday I lifted my head from the weekend papers, uneasy, suddenly aware of a subtle shift in our lives. Sitting in front of an empty coffee cup, the reason for my anxiety struck me. 'We used to spend so much time at Jane and Phil's house,' I said to Stéphane. 'I wonder what happened to those invitations. Why do you think we're not invited any more?'

'I don't know, but if you think about it your sister doesn't invite us any more either,' he replied. We both lapsed into pensive silence.

Mum came to our rescue, tactfully helping me to identify the cause of our social alienation. One evening she engaged me in an intimate conversation that revealed why close family and friends no longer invited us to their homes. Apparently they were irrationally apprehensive about preparing food for us, paralysed by our new-found competence, fearing rejection and criticism. I could not help but laugh – the thought of me being perceived as some sort of professional chef and culinary guru really was too much. Stéphane may have acquired a little more knowledge than most, but he would continue to derive the most pleasure from simple home-cooked family meals. I still counted the days until we would be sitting under the olive trees enjoying ripe, juicy tomatoes and basil, a hearty vegetable soup or a classic garlicky roast. It was strange that this anxiety did not spread to our French family but remained an exclusively English phenomenon. In France nobody seemed to mind serving last night's leftovers, recycled and reheated, often tasting better than they had the night before. Only in England did we experience a paralysing desire to impress and dazzle.

We were both determined to resolve this absurd dilemma. We began to arrange a series of invitations to our home designed to reassure our family and friends, suppressing any signs of sophistication, offering pure simplicity and an opportunity primarily to enjoy good company with a tasty meal – plenty of wine, no dazzle, no show, and no elaborate sauces.

One of these evenings involved a trip to the best fish and chip shop in town, keeping the parcels warm, slicing a few lemons, seasoning the chips. A tomato, olive oil and basil mix concocted by Stéphane in which to dip the chunky fries, the chilled Pinot Blanc removed from the fridge, and our feast was ready.

Another friendly meal of pasta with pesto sauce thoroughly coating each pasta shape caused a few bewildered glances. 'Eat up! This is it!' boomed Stéphane, delighted by the astonished faces.

Cold meat platters, garnished with gherkins and olives and followed by cheese, surprised another group of friends, in whom I detected a hint of disappointment; perhaps they had anticipated a free restaurant-standard meal.

For some the disappointment lingered and invitations still did not follow; with others, our real friends, we can now giggle over this period of estrangement, and the invitations have started up again. Very often we all prefer to gather in the kitchen, helping with the *mise en place*, informally enjoying the night, certainly not assessing the food for future reference.

We were now an established, recognised couple, running our personally tailored business, suited to our needs, fulfilling our hopes and dreams and, luckily for us, also appealing to a wider audience. The only disappointment lay in my relationship with France. I was still suffering deeply from my failure to develop a bond with this family, to secure acceptance, achieve a sense of belonging and attachment. I wanted to shout out my worth, show them I could be a real islander, I could fit in. I had learnt so much and come so far – surely they could give me a chance. Their visits to England had dwindled, removing any opportunity to unveil my understanding of their regions and traditions. Our visits to France were reduced to business trips or rare mini-breaks with the children (who brought an additional dimension to the problem) during school holidays. I resolved to address some of the issues during our next visit to Corsica, a month of healthy island living, plenty of time in which to air my concerns, to sort out this niggling personal business once and for all.

SEVEN

Picnics and Parties

AS WE INCHED laboriously closer, the children were tugging excitedly at our loose cotton trousers, pleading with us to pick them up and let them see. I loved the island like this, so close and yet far enough away just to sense it, feel the goodness of its *maquis*, without any of the heaviness – the sea separating us from its tight, constricting blanket, which lay brooding, ready to envelop our extended family unit. On previous visits we had shared the family home and experienced unbearable, claustrophobic tension as our active young children turned the house upside down, leaving it in sandy chaos. In some ways I felt stronger in their reassuring company, a welcome diversion from island gossip and traditions. We could escape together, fritter away the days at the beach without the worry of impending kitchen duties. I could lose myself in their care – a worthy, justified occupation which didn't leave me open to criticism. But we desperately needed more space in which to experience this glorious land together as a family. For the first time we deliberately caused upset to make sure we could experience a proper family holiday by breaking free, leaving the sacred family base.

This trip certainly felt different from the others now that the children were here and our own rented villa awaited. It was like a new beginning. It was my opportunity to bring change to this island, to shine a liberal light over these people, who were an integral part of my life, not likely to disappear. They deserved a second chance. Everyone had moved on, particularly Stéphane and I, who were coming back to the island a family, a team, brimming with culinary confidence.

I lifted Pierre up high over the deck rail, letting him feel the sea spray. 'Look, can you see those mountains? We're going to climb them all, swim in their rivers, gather their fruit and stroke the wild animals. This will be the best holiday ever.'

Our villa was superb – a spacious tiled haven with a wide-angled view over the still, glistening sea. The outdoor terrace, protected by an exotic bamboo shelter, looked down over this spectacular panorama in which, on a clear, cloudless day, the outline of the Cap Corse hazily unravelled. A little path led away from the long terrace table to a hand-built barbecue, making sure you remained transfixed by the open sea, and were not forced to hide away in the kitchen.

The villa was situated a few minutes' drive away from the village on a stretch of private land reserved for the building of select, beautifully landscaped residences. Within this hidden enclave of gorgeous property lay a couple of small protected beaches, one of which became a useful option when the island winds got up and white-backed *moutons* galloped out at sea – the telltale sign of dangerous, powerful waves. This particular beach was so positioned that the sea here was blissfully calm, its surface only gently disturbed by ripples, allowing us from our sanctuary to admire the frothy mass whipped up by the angry island wind.

One of Stéphane's aunties lived not far away and kindly offered to babysit, suddenly making me think that yes, maybe for the first time we could go out, eat at a restaurant, not be tied exclusively to family meals, dinner invitations and obligatory lunches. I gave a liberated squeal of joy and joined in the children's exuberance, running around the garden, exploring what would be our home for the next few weeks. Stéphane unwittingly put a damper on my spontaneous enthusiasm. 'By the way, tomorrow we're having lunch at my parents'. They've invited a few people round to welcome us back.'

It was starting again. I sensed myself on a mountain slope, desperately trying to retain my footing, abruptly realising its violent steepness. It might be steep but I was determined to find my way down gracefully, assertively, without stumbling, keeping a tight rein, totally in control. 'OK, that's fine. But let's get one thing straight. We decide when the next dinners will take place. We will organise all remaining invitations,' I said, clutching the airy beach ball, keeping it firmly within my grasp, unable to bounce it away.

Babbò and Mina. These are the Corsican names for grandma and grandpa, and this is how they had chosen to be called by the children. Babbò had been out on one of his intimate fishing adventures with his closest pal and was beaming proudly as we climbed the steps to the house, overtly pleased to see his grandchildren and share his freshly caught plunder. It had been such a lucrative trip that a bubbling pot of fish soup had been prepared, with plenty of fish like *rougets, pageots* and *pagres* to spare, washed and wrapped, ready for us to take home. It was certainly a triumphant haul, attractive, glistening Mediterranean fish making a pleasant change from the vicious sea snakes that usually made up a major part of his catch, much to Mina's despair. One day, after the third consecutive trip had brought nothing but *congres* and *murènes*, ugly, slimy sea eels, Mina declared that enough was enough. No more eels. She took out of her pocket a tiny sign with the words *'Congres et murènes s'abstenir'* carved roughly into the wood.

'Attach this to your hook and hopefully those beastly creatures will take heed,' she suggested jokingly.

Once we were seated around their table, within easy reach, they could begin to weave the ensnaring web of family commitments. 'You will make sure you take the children to see *Tata* Francesca. She's back from the mainland now and she will get better much quicker if you visit soon,' implored Mina, avoiding my gaze, aware of my critical eye. She knew how I felt about these imposed visits, parties and dinners, and yet she just could not help herself, fearing embarrassment and social scandal if we did not conform to recommended orders.

While we remained trapped within their territory, the irritating island ways and the domineering whispering would continue. I had promised myself and the children a new start and so I resolved there and then to test my confidence and unleash the newly polished, organised, professional entertainer. The rehearsals were over; let the performance begin.

Now that he had tasted the delectable freedom of our own space, absorbing the beauty of his island with fresh, relaxed eyes, Stéphane was more willing to cooperate and make changes. Without the constant burden of family commitments weighing him down, he remained the man he was back in England. This time there were no macho transformations; shopping, cooking, bathing – we continued working together as a united team. He relinquished the male ritual of the *boules* club, sometimes begrudgingly, but finding solace in a custard-thick Ricard once the rhythmic breathing of innocent slumber blessed the house.

We wanted to welcome family and guests – they could not be ignored – but we would do this on our terms, leaving time for us to be together, a foursome, getting to know each other away from the pressures of work.

Thus we turned the indispensable French tradition of the aperitif in our favour. Rather than allocating an entire evening to family dining, we invited aunts, uncles and cousins to our terrace just for aperitifs after an afternoon at the beach. After a quick shower to wash away the crusty salt and the day's sand, a mismatching collection of glasses and clanking bottles were thrown on to a tray ready for a refreshing drink before we jovially split up and went our separate ways for dinner. The children could play happily, not trapped for hours at a table.

I remember teasing Stéphane over his choice of drinks, because he would always insist on bringing out the whisky and port bottles. 'They're after-dinner drinks. You cannot possibly offer these just before eating!' But numerous aperitifs enjoyed in a variety of French homes and circumstances have proved the opposite as I have become increasingly accustomed to the sight of these late evening alcoholic beverages just before dinner.

We made cute canapés with thinly sliced rounds of baguette spread liberally with moist, spicy pork *rillettes*, decorated simply with a *rondelle* of gherkin, or thin slices of peppery Corsican *saucisson* and lean, chewy *lonzu* laid flat on the buttered bread. Others were covered with an aromatic pesto spread and embellished with an oven-dried tomato. We scoured the markets for the most appetising olives, tasting and deliberating before making a selection of four or five tubs, some floating in herbs, others spiced with chillies and peppers. Kept in the fridge, olives were always available for our increasingly popular pre-dinner soirées.

PISSALADIÈRE

When we had time, Stéphane enjoyed rustling up this savoury cross between an onion tart and a pizza, delicious cut into mini-squares – perfect aperitif fare.

This can be made with either shortcrust pastry or, for a more authentic pizza flavour, with a yeast pastry. This recipe would serve about 8 people.

To make your yeast pastry, place 250g of plain flour in the bowl of an electric mixer or food processor (preferably one with a dough hook). Dissolve 15g (3 teaspoons) of fresh yeast in 125g of lukewarm water; blend and pour into the bowl with the flour in. Add 3 tablespoons of olive oil, a pinch of salt and mix until the dough is well blended and begins to leave the sides of the bowl wall to cling to the dough hook. Remove from the mixer, knead into a ball on a floured surface, then transfer to an oiled bowl; cover and leave to prove (rise) for 1 hour.

Preheat the oven to 220°C/425°F/Gas Mark 7.

Heat 100ml of olive oil in a pan and briefly sauté 1kg of chopped onions. When the onions are well greased but not brown, add 3 sprigs of fresh thyme. Reduce the heat and cook the onions slowly, stirring occasionally, for about 40 minutes or until completely softened. Roll the pastry into a circular disc about 28cm in diameter or into a large rectangle depending on the shape of your baking tray. (Note: if baking in a large rectangular baking tray – 25cm x 30cm – then use 2kg of onions and increase number of anchovies and olives accordingly). Place the pastry on to the baking tray. Season the onion, salting only lightly because you will be adding anchovies. Spread the onion over the pastry base. Arrange approximately 12 anchovies in a criss-cross pattern on the top and dot with 15–20 Niçoise olives. Bake in the oven for 30–35 minutes. The beauty of this nibble is that it can be enjoyed hot, warm or cold.

Some days were gloriously lazy as we dipped in and out of the sea, lounging on the sand, engrossed in books, clutching well-thumbed, soggy pages, wandering the length of the beach, gazing entranced at every grain of sand, hoping for a glistening shell to sparkle, begging to be picked up. As the sun's rays became less hostile, we resisted the steep climb back up to the house. This was the perfect time to soak in the beauty of this island. We felt like castaways, alone with our sand and sea, the crowds long gone, preferring the intense midday sun in which to top up their tans. I loved this time, no longer worrying about protecting the children's pale, fragile skin, the sun disappearing fast but its warmth still leisurely lingering. Stéphane called out to our screaming, soaking children, coaxing them back to get dry, conscious of the looming aperitif party needing our attention. I sulked, unwilling to drag myself away from the cool, sensual sand. 'Just five more minutes,' I begged, desperate to prolong the glowing, contented solace.

Stéphane decided to go back and start getting things ready. He said he would come and fetch us once he was organised.

My bold island man surprised and enchanted me that evening, filling me with renewed energy with which to cope with his tenacious family. He appeared back at the beach, breathless, loaded down with a packed, cumbersome icebox, my tatty market basket full of plastic tubs and pots, lanterns, cushions, folded tables, linen napkins and chequered cotton cloths. He threw down a couple of downy shawls and old comfy jumpers for the children and excitedly declared that tonight's aperitifs would be served here on the beach.

We lit the mosquito spiral, protected the flickering candles in empty jam jars, arranged the nibbles, buried the bottles safely in the sand, and calmly waited for our guests. They looked horrified, outraged to have been made to trek down to the beach at this hour. This was breaking the rules, too informal, too exposed. This, however, was just what I wanted to see – islanders back in touch with their island, close to its beauty, letting the regular tempo of the sea, its hypnotic ebb and flow, and the caressing sand work their peculiar magic. They so often enclosed themselves tight in their homes, fearing the invasion of tourists and noise, peering out from behind salt-damaged shutters, unwilling to share. The tourists had now long gone – with darkness descending they would begin to invade the restaurants and bars, bringing the sleepy village to life. We were safe, the beach was empty, and we could reclaim our territory, savour its salty splendour.

Eventually my Corsican guests loosened up and listened, entranced by my frank discussions with the children. I struggle with these cloistered island people because of their difficulty in expressing emotion, their reluctance to speak honestly about events and problems for fear of gossip, judgement and criticism. Children are frequently told half-truths or even inappropriate lies, inaccurate stories to keep them quiet, safe from sober adult responsibilities. Stéphane has never been able to tell me how his grandfather died. He was never told as a young boy, and to this day he still does not know.

As we drank and picked politely at enticing morsels under the flickering light, faces shimmered and smiled, children squealed and squawked like greedy young birds, everybody was visibly relaxed. I sat facing this familiar group, my husband at my side, our arms securely entwined like those of young lovers, as one. Out in the open air, with no constraining walls, customs or traditions, no gender divides to harm us, we silently proclaimed our way, a new start.

APÉRITIFS À LA PLAGE

These are the simple aperitifs we enjoyed that night at the beach.

Ricard
Stéphane's favourite aniseed drink.

Kir
Chilled dry white wine with *crème de mûre* (blackberry liqueur), but it can also be served with *crème de cassis* (blackcurrant).

Olives Niçoises
These are my favourite black olives, rich and intense, greasy and oily, soaked in aromatic herbs such as thyme and rosemary.

Charcuterie Corse
A Corsican aperitif would not be complete without a few slices of *saucisson* and lean, chewy *lonzu* ham.

Tranches de pain grillées à la tapenade
Tapenade is a spread made by crushing together black olives, anchovy fillets and capers with olive oil, a little lemon juice and pepper.

Fromage blanc aux herbes
Mix together *fromage blanc*, crème fraîche, olive oil, a little white wine vinegar, salt and pepper. Snip some parsley, tarragon, chives, mint and chervil and mix well into the *fromage blanc* and cream. Adjust the seasoning and chill.

Batonnets de légumes crus du jardin
Sticks of raw fresh vegetables such as carrots, cucumber and celery.

We loved to bring out the champagne whenever there was a birthday or anniversary, or simply because we fancied a glass of champagne. This is my favourite aperitif; I prefer to indulge in a bubbly, tickling glass of this refreshing delicacy before rather than after eating. The French, however, do love to luxuriate in a glass of champagne at the end of a cele-bratory meal with dessert or a festive cake, a habit that always saddens me, as I know I will struggle to finish even a glass after a copious, rich meal. Consequently, whenever champagne is required, I will endeavour to pop the cork while tummies are still empty, accentuating the luxury of this special drink by serving rolls of smoked salmon, freshly dribbled with lemon juice, canapés of jet-black lump fish, or tiny smudges of easy-to-spread duck *foie gras*.

This year I was in luck; lots of champagne was in store thanks to an unexpected wedding invitation. Marie-Paule was the youngest sister of Stéphane's two best friends from his years growing up in Paris, from a Corsican family who coincidently happened to live in the neighbouring Parisian apartment to the Luiggis'. She was to be married in her home village, high up in the stunning mountains behind the ancient port of Bastia. Tragically, one week before the wedding, we heard that her uncle, her mother's brother, had died. He had been diagnosed with cancer but nobody had prepared them for such a rapid deterioration. The family was in disarray, now scurrying around to organise a funeral in the very same church where just a few days previously they had been joyfully planning a wedding. In Corsica these matters are dealt with swiftly out of cruel necessity. There is no sophisticated means of preserving corpses in such destructive heat, and so burials are usually carried out one to two days after the death. Whispering, gossip and conflicting stories filtered down the mountainside, reaching family ears, ready to be distributed and discussed secretly, in furtive huddles. Would the wedding go ahead? The older generations shook their heads disapprovingly, opting for a respectful cancellation, riling the young into opposing anger. It seemed so bitterly unfair for poor Marie-Paule, who was violently torn between contrasting emotions, her moment of happiness left in the unpredictable hands of her family, completely out of her control.

I was relieved to hear of the sensible compromise reached by Marie-Paule's parents. The wedding would go ahead, but the celebratory party would be toned down out of respect for the mourning family. It was no longer to be held in a luxurious marquee with a dance floor and orchestra but would now take place outside in *Tonton*'s orchard and garden. I felt relief for the bride, and looked forward to joining her in making the day memorable.

It was a hazardous car journey up the winding, forest-rich mountain. Fires had not scorched the landscape as violently here as they had on our own blackened, tree-barren mountains. It was lush and green, providing welcome shade from the mid-morning sun as we were tossed from side to side, mutely praying for the car to stick firmly to the road. We were dressed smartly in suits and hats, occasionally raising a buttock to pull out the creases slowly forming on the car's sticky seats. It felt unnatural wearing so many clothes after weeks of wandering free, baring flesh, wiggling toes, cool and relaxed. I longed to reach the village and shake myself loose, like a dog after a brisk soaking in water.

There was a bustling, chattering crowd outside the crumbling church that stood high above the mountainside,

COME TO THE TABLE

reminding the scattered villagers below of its unquestionable omnipotence. We seemed to hover in the sweltering heat for an interminable length of time, waiting for the couple to emerge from the minuscule town hall. All French weddings require a civil service at *la mairie* at which the register is signed. Church is clearly differentiated from state, standing alone within the community, excluded from schools as well as ceremonies such as weddings. And so we shuffled, lifting the dust between our toes, uncomfortably squeezed together under the shade of a magnificent plane tree that must have witnessed numerous occasions like this one.

Eventually we proceeded into the cold, atmospheric church. The chill hit everyone as if we were in an air-conditioned hotel, stirring a busy movement of shawls, scarves and shivers. Initial relief at the sudden drop in temperature soon receded as a synchronised rubbing of hands and stamping of feet could be heard throughout the church. This was a mass gathering of friends, family and local villagers packed into the impressive building, all eager to participate in this major social event, rousing the entire village, raising their dampened spirits to unprecedented levels.

Deep, harmonious male voices suddenly hushed the whispering congregation. I had never heard these famous Corsican voices before; moody, haunting tones whose awe-inspiring potency left me emotionally drained, yet at the same time uplifted, spellbound. This was *la polyphonie*, rich, deep and immensely beautiful. They sang the mass in Latin, an incredibly moving experience made even more dramatic by the fact that we could not see them. The voices seemed to seep out of the ancient sacred walls, bouncing spectacularly off the thick, cold stone, their source a disconcerting mystery.

A slow ceremonial procession made its way to the altar to congratulate and kiss the bride, groom and parents, indicating the end of the service. A tumultuous mix of emotions was felt by everyone – a mixture of happiness and profound sadness evidenced by watery eyes and soft, unwiped tears. We all scrambled out of the church, an untidy, undisciplined rabble, like a frenzied crowd on the first day of the sales.

A shower of delicate rose petals and rice was launched over the giggling, kissing couple. Suddenly the ear-splitting boom of large hunting guns ripped across the valley. Four traditionally clad men were standing facing the hills and firing a deafening blast of shots. This is the Corsican method of announcing to all the surrounding villages that an event of some significance has taken place. No musical ringing of bells here. Each explosion left me feeling shattered. I found this outburst of gunfire disturbing and offensive, out of place as the fragile petals fluttered peacefully in the breeze. I longed for their intrusive, masculine aggression to stop, but male Corsican authority reigned and four precise gunshots turned into a trigger-happy ricochet of continuous noise. Another very long wait outside the church began while the happy couple were whisked away for the customary photographs.

Eventually the party could begin, and the procession of cars weaved its way precariously back down the mountainside. We all followed each other slowly as the last-minute planning meant that no one knew where the party was to be held except the family in the leading car. French weddings are crazily unorganised, uncomplicated affairs compared to the pompous, formal parade of etiquette and ritual that takes place in England. The wedding car is often not a hired sleek white limousine but simply the parents' car decorated with ribbons and bows. Some people wear hats, some don't. It is guaranteed that you will spend hours standing around, no one sure about the arrangements or the timing. In fact no one really cares about the time, because everyone knows the party will eventually get under way and that the food and wine will inevitably be well worth the wait.

Waiting is exactly what we did that day. On the way down the mountain, someone unfortunately misjudged a bend and dropped into a ditch. A mad, unorganised commotion developed around the stricken vehicle, involving the priest, who stood grandly presiding over the rescue operation. Quickly irritated by the fact that his advice was being blatantly ignored, he jumped back into his car and the procession continued, leaving behind the stranded invalid.

I think we were all expecting a sombre, subdued function, given the profusion of apologies previously offered by the grief-stricken family. On arrival at the prettily decorated orchard, with lanterns flickering from every tree and welcoming tables dressed under each arbour, we encountered a seemingly endless trestle table piled with colourful, appetising dishes. It was hard to believe this was second best, a compromise on the part of a mourning family. There was no dancing, no intimate tango or traditional sweeping waltz, but this delightful setting will remain fixed in my memory for a long time. The champagne did flow, and we deserved every drop given the long, thirst-inducing delays we had endured during the day. The feast was simply prepared, a delectable selection of cold, tasty dishes: couscous, spicy stuffed peppers, lean slices of *gigot*, a variety of savoury *tartes*, bowls of bright, enticing, island-grown fruit, sensationally presented, all made memorable by this magical garden.

I have been to many French weddings, each special in its way, but all possessing a similar haphazard charm. When I think back to my own French matrimonial celebrations, it seems to me that my own family must have found such chaos unbelievable, although they never once complained or commented on the disorder. I suppose that's family love for you.

The next day, after our long evening of champagne, feasting and reminiscing, we sought repose away from the crowded, stifling heat of the beach up in the cooler heights of the mountains. A dip in ice-cold river water was guaranteed to bring us all back to life, sharpen our senses and allow us to shake off the after-effects of wine. We decided to pack a picnic and take to the hills. Our trusty icebox was packed with favourite Corsican picnic fare, easy-to-eat snacks designed to be manageable when balancing on the uneven, glassy surface of huge river rocks.

We set off for the beautiful hidden Forêt de Bonifato, about an hour's drive from the coast and a relatively easy descent, even with young children and a cumbersome box of food, to reach the tumbling, lively river. Stéphane scrambled ahead in search of the ideal spot. We sought a deep, perfectly formed river pool for swimming surrounded by large polished rocks with flat surfaces on which we could spread out our picnic and dry towels and wet articles of clothing, preferably with a waterfall under which to massage our shoulders, feet and toes – and, for the very brave, their heads.

I sat with the children under the limited shade of a spiky tree, waiting for Stéphane to reappear and escort us through this perilous terrain of awkwardly positioned rocks and boulders. He was free and energetic up here, his true personality released as he pranced goat-like along the edge of the river. 'I'll be back soon. Wait there. Don't move,' he had instructed us, struggling to be heard above the crashing sound of a nearby waterfall.

Sometimes he frightened me, his confidence overbearing in the face of my own ridiculous vulnerability. These immense snowcapped mountains, the lethally sharp stones, the icy, forceful water, thundering along its chosen path, reduced me to a feeble, defenceless individual. I could enjoy nature's beauty, relish it from a distance, but close up like this I inexplicably feared its intense strength, instinctively protecting my children, the three of us huddled like sheep, petrified to move. He disappeared for what seemed an incredible length of time. My thoughts tumbled irrationally and deliriously, conjuring up images of an injured man, stranded with a twisted ankle, a cracked skull, alone, unable to be heard above the deafening crash of water. I even considered abandoning the children to begin a tearful search for my lost, wounded husband. Then miraculously I caught a glimpse of his spidery feet sliding down the facing rock, and a gloriously elated face appeared. He had found the perfect spot and was totally unaware of the agony I had been suffering, sitting here surrounded by all this threatening beauty. He had been totally immersed in his quest for the ideal swimming location, deciding to check out each tempting bathing pool, climbing increasingly higher, farther away from his forlorn, rejected brood, eagerly anticipating an even greater find beyond the next group of rocks. In the end we settled for the first idyllic setting he had spotted, just a couple of minutes' climb away. Even today he cannot understand why I greeted his return with such a furious expression, beating his bronzed back uncontrollably with tense, clenched fists, releasing my relief and anger.

Corsican mountain water is pure, icy and numbingly invigorating. The children launch themselves into this spectacularly clear pool water immediately, with no hesitation, while I need several minutes to acclimatise my toes, then my feet, admiring the towering mountains rearing up around us, protecting our private pool from the whistling winds that can appear from nowhere, dispelling the calm of the day. A gentle sprinkling of water over shoulders, face and hair, and then I can dive in. I always scream, horrified by the shock of the cold, sinking into its sharp magnificence. Skin and hair are conditioned to a baby softness never felt before. This is the most effective beauty treatment – free, fresh and energising.

Here are some of our river picnic ideas, many of which I also use at home for children's school lunch box ideas.

I use plastic tubs with lids for sliced tomatoes, salt and olive oil, easy to eat with a slice of baguette and a little fork. Cold ratatouille in tubs is also delicious, eaten either with a fork or just scooped up with chunks of fresh, crunchy bread.

Eggs are always a picnic favourite. We like to make *oeufs farcis*, little stuffed eggs. These are very easy and quick to make. First hard-boil 6 eggs for 10 minutes. Cool them in cold water and peel. Cut them lengthways and remove the yolk. Mix the yolks with 1 tablespoon of mayonnaise, 2 anchovies and a tablespoon of freshly chopped herbs. Fill the whites with this mixture and coat with a thick tomato *coulis*. Sprinkle with paprika but avoid salting too heavily because of the anchovies.

The children also adore our *petites brochettes de poulet aux herbes*. These are little skewers of chicken pieces that have been left to soak up the flavours of a marinade. In a large salad bowl prepare the marinade with 500ml of olive oil, the juice of 2 lemons, 2 bay leaves, 2 sprigs of thyme, 1 branch of rosemary, 2 cloves and 4–5 juniper berries. For 6 people, put 1.5–2kg of uncooked, skinned, white breast of chicken cut into regular pieces into the bowl and soak in the marinade for 24 hours. Prepare the *brochettes* by threading the pieces of chicken on little wooden or metal skewers. Grill well on the barbecue, then sprinkle with salt, pepper and thyme.

We also take along tubs of dips for the chicken and crunchy batons of carrots, peppers, celery and cucumber – sauces such as *aïoli*, a garlicky mayonnaise; pesto, an olive oil, garlic and basil sauce; and something tomato-based blended with lots of freshly chopped herbs from the *maquis*.

The best picnic dessert is a colourful assortment of fruit – juicy quartered melon, apricots, peaches, strawberries and plums.

We take a final plunge into the river water to wash away the fruit stains and cleanse ourselves one last time, signalling the end of our invigorating mountain picnic. So close to the island's heart and soul, enjoying its colossal beauty, I could contemplate more lucidly my troubling dilemma – how to bring myself closer to its people, connect with my family, loosen up in their company, appreciate their culture as much as I unashamedly manage to appreciate their land.

I could hear *Tata* Francesca's name still ringing in my ears, a gentle reminder that she was back home, needing a visit.

This quiet, gentle lady is one of survivors of the older generations, independently clinging on to her home, her pride and life. Somehow, up here in these wild, noisy mountains, I knew that she would be my saviour, pointing me in a new direction, innocently laying before me the solution to this complex Mediterranean island puzzle.

Tata Francesca has always been a favourite – a small-framed lady, stooping as old ladies do, hobbling awkwardly over the cobbled paths, with creased, pale skin that has rarely been exposed to the harsh midday sun. She is Babbò's aunt, his deceased mother's sister, the last of that generation, able to provide an insight into island life, to offer explanations, help me understand and possibly be more forgiving. *Tata* Francesca still lives in the family's original home village, a cluster of houses carved into the rock face, clinging precariously to the stony edge of the craggy, steep mountain above the coast. The village can be reached only on foot – a slow, steady, twisting climb until the main plateau opens up, allowing you finally to raise your eyes and steady shaky limbs. Here in the open you can breathe again and recover lost energy.

For many years *Tata* Francesca lived in a cave-like house at the top of the spiralling village, until a nasty fall damaged her hip. Somehow, miraculously, she was allocated another house at the bottom end of the village, closer to neighbouring help. I don't know whether this was a community or a family decision, but it certainly impressed me. I was more accustomed to the ways of a self-centred society that quickly locks the old away in purpose-built homes as soon as they display the first signs of weakness or time-consuming, inconvenient illness. Neighbours, family and friends frequently call to take her down to the coast for family gatherings and to buy groceries. She still dresses in the distinctive uniform of Corsican mountain women – a light cotton overall, often of a fresh, sky-blue, flowery design, with one wide pocket across the front, ready for cleaning or cooking action. *Tata* actually does very little, struggling to lift herself out of a firm, cushioned dining chair, but always coping admirably, tucked away in her own space, surrounded by cheeky, smiling photographs of her ever-increasing line of grandchildren, nephews and nieces.

She smiles freely, but occasionally moans as she remembers the past. 'It's not the same, you know. Everyone has left the village. In the winter I'm here on my own. It's hard now, not like it was before.' In her mind the past is vibrant, perfect, and she forgets the tough, anxious times suffered in the struggling mountain households. *Tata* would often help out her sister, who had one of the largest families – six children all squeezed into a minuscule house by the railway. Their railroad income was pathetically low for the number of hungry mouths and growing feet, so they were quickly forced to become self-sufficient by exploiting every inch of their small plot of land, feeding the family with home-grown vegetables and fruit. *Tonton* Antoine, the eldest son, had often told us about his early-morning garden duties, obediently assisting his father, without protest, understanding from an early age his role and place within the family structure. Physically he wore himself out significantly more than the other children, tending the soil, nourishing the dry, brittle land. He would be the one to endure the painful trek by foot up the winding steep road, head bowed low to avoid the glare of the sun, climbing steadily to the highest mountain villages to seek out scarce commodities such as olive oil, sold selectively by astute villagers to those who could pay or who were in favour with their family. The young Luiggis appreciated their older brother's commitment and tenderly did what they could to help him. Bread was home-made, delicious and scarce. A slice each was the ration, a cruelly inadequate amount, particularly for Antoine, who was the greediest of the six. His brothers and sisters each saved a portion from their ration and passed it round the table, calmly, quietly, conspiring together to support their brother and maintain his strength.

Tata can be forgiven for forgetting these hard times – many years have gone by, many changes have taken place. She is a simple soul, appealing and approachable. As the youngest family member she did not suffer the onerous pressures of watching over the entire brood, as did her eldest sister, Stéphane's grandmother. As a result *Tata* turned into a cool, calm character with a likeable laissez-faire attitude that immediately endeared me to her. I can hold her close and squeeze my love into her, always causing one or two silent tears to marble her weary, lined face. I wonder sometimes to what extent she appreciated my anguish before I shared my innermost thoughts with her. She seemed to understand long before we talked. We had similar spirits, and her audacious eyes, which protected her secrets, stared deep within me, beyond my confident foreign exterior.

Late one Sunday morning I slipped away to *Tata* Francesca's house. The church bells were pealing out among the tightly packed, shuttered buildings; even the warm, uneven cobbles resonated with the sound of their Sunday-morning calling. I pulled back the beaded cords hanging from her door frame, keeping out unwanted animals while letting the cool air filter through the doorway. *Tata* was sitting in front of the television, following the morning's mass, praying silently, maintaining her Sunday ritual in the comfort of her own home. As soon as she saw me she uneasily switched the television off, embarrassed to have been caught participating in devotional matters in her armchair rather than battling her way to the cold, uncomfortable benches of the church. I begged her to carry on but she insisted it did not interest her. We made coffee together and took it into the cavernous sitting room, dominated by an immense round table and the enormous television set. I think she knew why I had come to see her alone. She looked at me knowingly, the dark pools of her eyes safeguarding her secrets, veiling the anguish deep within her mind. Today, however, she let her anguish spill out, letting go for the first time, allowing me to step inside her mind. We looked like conspirators, locked in our mountain cave, plotting, as *Tata* offered explanations and justifications for immutable island customs, traditions and beliefs, as well as revealing a few buried family stories.

Almost unbelievably, *Tata* had suffered as the black sheep of her family for many years. She had spoken out passionately on numerous occasions, contradicting and challenging her family's decisions, and so developed a reputation for unpredictable, nonconformist behaviour which not surprisingly led to considerably reduced freedoms. She spoke calmly, coherently, sympathetically, recounting her experiences, displaying a remarkable capacity for forgiveness and understanding. I listened with admiration, filled with a desire to emulate such stoic appreciation and love of family and island ways, in spite of punitive parents. Only once did her tone sharpen and her frail frame tense, ready for battle. She was talking passionately, almost aggressively, for the first time, revealing signs of the defiant young girl who had so fervently shaken up and deeply embarrassed this united family.

Her nephew had fallen madly in love with a pretty young local girl who had the tragic misfortune of belonging to a reclusive neighbouring family, driven to alienation, labelled outcasts, despite numerous desperate efforts to hide the existence of their severely hunchbacked aunt. *Tata* had protested vehemently against the contentious decisions made at this time, attempting to defend her poor defenceless relative, who was distraught and helpless. Ignorance and fear are inbuilt island traits and extremely difficult to override; everyone believed that this ugly, frightening condition was hereditary. Consequently it was decided to ban any form of union between the two families.

Tata's nephew eventually left the island for Marseille, taking his unhappiness with him, inevitably unravelling a chain of emotional turmoil and unstable relationships that surrounded him until the day he died. He did not win this battle but the hurt, injustice and guilt remained within *Tata*, strengthening her resolve to enlighten her family and be a calming, peaceful influence.

Food plays a major role in placating, controlling and expressing love. *Tata* knew this better than anyone. For the first time my misgivings about the controlling influence of mealtimes began to make sense as I listened keenly to her sensitive descriptions, her resourceful analysis of the food dilemma. *Tata* had learned how to cope with her family without the tantrums, realising that there could be no escape for her and so a certain amount of conforming would be needed. Sharing in the creation of food with her family helped to calm *Tata*, showing her the way to placate her angry parents. She would willingly volunteer to make the infamous *torte* for large family gatherings, proudly receiving the compliments, enjoying the feeling of giving and sharing. It was then so much easier to slip unnoticed down to the village and meet up with her friends as her parents happily chatted, relieved at the emergence of their newly temperate daughter – a clever ploy that made sure she could now enjoy unlimited freedom.

Tata's anguish eased with maturity as she grew to understand her parents and family. Deep down she knew they all meant well; they loved so intensely that they feared separation, a sudden, impetuous departure from the island, feared being abandoned – destructive emotions that seemed to encourage all these unreasonable battles and sadly produced the very result they so desperately wanted to avoid. Most of the young will leave the island. On the whole this is for economic and career reasons, but inevitably many are drawn to the mainland in search of freedom and independence, and in particular the longed-for release from the clinging hold of family.

Tata believed firmly that the future depended on converting the young, winning their hearts, bringing them closer to the beauty, the soul of their island. She also knew this was where her strength lay; she could be a subtle, gentle influence, someone who could maintain the fiery island spirit while encouraging the quest for freedom. 'You have a gift to offer now, both you and Stéphane,' she told me. 'Now is the time to use it. Bring everyone together. I'll be there. The older island face issuing approval. It'll work, trust me. Corsicans love a good family party with lots of sweet, rich food.' She giggled, twisting her arthritic hands with glee. 'I'll make the *torte*. There will only be one. Be firm and guide everyone towards their strengths. *Tata* Mimi will love it if you request some of her *vin d'orange*. Let Francette bring her divine roasted almonds. Everyone needs to be involved. Let them all bring gifts.'

I could feel a sense of triumph washing over me. I had a party to organise. A Corsican party with Stéphane and me leading the way, hosting, welcoming, demonstrating our culinary skills. This would be different from the failed christening celebration because this was to take place on their territory, with everyone involved, young and old, and with my beautiful table presided over by a respected island figurehead.

Word spread quickly: the English girl is holding a party and everyone's invited. Stéphane allowed me the pleasure of organising the food, planning the menu in all its intricate detail, as he stood by, observing, resisting the temptation to interfere, stepping in only with helpful tips on feasibility now and again, which I managed to accept. As usual I left the choice of wine and champagne completely in his competent hands. Stéphane sensed how much this meant to me and collaborated sensitively, allowing me an independence that demonstrated just how far he had come in acknowledging and respecting my understanding of his food and culture. I could do this – easily, without stress or anguish. I knew them all, had learnt the sorrows, joys and triumphs of every single invited guest, as their stories had been divulged at dinner parties, their tongues loosened by potent Corsican wine. I could please them, bring to table their favourite indulgence – figs, chestnuts, fluffy apricots, dark, rich chocolate. Let them luxuriate and mellow, like warmed butter, easy to spread and mix. No one would be able to escape my charm, a magical recipe tailored to each and every personality – surprising, maybe shocking, but clearly expressing my perceptiveness, appreciation and love for them all.

Our terrace was beautiful in the early evening as the rapidly disappearing sun reddened the sky, casting a shadow over the flickering sea. The setting was perfect for a party of such immense importance. The main terrace could be set with tables and chairs, leaving the garden scattered with deckchairs, their faded fabric flapping like the sails of solitary dinghies in the late-evening breeze. A hefty stone bench had been thoughtfully positioned at the bottom of the garden, ideal for solitary contemplation and absent-minded gazing over the rough, wild terrain and the vast expanse of water curving away below. So much space – room to wander, to huddle together around a table, to escape to the bottom of the garden and digest, to sneak a surreptitious smoke in an isolated corner. For now, there were no mingling, chattering guests. Our preparations were almost complete and the garden was still exquisitely quiet in all its exotic beauty and tranquil, seductive calm when suddenly the silence was abruptly broken by the clattering of enormous chunks of ice hitting the bottom of a huge round bin, ready to receive the bottles of champagne and rosé wine shortly to be immersed in them. Having lit the last candle in its protective glass shell, I dipped my hands into the icy freshness, startled by the stinging pain of the cold. I jumped to attention as the bright headlights of the first visitors wound cautiously up the long, winding, potholed drive. I ran over to welcome them, kissing their smiling faces warmly, leading them down to the twinkling terrace, placing a glass in their hands, manoeuvring them into position. Everyone was carefully placed in front of subtly selected and strategically positioned dishes of appetisers.

To follow there were spicy *merguez* sausages, barbecued until black and crunchy, for Antoine; a refreshing *taboulé*, with its citrus, minty blend of couscous, tomatoes, peppers and onion, for Madeleine; crisp, salty sardines for Babbò; *saucisse en brioche* for Chris to capture nostalgic memories of home in Lyon; a traditional Corsican classic for Francette, her sweet tooth drawn to a well-made *Fiadone* (*gâteau à la brocciu*). Mimi is always won over by something Corsican – I knew *beignets de courgettes* were her favourites – while Mina adores *côtelettes de porc grillées*, freshly cooked on a hot barbecue and sprinkled with sage. There was lots of Babbò's fish, a fitting tribute to the island and its people. Encased in foil parcels, resting gently on the glowing embers, these were my surprise gifts, freshly caught presents from the sea, delicately seasoned with fennel, lemon and tomato.

The children's cheeky, happy eyes sparkled, drawn to a collection of bright, shiny bowls filled to the brim with naughty sweet treats: diamond-shaped almond delights, tiny, white *calissons d'Aix*, *nougat blanc, nougat noir*, red, juicy strawberries sprinkled with lemon juice and covered in chopped mint, glowing Corsican oranges and clementines, freshly picked from the tree, proudly retaining their stalks and leaves.

This was an informal progression of flavours combined with an unusual blend of aromas drifting headily through the mingling guests, cajoling this familiar group into peaceful harmony. I suspected that they were amused and pleasantly entertained by my bizarre, eclectic choices, which rekindled memories, bringing wry grins to some faces, hearty gratitude to others. This was not a *soirée découverte* of perfect food and wine partners, sophisticated flavours and harmonies to dazzle the taste buds, but a friendly offering of gifts, tasty and succulent, lovingly created, like a well-planned Christmas.

Tata Francesca was there as promised to smile and greet the guests, sitting proudly at the head of the main dressed table, reassuringly close by my side. Together we watched our gathered flock, having led them to their individual plates and allowed ourselves the privilege of being in control. Tonight we were the leaders, the decision-makers, and we both quietly revelled in this magical evening.

Soft, gentle music caressed our ears as everyone settled, some at the table, others hovering, wandering in front of the spectacular panorama, now glimpsed only dimly under the fairy-tale night lights. Sparkling glasses were filled generously, the wine working its enchantment over the party. I do not think it was the just the wine's influence which drew *Tata* Mimi over to Stéphane and encouraged an animated exchange of recipes. For the first time our skills were seen and appreciated. It's true that the men still had a hard time overcoming their astonishment at seeing a Corsican man talking women's talk – kitchens, shopping, ingredients and baking. I was not yet allowed into these intimate discussions, but I did manage to create a moment of awed silence as I articulately and professionally described the wide range of cheese varieties on display. Many French people do not possess the depth of cheese and wine knowledge we expect from such a rich food heritage. The English naively assume that all French instinctively understand these culinary matters, are able to name and distinguish varieties and brands with natural, inborn ease. I recall my horror at two of our French students, who not only knew nothing about cheese but also hated it with a passion. Many years ago, long before we opened our business and acquired our knowledge of wine, the inexplicable influence of a few French words spoken surreptitiously in an English supermarket bewildered me. While choosing a bottle of wine, Stéphane let slip a little French, loudly enough for a gentleman hovering indecisively nearby to hear. This man turned towards Stéphane and asked whether he thought the wine was good. He confidently selected his bottle on the basis of my inexperienced French husband's word.

I was accustomed to knowing considerably more about cheese and wine than many of my French family, but this was the first time I had dared reveal my secret. They were not embarrassed to be told about their cheeses by a foreigner. They smiled proudly, beguiled by the crazy paradox of an Englishwoman extolling the history and virtues of a French cheeseboard. I felt myself being drawn in and accepted by my island family as we shared the goodness of the *maquis* and the satisfaction of a lazy, enriching feast. Corsican utterances juxtaposed with loud, raucous belly laughs filled the star-spangled night air. *Tata* Francesca reassured me throughout the entire evening, nodding her approval as promised. She sat there, regal and splendid, fulfilling her dream as the young teased the old, as defiance and courage led the way, momentarily stilling the harsh, traditional, ageing voices, opening their eyes so that they could see, dispelling their fears so that they could hear. She knew her task had been accomplished in style and harmoniously – no battles, no shouting or anger were required. Just a magnificent, creative feast.

Entertaining outdoors is an excellent way of introducing informality and creativity. Barbecues do not always have to mean burgers and sausages thrown indiscriminately on to a grill. Try using marinades for meat before grilling, roasting vegetables as well as meat, and don't overlook fish, superbly moist and succulent when cooked in foil parcels on a hot barbecue.

BROCHETTES DE BOEUF AU BEURRE D'HERBES

Cut about 1kg of entrecôte or rib-eye steak into regular-sized cubes and push them on to skewers. Place them on a hot barbecue grill for approximately 10 minutes, turning them from time to time.

Put 100g butter in a bowl over a *bain-marie* with salt and pepper. Add 2 tablespoons of strong Dijon mustard and 1 tablespoon each of finely chopped parsley, tarragon and chives. Mix well and wait until the butter begins to melt. Do not let it boil.

When the kebabs are cooked, arrange them on a plate. Sprinkle with salt and pepper. Pour the butter sauce into a sauce dish and serve separately.

SALADE DE LÉGUMES GRILLÉS

For 6 people, cut in half 5 green and 5 red peppers and remove the seeds. Place them on a hot grill. Once they are softened, remove the skin, which should come away easily, and then cut into fine strips. Keep to one side on a serving plate.

Cut 5 small aubergines and 5 courgettes into thin slices. Pour some olive oil over them and sprinkle with salt and pepper. Put them on the barbecue grill and, once they are soft, serve all the vegetables on a serving platter. Pour a liberal quantity of olive oil over them and sprinkle with crushed garlic, chopped parsley and chives. Serve well chilled.

Following our big party night we received an endless stream of gifts: home-made jams, preserved fruits, tarts, quiches and oddly shaped garden vegetables. My aversion to sugar was thoughtfully considered by Mimi, who sent a beautiful gift box of chocolates, sugary *beignets* and Corsican biscuits, with a handwritten note inside sitting next to an individually wrapped parcel. 'And this parcel is for you, Louise. Please take care of my home-made olive cake as I know you will appreciate it much more than these sugary treats.'

This kind-hearted gesture overwhelmed me more than any of the amiably delivered words and cards we had received during the last few days. I had recognised everyone's foibles, weaknesses, loves and secret desires, and now they could see mine. This was the Corsican way, a sharing of harvest surpluses, whether from the kitchen or the winery. We were now a part of this world, and my independent spirit somehow seemed able to accept these generous gestures with gratitude and love. But it still seemed strange, everyone watching over me like fussing, protective parents.

One day I thought I saw Dad down on the beach in his favourite faded denim shorts, wandering towards me, his strong, prominent nose lifted to the salty smell of the sea. It was an uncanny, almost creepy resemblance that made me shiver and gasp out loud, taken aback by the freckled bronzed arms, the gummy, childish smile, the thin, baby-soft hair flopping untidily over a happy face. I looked again and he was gone. It was ten years since Dad had died, and not once had I hallucinated in such an eerie way. Why now?

Maybe he was also watching over me or trying to tell me something. I knew exactly what he would have hated here in Corsica and what he would now be saying. The interfering, the fussing, the stifling of independence would have irritated him beyond belief. I hoped he was not judging me as I struggled to find a happy balance. I had not compromised any of my free spirit; on the contrary, I had successfully shown my individuality, self-sufficiency and ability to organise and cope at my party. Receiving and accepting islanders' gifts, their gestures of help, did not mean defeat, just acknowledgement of their care. They could not hold on to me, keep me locked up on the island, with their generous offerings. They knew we had already made our escape. I now understood, but the ghostly apparition still shook me, casting my mind back to childhood, to memories of my varied holiday and weekend jobs – folding jumpers into neat piles to have them rummaged through and soiled by frenetic hands; sorting out books by ISBN numbers; serving tea and cake to trembling pensioners at the local garden centre; picking raspberries and strawberries, enduring painful cuts and scratches, at a nearby fruit farm – taken to allow me to pay back loans, however laboriously. Dad was resolute in his determination to make me pay my way. I remember thinking how cruel this was at the time. There were no easy handouts with my family, just lessons in being able to cope without parents, developing an independent spirit, understanding the value of money. I know this is why I initially found it so hard to cope with the Mediterranean island way of exuberant, unnecessary generosity. My pride was hurt by this desire to fulfil every whim and fancy, not allowing me to pay my way at restaurants or shops during our rare island visits. 'I'm not sinking in the quicksand of Corsican family life; I'm just trying to understand and belong.' My thoughts sped on unbidden as my watery eyes chased after the familiar, blurred figure of the stranger on the beach, hoping to sneak another glance. Oh, how I missed Dad. I so longed for him to be here now to guide me, offer some reassurance, make me laugh at these family predicaments. He was always so quick to spot the funny side to a situation, lightening the mood and finding the appropriate joke. I so wanted him to be here with me now, to enjoy my new-found family, their food, their traditions, and make us all laugh.

I do not know where this inexplicable surge of nostalgia came from, or why, but somehow it helped. Memories of home, Dad, Mum and England resurfaced during this time. Family memories I had buried, stored away in the darkest depths of my mind, hoping to protect my soul, keep me whole, stronger, less vulnerable, were suddenly released uncontrollably as I surveyed my island-grown gifts. Baskets of oranges, peaches and nectarines, small punnets of strawberries and raspberries, wafted a nostalgic scent of brambles, damp hedges, spicy red wine and bubbling pans of sugary fruit, apple compote, cloying home-made jam. I remembered my childhood adventures down muddy country lanes, a grey, threatening sky bringing premature darkness during our search for ripe, juicy blackberries. We reached dangerously, precariously high, lifting each other closer to those difficult-to-reach, succulently large berries, ignored by others, left for our reckless, sore hands. We would return home stained and triumphant, scattering our meagre harvest on the kitchen table. Mum would never laugh or dismiss our innocent hunting instincts. She always managed to bake the most delicious crumbles and pies, supplementing our berries with a selection from the fruit bowl. I loved the sensation of miraculously creating a pudding from a strenuous, treacherous outdoor treasure hunt rather than simply visiting the local supermarket.

I was inspired to make some English crumbles and fruit pies with my gifts and then invite a few aunts and uncles for tea. I also distributed my creations, feeling extremely Mediterranean – confident, almost brash, in my giving. *Tonton* Antoine made me giggle after we had devoured a particularly delicious crumble. 'For an Englishwoman, you might make a Corsican yet!'

Everyone had enjoyed the party, and most importantly they had all taken away a memory. From that day onwards things changed. Beach talk began. Our favourite beach hideaways were no longer a secret as everyone watched the sea, checking its movement, its temper, and then logically working out where we could be found. One of Stéphane's cousins silently appeared under our parasol one warm, calm day and threw his towel down next to ours. After a few minutes of general chit-chat he began to talk more seriously. It was the usual island stuff – claustrophobic love and stifling protection. With this particular cousin I did not hold out much hope for dramatic change; he was now at an age where he would be content with peace and quiet rather than radical reform. However, he certainly looked happier for having spoken, expressing emotions freely, speaking openly to others who were detached and non-judgemental.

Others, however, did want to make changes. A number of the younger teenage family members also began to creep down to the beach to join us and talk. It became their ideal meeting place, lounging under the shade of a large Kronenbourg parasol, as many parents and older aunts and uncles kept away from the suffocating sandy heat and the noisy beach activities. Here the young could speak freely – they were safe, in no danger of being overheard. They giggled and chatted, occasionally playing with the children's luminous plastic toys, creating spectacular sandy works of art to the wonder and gleeful delight of Nina and Pierre. As they dried themselves after a cooling dip, eyes closed against the sharp, painful brightness, talk of travel, discovery and exploration would begin to flow. 'I've always wanted to go to England,' declared Pascal, prompting a chorus of agreement from the rest of the troop.

They were not very subtle or particularly clever at hiding their underlying wishes, but couldn't bring themselves to boldly request a trip back to England with us, skirting around the issue, flirting, hinting, suggesting, their Corsican characteristics already deeply ingrained. But we knew exactly what they were after. A way out. An escape.

I warned Stéphane to tread very carefully with these Corsican refugees, not wanting to risk damaging my newly acquired acceptance. I certainly wanted to help these youngsters and bring some independence and adventure into their cloistered lives, but I did not want to carry the blame for luring them away. A couple of work placements were arranged at French Living with parental consent, the departure and return dates fixed precisely so no ambiguity threatened. I'm not sure their English improved to any great degree, but these kids experienced a few months of liberty, free expression and a contrasting culture. A few months of change can sometimes be just enough to help young minds work out for themselves their future direction. I know au pairing in Paris was my escape, calming my impetuous urge to abandon education, giving me space to reflect away from the pressures of home and school. With our guidance, a few whispered comments and observations, they returned home with fresh eyes, for the first time viewing their island as independent young adults, perhaps now able to appreciate its beauty, seeing home, family and friends in a more favourable, understanding light.

Our Corsican holiday was drawing rapidly to an end. This had been a triumphant visit, relaxed and calm, with invitations limited and our freedoms extended. I yearned to experience more of this heavenly place, made all the more enticing by the loosening of our family ties. Our understanding of its food and culinary traditions had been seriously limited to home family cooking. I felt this deprivation probably more than Stéphane, who had only ever known family favourites and had never until now imagined he could widen his horizons through restaurant dining.

Hitherto undiscovered countries are more thoroughly unmasked and more completely understood by an appreciation of their food; regional specialities and local produce can reveal perfectly the characteristics and charm of a country and its people, and are often accompanied by eccentric tales and anecdotes which explain their origins, magically bringing a place to life. I knew we had not experienced the full potential of Corsican cuisine, having tasted only the familiar traditions of the Luiggi household; admittedly these embraced a wide variety of Corsican classics, but they also shunned anything that required time, expense or ingredients not appreciated by the head of the house.

And so we began our restaurant crusade, searching out hidden treasures, looking for superb locations and atmosphere as well as carefully executed meals. We prised the

232

names of the best from family and friends, listening to their advice and judgements with care, soon learning how to interpret their criticisms, which always tended to be extremely severe. No one could make a better *beignet de courgette* than Francette; even the most refined professional touch and creative flair could not inspire anything more than the barest acknowledgement of worth: 'It's not bad.' This was a frequently repeated comment that would ensure that Stéphane put the restaurant in question high on our list. He recognised the signs, realised that there would never be any more flamboyant expressions of enthusiasm.

We began sampling in the village, taking the children with us to enjoy simple family fare at the welcoming and friendly terrace of Le Chariot. Freshly cooked *sauté de veau aux olives*, dished up with plenty of pasta, proved to be a favourite. This was the cuisine I knew and relished at my Corsican home, a hearty, flavoursome collection of rich stews and pasta – the solid peasant cooking that underpins many of the local dishes. Refinement is limited, even with increased tourism and easier access to the mainland, the dishes remaining simple, not enhanced by more exotic mainland ingredients. Traditional island food has not really experienced any change over the years, the Italian influence ever-present and home-grown island produce continuing to form the basis for most menu planning. Obviously tourism has nurtured a greater demand for restaurants, many of which open only during the summer season. What they offer alternates between very basic, anonymous tourist catering and excellent *auberge*-style dining. These delightful rustic *auberges* also feed the locals and are used by islanders all year round. They tend to be off the beaten tourist trail, and can often only be reached after a long, nauseating car journey up into the mountains, well away from the bustling, high-priced seafront. Many do not even have a menu but serve a selection of dishes of their choice, whatever is fresh and available that day.

Such establishments certainly do not cater for devout vegetarians. I recall one such *auberge* which we reached late one afternoon, not even sure that they would still be able to serve us. They sat us down, happy to receive us but extremely apologetic, regretting that they did not have a great deal left to offer at this late hour. An enormous bowl of Corsican soup arrived which I mistakenly tucked into greedily, taking several helpings. Crisp fried river trout followed with a platter of *beignets*. I was convinced this was the main course, until to my horror an enormous platter of meat was ceremoniously placed on our table. This included a bizarre array of veal, chicken, goat – roasted and herbed, moist and succulent – with a few pork chops thrown in. It was delicious but ridiculously generous. I learnt a hard, sickening lesson that day about the Corsican *auberge* and its hospitality, recognising that bountiful, multiple courses are an integral part of its character. I no longer ever feel tempted to refill my bowl with gorgeous scented soup.

One of my favourite rustic establishments is the Auberge de Tesa on the road towards the Regino plain. This pretty restaurant and hotel sits next to a beautiful river, and while retaining the traditional peasant mountain fare has also introduced an element of sophistication, particularly in the presentation. Locally produced pottery manages to lift the olives, anchovy spreads and salty appetisers to a refined level of finesse. The pastel tones of the yellow and green linen table coverings feel luxurious and special. The filling procession of platters is familiar, but the pace is slow and civilised; you have time to daydream outside on the terrace, to be brutally roused by the piercing cries of the wildlife scooting around on the river. The beauty of Tesa is the availability of a bed if the thought of the black, spiralling roads threatens to spoil a magical evening.

Back in the village we would stroll down towards the beach and initiate the children into the skills of dismantling a lobster at the more sophisticated Le Beau Rivage. The cracking and fracturing of the shell, the sucking and yanking of flesh out of the fierce orange claws, intrigued and fascinated our eager young guests. The children were attracted to all those dishes that entailed involvement and the dirtying of face and hands – spreading spicy *rouille* on platefuls of crusty *croûtons*, sprinkling them lightly with grated Emmental cheese, then waiting for the steaming, aromatic fish soup to arrive. This marvellous routine of anticipation enchanted the children. Some friendly waiters let the children leave the table and watch the fish being filleted close up, sometimes letting them help with their chosen fish, which for a long time led to them both always insisting on ordering fish at every restaurant we visited.

These were intimate and special times with the children, moments where we could share our offsprings' thoughts and indulge in silly conversations that only we as parents could ever appreciate. I treasured this time we spent together, relishing the children's closeness, for once not having to distribute them among doting grandparents, aunts and uncles. Restaurant dining away from the family table gave us wonderful occasions of selfish intimacy, allowing us to educate the next generation in the delights of the table.

Lunchtimes, private and informal, casual and fun, were spent with our children, while we reserved some time when our contented brood slept for romance and personal closeness. I called upon *la famille* to babysit as we galloped away to coastline terraces, protected courtyards and on-the-beach tables. The night of my birthday Stéphane promised to whisk me away for a particularly memorable meal. I had never seen the sophisticated side of Corsica before, not even convinced it actually existed. Somehow I didn't want to believe that my rugged, earthy island could possess the elaborate worldliness and trendy refinement I had left behind in England. I liked simplicity and hearty, wholesome cuisine. I did not need sophistication.

We drove in the direction of Calvi, turning towards the airport, and then left the road for a bumpy dirt track, finally sweeping into a beautiful tree-lined, floodlit drive framed by ornate open metal gates. This was the historic La Signoria, a luxurious hotel for the rich and famous which housed a restaurant also open to the public.

It was a warm, still night as we drove through a Mediterranean parkland of eucalyptus, towering palm trees, ancient olive trees and scented pines. Here stood an eighteenth-century home, a former *domaine génois*, now a superb hotel with individually styled rooms and suites. We were here to dine on the terrace overlooking the pool, to taste a part of Corsica's aristocratic past, sample some *génois* sophistication and soak up a little kingly service and attention. In spite of my misgivings about Corsica trying to offer gastronomic refinement, I hold both hands up and admit to having been proved wrong. I experienced the most memorable meal of my life during our three-hour visit. The food was not clever or overly ambitious but it was fresh and perfectly executed. I have never tasted such intense, lingering flavours, enhanced by the most regal backdrop – a neat

row of thyme and rosemary lining the terrace, which overlooked a motionless, floodlit pool, invitingly tranquil,
surrounded by tropical dried-grass parasols, a serene,
special place in which to luxuriate in the astonishing quality
of cuisine, table dressing and setting.

TIAN DE MOULES AU CÉLERI
Stéphane enjoyed a spicy mussel and celeriac starter. He
relished and memorised every flavour that night, and now
often reproduces this exquisite appetiser for dinner parties
at home.

It's a matter of preparing a celeriac purée, then cooking
and seasoning mussels and bringing the two together.

Preheat the oven to 190°C/375°F/Gas Mark 5.

For 4 people, you will need 500g of celeriac after it has
been peeled, chopped into small pieces and boiled in water
until very soft. Purée well, blending with 100ml of olive oil.
Season with salt and pepper.

Scrape and wash 2kg of mussels. While doing this check
that they are alive and well (they should be closed up – if
they are ajar but close up when you squeeze them, that's
fine). Put them in a large casserole dish with a glassful of
dry white wine (do not add salt; they will release plenty of
that in the pan), cover and cook for 5–10 minutes until
they are all open, shaking vigorously every 2 minutes. If a
mussel does not want to open, throw it away. Never force
a shell open. Take the cooked mussels off the shells (keep
the juice as stock to make a tasty fish sauce for later).

Fry 2 teaspoons of thinly diced fresh ginger for about 1
minute on a low heat. Add 2 teaspoons of ground cumin
and mix in the mussels, coating them with the spices. Take

off the heat. Blend the mussels with the celeriac purée and place in 4 oven-proof ramekin dishes. Serve immediately.

FILLET OF DORADE

My main course was a succulent, moist fillet of *dorade* (sea bream or sea bass, or equivalent), placed delicately on a bed of shredded vegetables soaked in olive oil. This dish can work with most fleshy fillets of fish, including tuna and even a thick fillet of fresh cod.

The secret is not to overcook the fish to ensure the flesh retains a moist, tender flavour, and is not dry and tough. Just 2 minutes in a pan on each side (lightly floured) or a maximum of 12 minutes in the oven (190°C/375°F/Gas Mark 5) will achieve this.

Prepare a selection of vegetables such as aubergines, peppers, courgettes, fennel and celery, cutting them into thin, long batons. The quantity will depend on how many people you are cooking for.

In plenty of olive oil toss the vegetables in a wok, season with salt and pepper and herbs (fresh if possible), making sure they retain their crunchiness to contrast perfectly with the delicate flesh of the fish.

It frightens me to think that I came so close to being repulsed by this gorgeous gem of an island. I sat at this perfect table surrounded by classic architectural splendour and lush scented plants and declared how lucky I was to have experienced such perfection.

On the way home, relaxed and glowing, Stéphane turned the car into the *marine*, where our rented villa stood. He pulled over on a dusty verge in front of a wasteland of weeds and thistles, a gently sloping field that led down towards the sea, and told me to get out of the car. From here there was a magnificent view of the Ile Rousse, the russet island that sits out to sea, giving the next-door town its name. It shone eerily in this late night glow, the town's flickering restaurant lights bouncing off the sea and illuminating the jagged red rock. From the road, at the top of the wasteland, the sea was visible, and tonight it was calm, shimmering enticingly.

'Why are you stopping here?' I asked, confused. This was not exactly a recognised beauty spot – a neglected field covered in overgrown olive trees and prickly weeds, with the remains of a boat, dangerously exposing its rusty nails, and a derelict shepherd's refuge slowly losing its shape as the stones crumbled into a sad rubble. The cool night air had started to filter through my light cotton wrap, and the wine I had drunk was now making me sleepy and irritable. 'Come on, Stéphane, I'm tired and cold. Let's go home,' I moaned, heading back to the car.

He pulled me back firmly, seemingly astonished that I could not see why we were standing here. He was about to surprise me. I knew the signs – the familiar tone and the reckless mood that always managed to unnerve me. I almost dreaded his next words, tensing my arms across my chest, stubbornly refusing to be drawn back, annoyed because I was completely unaware of what this could all be about. What on earth was he plotting? It couldn't be anything to do with the business. That was now flourishing and prosperous, with an ever-increasing number of regular, devoted customers, a comfortable cash flow and a steady routine. But his voice had the same deep, serious inflection he always adopted when discussing new business ideas or talking about menus, trying to hold back his excitement and resist the temptation to squeal like a child with enthusiastic delight at his secret news. His twinkling, devilish eyes brought back memories of the day when, flushed with elation, he announced the restaurant project.

'Look at this land – from that tree over there down the field to the low line of bushes at the bottom. This is ours. It belongs to us. A superb-quality building plot,' he announced proudly.

I could not speak. I stared at this ordinary field that had in the space of a few seconds been turned into an area of major significance. Dumbfounded, lost for words, I was once again struck by this man's audacious ability to throw such momentous revelations at me and expect a calm, rational response. My mind was racing, deliriously leaping from one thought to the next, uncomfortably absorbing this weighty news.

'It's my inheritance,' he continued. 'I wanted to tell you before but now it's official and you seem so much more at ease here, with the family and everything . . .' He was babbling, justifying, hoping, not really wanting me to answer. He knew me well enough to understand that I would need some time and a whole range of questions answered before he got his reply.

For now, I wanted to go home.

EIGHT

Chocolat

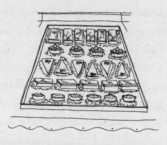

SEPTEMBER IS A month of new beginnings. We are fresh
from a summer's repose, eager to return to the regular
rhythm of reality. There is always a wonderful sense of
anticipation as preparations are made for our return to
normality, to everyday monotony and daily routine. There
was to be a fresh start for Pierre, now starting school,
proud of his new independence. Homework and more
serious application are in prospect as Nina graduates to the
next level of her educational career. Autumn menus are
finalised, decorated with flowery, dashing embellishments.
Home improvements are enthusiastically undertaken before
this dynamic momentum and exceptional high spirits are
extinguished as the months slide wearily by, reducing us to
apathy.

I loved this return to secure familiarity, always impatient

to introduce fresh ideas to both home and business. I looked forward to settling the children into a solid routine, calming their over-exuberant spirits and re-establishing tranquillity in our lives. Following our return from Corsica I felt an even greater desire to return to normality and familiar faces. Like my children, I needed to be comforted and welcomed home. I knew why I felt so much disquiet. Stéphane's revelation had thrown me into disarray. I did not want to talk about this newly acquired land, almost fearing the outcome of such a conversation. If I said nothing maybe it would go away.

Meanwhile I worked hard at establishing our routines, launching myself into a frantic schedule of work, losing myself in the humdrum reality of daily activity.

Both Pierre and Nina now attended a small village school, which had considerable benefits but unfortunately meant that I lost control of their mealtime routine. This loss upset me because I had worked hard while they were toddlers at home to activate their taste buds and excite their receptive minds with a desire for imaginative, tasty food. Unfortunately, the school seemed incapable of offering inspiring meals. My memories of the Ecole de Commerce student cafeteria in Toulouse were of fresh, wholesome dishes. Hot meals, salads, fruit and desserts were always available, all delicious and eagerly queued for at the regular *midi* slot. Sadly such attention to achieving a balance between healthy nutrition and flavour is not a priority in our schools. I would therefore have to focus on their lunch boxes. I revived our Corsican picnic ideas, and filled their colourful boxes with tubs of ratatouille; seasoned ripe tomatoes, drizzled with olive oil, layered with fresh basil; couscous mixed with peppers, chopped tomatoes and mint;

roasted chicken pieces, sprinkled with tarragon and a herby *fromage blanc* dip; pasta shells and crunchy broccoli seasoned with coarse sea salt and Provençal herbs; chopped fruit with a few drops of lemon. My imagination was fired by this mission. I certainly was not going to let my children's love of good food be destroyed by disappointingly bland school dinners.

Every action and decision, my every thought, seemed to be centred around making England a decent place for us to be, justifying my choices, finding ways around problems, striving for solutions. I had eliminated the school dinner problem, preventing any fuss, ensuring that the children would have no reason to complain. I had resolved the issue; it had gone away. I would snap defensively at Stéphane if he made the slightest derogatory comment about home, England or the English. I was sensitive and tetchy, turning into a neurotic, obsessive witch. Protective and afraid, rapidly losing my sense of humour, I felt like a lost soul, anticipating the worst, petrified of the truth. I had no idea what Stéphane's intentions were, how he planned to use his beloved inheritance, because since our return we had avoided the subject. No one dared mention the land. I naturally assumed he wanted to build a home and move us all over to his dream island. And so I nervously waited for his next momentous announcement.

Meanwhile I spoilt the children, extravagantly indulging their childish pleasures. I wanted to recreate French lux-uries and triumphantly show everyone we could enjoy France here at home as well as at work. We didn't need to live there. My children could still reap the benefits of France. I certainly didn't want them to conspire against me and plead to be taken back to their treasured holiday island.

243

And so I turned my kitchen into a French paradise of sugary treats, with sticky caramel pans leaving behind their distinctive cloying aroma, melted chocolate on wooden spoons, demanding to be licked clean, hot *chocolat chaud*, always ready to warm through cold, tired bones. I surrounded the children with naughty French temptations, selfishly relieving myself of my inexplicable guilt. Stéphane looked on bewildered yet inwardly delighted at my sudden interest in sugar. Nina and Pierre revelled in this child's sweet shop of pleasure, helping me stir and whisk, coating their fingers and mouths in sticky, irresistible glue, furiously licking and devouring before it could be cleanly wiped away. Like most children I know they both adored sugar and fell hopelessly in love with my *crème caramel* and *mousse au chocolat*.

CRÈME CARAMEL

Preheat the oven to 190°C/375°F/Gas Mark 5.

For 4–6 people, cut a vanilla pod in two lengthways and scrape the seeds into a saucepan containing 1 litre of milk. Add the pod and bring to the boil. Take off the heat and allow to cool.

Beat 6 eggs, 2 additional yolks and 175g of caster sugar in a bowl until completely blended. Remove the vanilla pods from the milk and gradually pour the tepid milk into the egg mixture, beating firmly with a whisk.

To make the caramel put 100g of brown sugar in a saucepan over the heat and cover with 4 tablespoons of water.

When it reaches a golden-brown colour, quickly pour the caramel into ramekins, tipping them to ensure that all the sides are coated. (At this point fill the dirty saucepan with water and bring to the boil otherwise you'll be forever trying to wash it!) When the caramel has cooled add the egg mixture and place the ramekins in a *bain-marie* over warm water. The water should reach to almost the top of each ramekin. Put in the oven for approximately 1 hour but you need to check that they don't boil. Before taking them out of the oven, slide the blade of a knife into them to make sure they are not too soft. The blade should be clean when removed.

Remove from the oven and allow to cool. Put them in the fridge only if you will not be eating them within the next few hours. They are best enjoyed 1 to 2 hours after being made.

MOUSSE AU CHOCOLAT

For 6 people, put 100ml of water and 300g dark bitter chocolate pieces (preferably at least 50% cocoa) in a *bain-marie* and let the chocolate melt, mixing well.

Mix in 50g of caster sugar and a couple of drops of vanilla essence.

Take the pan off the heat and allow to cool down slightly. Separate 4 eggs and add the yolks to the mixture, gently stirring them in.

Beat the egg whites, add a pinch of salt and then whisk until firm. Incorporate the whites into the chocolate, gently folding with a spoon in order to prevent the whites becoming liquid.

Let the mixture cool in the serving bowl in the fridge for 2 hours. It is even better if eaten the next day, and superb with delicate, crumbly biscuits such as Les Gavottes, a Brittany speciality of folded crêpe biscuits.

Preparations were being made for Christmas, a frantic period in the retail and restaurant calendar. We were however improving each year in the handling of these festivities, adapting, understanding where tricky situations could arise and learning to avoid them. French festive luxuries were brought in directly from our suppliers in France, filling our shelves, squeezed into every available display space. Traditional Christmas savoury flavours such as *foie gras, confit* and *marrons entiers* arrived, and we stacked them high in exotic pyramids, declaring their importance in the French scheme of things. Sweet Christmas treats were also unpacked and displayed with carefully translated labels, explaining the value of these sweets for the benefit of our inquisitive customers: *nougat blanc au miel de lavande* in bars as well as loose, individually wrapped pieces; pretty diamond-shaped *calissons d'Aix*; boxes of sticky *caramels au sel de Guérande*; traditional *marrons glacés* individually wrapped in luxurious metallic gold paper – all transforming our shop into an enchanting cave of mysterious delights.

Les treize desserts of Provence would spring to mind as I transformed the shop into an enticing, sparkling paradise of gifts. These thirteen desserts were served to us as part of a colourful ritual on a long, exquisitely dressed table at Stéphane's cousin's house one Christmas in Aix-en-Provence. She had married and left the island to be close to her parents in Provence. An artist and dreamer, she was a strange combination of tradition and modernity, rebelling against the customs of Corsica, sneaking away to marry privately and alone, leading a bohemian painter's life of free expression and yet proudly laying out a traditional Provençal Christmas for family and friends. I was intrigued by this appetising display of treats, recognising many items familiar from an English Christmas. Traditionally there would be dried raisins, figs, almonds, walnuts, hazelnuts, pears, apples, plums, *nougat noir, nougat blanc*, the flat, round, olive-oil-soaked bread – *fougasse* – *confiture de coings* (quince) and *confiture de pastèques* (watermelon). Nowadays the traditions are adapted to include specialities such as *calissons*, widely available fruits such as oranges, mandarins and dates, and the closest the French have to our crackers, *papillotes*. These are individually wrapped soft nougat sweets coated in chocolate with a joke hidden inside the wrapper.

Adapting, experimenting and improving are exactly what I love to do with the customs that seem to have accumulated around me. Replacing flavours with more familiar ingredients, taking the basis of a tradition and making it my own, has liberated and strengthened my cuisine and suits my haphazard methods. Having never grown up with set rules and regulations concerning mealtimes and kitchen techniques, I was not restricted by a family code. Today, having been rudely awakened to French family practices and kitchen etiquette, I also no longer feel the need to copy my adopted family's methods. I am brave enough to listen to my instincts and adapt the wonderful selection of recipes now firmly implanted in my head. These are my culinary memories, gathered over the years through my French family dining experiences. Only now do I appreciate the gift I have so kindly been given.

Christmas tradition, however, dictated the range of gifts we put on offer in the shop, and a top-class *chocolatier* from Paris was contacted to supply an essential range of tempting chocolates. Varying sizes of *ballotin* assortment boxes were individually gift-wrapped in textured white paper and secured with a delicate blue ribbon engraved with the name of the *chocolatier*. The heady aroma of rich, bitter cocoa swept over me as I opened up the large container full of boxes of intoxicating chocolate. I lost myself in its soft, erotic smell. We had never before received such quantities, filling our tiny shop with a powerful, bitter scent of vanilla and cinnamon. I realised that I was enjoying immersing myself in this confectionery. I felt no repulsion in handling these perfumed boxes, bows and ribbons. I closed my eyes, breathing the delicious scent in deeply, and recalled my childhood trips to the local sweet shop to buy a quarter of boiled sweets – messy sherbet dips, colourful liquorice allsorts – reminding myself of my addiction to this unhealthy routine. I had clearly not always suffered from an aversion to sugar. Now this spicy, aromatic scent inspired reflection.

December was a frenzy of revelling party-goers, high-spending shoppers and overexcited children, raising my stress levels to unprecedented heights as I juggled precious time, torn between an increasingly demanding school social calendar and extended shop hours. Stéphane was forced to work in the restaurant every evening as large groups of jovial office workers gathered to eat and drink, wear silly hats and cajole each other into a frivolous celebratory mood. I'm not sure they really remembered what they were celebrating, most of them having been dragged along to this foreign place, not understanding the food, turning their noses up at the strange assortment of dishes placed before them. It was a testing time of the year for Stéphane and his staff, but they continued to smile, dutifully translate and describe, and occasionally laugh at the ridiculous transformation in their clientele.

Late nights and early-morning starts would start to show on his tired, drawn face as we met briefly at the breakfast table. A cursory glance at his darkened weary eyes was enough to make me thoroughly miserable, as I realised there was nothing I could do to take away his tiredness. He was needed at the restaurant; his organisational skills were a vital component in its smooth operation at this exacting time. This was a problem I simply could not remove. Poor school dinners, impersonal supermarket shopping, undressed salad accompaniments, the existence of cress, the hasty removal of a bread basket once the starter is finished – these were all superficial, irritating English habits that I could handle and control, knowing that they annoyed Stéphane. His prolonged tiredness, brought on by our overexcited Christmas customers, was another matter, and it left me feeling vulnerable and exposed. I wanted Stéphane to be strong and happy, to enjoy his work, to want to stay in England.

My search for comfort and happiness took me farther along the path of sweet extravagance. I indulged my husband in the sensual beauty of dark bitter chocolate and rich sugary desserts, coaxing his jaded appetite, acknow-ledging his Corsican love of puddings. I had always avoided this finale to mealtimes, focusing my attention on the savoury dishes, hoping for the pudding to be forgotten. My gradual acceptance of chocolate had come about thanks to our fragrant collection of Christmas confectionery, suddenly encouraging me to wallow in its gorgeous creamy texture, producing sublime desserts that closed eyes, provoked gentle moans of pleasure and encouraged us all to drift away to a child's world of chocolate heaven. I did not eat my creations but became increasingly tempted by the divine, alluring aroma that seemed permanently to permeate every corner of my kitchen.

Here are a couple of my chocolate heaven desserts.

CHARLOTTE AU CHOCOLAT

For 6 people, lightly butter the bottom and sides of a 20cm charlotte mould (it is a high-sided, fluted cake mould – a trifle dish would do). Cut out a circle of foil and place it in the bottom of the mould.

Separate 4 egg whites from the yolks.

Break about 250g of dark cooking chocolate into a pan and add half a glass of warm water and 2 tablespoons of caster sugar. Place the pan over a *bain-marie* and let the chocolate melt, gently stirring with a wooden spoon. Gradually add 250g of softened butter and stir continuously until a smooth, firm cream has formed.

With a whisk beat the egg yolks and mix them into the melted chocolate mixture.

Add a pinch of salt to the egg whites and beat until firm. Carefully incorporate the whites into the chocolate by folding gradually until a smooth mousse texture develops.

Put a wine glass of warm water, 2 tablespoons of caster sugar and a wine glass of rum in a pan over the heat. Stir with a spoon until the sugar has dissolved. When a syrupy consistency has formed take the pan off the heat and let it cool for 10 minutes.

Soak about a dozen *biscuits à la cuillère* one by one in the syrup mixture and line the bottom of the mould, covering the foil with the biscuits, and then continue to position the biscuits around the sides. Squeeze the biscuits tight next to each other. Fill the mould with the *mousse au chocolat*. Add a final layer of biscuits on top and cover with a plate that is slightly smaller than the mould, placing a weight on top to ensure that the charlotte is tightly packed. Place in the fridge ready to eat the next day. Served with a runny *crème anglaise*, it is apparently *un dessert géant*!

Crème Anglaise

To make the *crème anglaise* put a large pan of water on the heat to make a *bain-marie*.

In a pan, bring 750ml of milk with a vanilla pod split in two lengthways to the boil. When the milk starts to boil, remove from the heat and allow the vanilla to infuse for up to 15 minutes.

Put 8 egg yolks with 150g caster sugar in a container that will fit in the *bain-marie* (it must be able to sit in the pan with the boiling water without letting the water spill). Whisk together until the mixture turns pale and frothy.

Remove the vanilla from the milk and then pour into the egg yolk and sugar mixture and mix well together. This container should then be put into the *bain-marie* over a low heat and stirred until it thickens. It must never boil! It should take 5–6 minutes and you will know it is ready because the spoon, when removed, will remain covered in the mixture.

Pour the *crème anglaise* through a sieve and then allow it to cool while continuing to stir it with a spoon. If you want to add a flavouring – like rum – now is the time to do it. About a tablespoon should be about right.

When the cream is cold, put it in the fridge for an hour or two before serving.

MARQUISE AU CHOCOLAT

This dish is very rich, so for 6–8 people, beat 90g of caster sugar and 3 egg yolks until frothy. In a *bain-marie* melt 300g of dark bitter chocolate and then add gradually the egg yolk mixture and a couple of drops of vanilla essence. Incorporate 180g of softened butter, stirring until completely blended.

Beat the 3 egg whites until firm and carefully mix them into the chocolate.

Put a 24cm flan mould under very cold water and, without wiping it, pour in the chocolate mixture and leave all night in the fridge.

Just before serving dip the bottom of the mould in hot water and release the *marquise* on to a serving plate. Surround with *crème anglaise*.

'Mummy, is it chocolate day?' Pierre excitedly enquired almost every morning before leaving for school. I had decided to reserve our chocolate treats for just one day in the week, sometimes making it two as Christmas approached and a soothing magic was required to see us through the week. The evenings were bitterly cold, with treacherous ice on the roads and blinding, hazy fog disorienting even the most focused driver. The children were longing for snow. I prayed for a mild spell, just until the Christmas rush was over, and then it could freeze, blow up a blizzard – I didn't care because our doors would be closed and we could hibernate in front of a blazing fire, safe and protected. I waited each night for Stéphane to return, sipping a glass of warm red wine, trying to distract myself with novels, films and magazines. Each night I tried to stay awake to make sure he was back, looking out for the flash of headlights sweeping across the window, listening for the door and his heavy footsteps making the stairs creak. He seemed to be returning later and later, which made me curse the jovial drunken groups that would selfishly hang on in the restaurant, loudly chatting and joking, ungraciously pleading for one last drink. My anguish always increased as I succumbed to tiredness and flopped exhausted on to my bed. The quiet darkness and eerie shadows teased my imagination, awakening my irrational fears. I could sleep for a few hours, my body depleted, surrendering to the warm, caressing softness. Then, for no apparent reason, I would wake, reach out to a cold empty sheet beside me and check the time, which only brought on panic-filled insomnia, drawing out the hours until I heard his reassuring steps. Only then could I sleep peacefully. Once his warm, heavy bulk was ensconced on his side of the bed I could let my mind rest and drift off effortlessly.

The sanding lorries had been round, leaving their trail of noisy gravel which spat and scratched, riling Stéphane, provoking him to anger. Logical reasoning seemed to be a disappearing commodity as the weeks progressed, but the end was in sight, only a few agonisingly long days and nights to go.

It was another bitingly cold evening, with a light sprinkling of snow resting enticingly on the pavements and roads, raising the children's hopes for a cartoon snow-filled Christmas. I was feeling pleased with myself, having effortlessly nurtured a raging fire, now blasting out an almost unbearable heat. Happily the children were snuggled up in bed as I began my nervous vigil. I had nearly reached the last of my vast mountain of books, flicking impatiently through the pages, racing ahead, realising late in the evening that the plot of this one had completely passed me by. I wandered into the kitchen, rummaged around in the fridge and came across a *ballotin* of chocolates. It had been sent as a sample by our Parisian *chocolatier*, a gentle inducement to purchase. Two gaps spoiled its perfect display, the remaining delicacies each sitting primly in their slots, waiting solemnly to be picked. The two missing chocolates had been hastily devoured by Stéphane as he was passing through the house one early evening, dashing in to change his shirt and rush straight back out again, turning to me with a wink and a nod of approval. I took the box and examined the contents closely, perusing the shapes, colour and texture, drawn to a dainty hazelnut praline, unexpectedly finding my mouth watering. I sat in front of the fire and ate the dark crunchy chocolate, sipped a soothing glass of wine, lay my head back and smiled, relaxed.

Later I woke abruptly to realise that Stéphane was still not home. There was no noise, no disturbance, just a silent empty bed. This emptiness seemed to wake me instinctively, prompting me to check the time. I tried hard to close my eyes and let myself float back to sleep, applying all my textbook relaxation techniques, breathing deeply, consciously forcing myself to succumb. The minutes were painfully long, the dark, bleak hours filling me with dread. Three o'clock passed and four o'clock approached. He was always back by three, half past at the latest. I got up and decided to try his mobile, leaving it as late as possible, not wanting to fuss or show my anxiety. His answer service kicked in immediately. I paced the chilly kitchen floor, trying to decide what to do next. My head was now spinning, and that single chocolate I had so appreciatively gobbled was starting to churn heavily in my stomach. Why didn't he answer?

What should I do if he didn't come home?

I stood miserably in front of the icy black window, shivering, waiting longingly for the crunching of tyres, the bright lights that would announce his safe return. No cars, lorries or tractors broke the silence to raise my hopes, however briefly; everyone was sensibly at home, safe and secure. I decided to try his phone one last time. Relief and tears flowed when I heard his voice. 'Where are you? Why have you taken so long?' I spat the questions out breathlessly, allowing no time for answers or plausible excuses that would soothe my overwhelming angst.

It was gone half past four in the morning, rapidly moving towards five o'clock. Soon the children would be awake and everyday normality would be resumed. Meanwhile Stéphane was stuck in a ditch, having lost control of the car on a lethal, invisible stretch of ice. A desolate stretch of road, a short cut through the country villages, was now the scene of a desperate struggle to pull the car back on to the road. He had spent the last hour with his taxi-driver pal, trying to force the stranded vehicle out of the tight embrace of a hedge. John, the taxi-driver, was used regularly by the restaurant for both customers and staff, and was the first person Stéphane could think of who would be awake at this hour and willing to come to his assistance. Luckily the car had been cushioned by the thick, prickly hedge, preventing him from rolling farther into the field. He was not injured, just shocked and annoyed because the car did not want to budge. They eventually admitted defeat and Stéphane arrived home, muddy, cold and exhausted.

My worst nightmare had come true. How would I ever be able to sleep again during these late-night shifts? Why did we put each other through such anguish and distress? Surely there must be another way. At that moment I could not envisage coping with many more years of stress and anxiety, long nights of lonely anticipation. We would need to talk very soon.

Christmas arrived and the horrendous nightmare was soon forgotten as we excitedly tore open our gifts. Stéphane was the specialist in unusual present-buying. He always managed to astonish me with his intuitive choices, revealing a discerning insight into individual characters, their likes and dislikes, their hopes and dreams. He had an almost female intuitive understanding of what everyone would like, and this year he surpassed even his own incredibly high standards. I unwrapped my gift, rolled and secured with a silky gold ribbon, to discover a picture of the romantic Pont Neuf, glowing mysteriously under its carefully targeted spotlights, accompanied by a list of dates, flights and accommodation. We were returning to Toulouse – a few days' holiday back in the red-bricked city where we had met and married. I had not returned since we had left fifteen years earlier, and Stéphane knew that I had secretly longed to go back for some time. I had such fond, relaxed memories of this city. It had been my first home in France, full of carefree happiness, with no constraints or ties. I had not been weighed down by family commitments at this time and absorbed France innocently, just like Dad on our Normandy camping expeditions. France was my English holiday-maker's paradise, and in Toulouse I was living the dream of many. I had been drawn into the romance of Gallic charm, bewitched by the *Ville Rose*, beguiled by my swarthy, enchanting Corsican. I did not know how I would feel going back, reliving those head-spinning days of first passionate love. I wanted to recapture my infatuation with France, sense how I used to feel, living and working, shopping and cooking, and try to rekindle a lost love.

I did not believe naively that I would feel the same. I was now a mother, almost twenty years older, more mature, experienced and maybe more perceptive, critical and wary. This would not, however, prevent me remembering. And I keenly wanted to remember the bustling, aromatic markets, our Sunday-morning dinner planning, wandering through the mounds of raw flesh, dirty vegetables and ripe, squashy fruit. It was hard to believe that all those years ago our innocent obsession with these food-rich markets would eventually lead to a professional interest. I wanted to go back to our beginnings, be surprised and motivated, share the enthusiasm of the larger-than-life market stall-holders, listen to their jokes and anecdotes, let them win me over and be captivated again by the simple presentation of honest fresh ingredients. I was seeking inspiration and guidance to take me on to my next risk-taking challenge. Filling my lungs with the raw air of student days, imbibing the courageous, flamboyant spirit of our youth, I hoped to see more clearly and perhaps be steered towards my future.

It rained heavily as we approached Toulouse, the wipers on full speed, hindering our vision. I so desperately wanted to be able to focus cleanly on every building and street, soak up the familiarity and devour the beauty. The dripping windows were not going to let this happen. Maybe this was the way Toulouse wanted it to be – hazy, steamy, unfocused. We missed our turning and had somehow forgotten about the crazy system of flyovers, narrow one-way streets and dim, concealed traffic lights. Tetchy and tired, we finally ran to the hotel huddled under our enormous striped umbrella. It never rains in Toulouse at this time of year! Ironically, and annoyingly, we had left Nottingham in glorious hot sunshine. Here we were soaked to the skin, in soggy shoes, unprepared and a little disappointed.

The next day the clouds were still hovering, dispersing a light drizzle, but we refused to be disheartened. We set off to search out our favourite shops, cafés and restaurants. The pattern of cobbled streets and wide, busy boulevards was imprinted in our heads, and we certainly did not need the help of a map. We were former *Toulousains*, or so we thought. An hour of struggling and arguing, frustration and wasted precious time, sent Stéphane scurrying back to the hotel to retrieve the discarded map. Toulouse hadn't changed, the roads had not been moved or street names modified – it was just our memories which were deceiving us, time playing tricks, transforming the past into a confused image of how we thought it should be. Fifteen years is a long time.

Chez Fazoul, our trusted restaurant, cheap and cheerful, warm and friendly, was still there, the father now replaced by the son. Exactly the same menu formulas, the infamous *salade Fazoul* of *gésiers* and spiky *frisée*, the carafe of wine and coarse pâté and gherkins, all so popular fifteen years ago, were still being served, the appeal surviving, the old favourites still working their magic in the same unpretentious, uncomplicated manner. The butchers' shops, bakers and fishmongers, my favourite *pharmacie* off the Place St Georges, were all there, as prosperous and busy as ever, as though we had never moved away. There was now a *métro*, its distinctive underground scent reminding me of Paris as I stumbled across the metal grille of a warm air vent. We didn't respond to this modernisation, preferring to stick to old habits, striding out from the Place de Capitole back to the Place St Augustin, crossing the Rue Alsace Lorraine more than twice in a day, and returning to the hotel with aching, throbbing feet. It was all slowly taking shape, the pattern of the old *centre ville* beginning to make sense again, bringing back a smile of satisfying recognition. We drank morning coffee in a brasserie on the Place de Capitole, with a wide-angled view of the majestic *mairie*, savouring the long red velour-coated benches, ornate gilded bar and hand-painted fresco wall designs. We had always gazed longingly into this luxurious, expensive café and never dared venture in, but now we were back, rich and grown-up, and no longer afraid or ashamed to indulge.

I was shocked by an increase in the defacement of monuments, shops and walls, which were scarred by ugly, obscene graffiti. Or maybe with adult eyes I suddenly noticed the damage. We reached rue des Arts, our street, the road with our rooftop *appartement*, home to our first dinner party soirées. I gazed up at the solid concrete balcony on the fifth floor and sighed. The building looked tired, a little neglected, the front door in need of some varnish, a pane of glass cracked – or was this again my mature, dulled eyes washing away the sparkle, highlighting the imperfections? I peered at the names listed next to the buzzers and cautiously prised away a curling, faded label that unexpectedly exposed the past. My maiden name in neat, characterless handwriting – 'Simcock' – could clearly be read, as though we had never gone away. I shivered, squeezing Stéphane's hand, pleading for reassurance, longing for him to guide me firmly away. It felt wrong, trying to recreate the experiences of our youth. It was time to move on.

Inadvertently we started to discover the Toulouse of today, the Toulouse that suited us now, abandoning the old and familiar, replacing it with the expensive, refined and comfortable. I realised we could not return. This trip was a sad, poignant journey of discovery, highlighting our differences, bluntly telling us we were no longer the same naive couple of those glittering *Toulousain* days, when life glowed with optimism; we had matured and grown, experienced a wider, more complex world, and there could be no going back. Our future lay elsewhere.

The next day we lunched in a bustling, highly popular café serving the local office workers, who were all desperately keen to fit in their *plat du jour* during the precious *midi* slot. The place was heaving, and I was in two minds as to whether to queue or leave. But Stéphane's astute eye had assessed the slick professionalism of the tight team of waiters, who dodged, weaved and danced around the tightly packed tables and chairs, and he persuaded me to stay. Everyone was squeezed in close, strangers dining with strangers, nodding and acknowledging the sharing of their space. They all, however, had something in common: they were sharing the secret of this establishment, participating in the appreciation of sumptuous lunchtime food, oozing with flavour, as if in a secluded, clandestine club. I watched a middle-aged lady, round and red-cheeked from too much daily wine, sitting alone, yet surrounded by diners, some momentarily making contact, excusing each other as they stood, squeezing through her space to reach the cloakroom. She devoured an *assiette de crudités*, copious and colourful, and patiently waited for the next course. Again, a beautiful fillet of fish confirmed a wise choice. She was clearly selecting light, reduced-fat options. Meanwhile we ate large bowlfuls of *salades composées*, with baskets of neatly cut bread and glasses of wine. I remained transfixed by this lady as she sped effortlessly through her multiple lunchtime courses. I was shocked by the speed with which she could eat. Admittedly she was alone and had only her plate as a focus, but her appetite and capacity to wipe her *assiette* clean in a short space of time astounded me. The organisation and skill of the waiters, juggling carafes and plates and coping with additional requests, kept Stéphane preoccupied while I analysed the dining workers. Lunch boxes, filled baguettes and sandwiches on the hop were simply not an option here. The French are fortunate in possessing a plethora of smart cafés, brasseries and restaurants geared up for an intensive two hours of cooking, serving and clearing. Why bother with a bland, over-refrigerated sandwich? As we struggled over our last mouthfuls of salad, our lady had not only swiftly devoured a *tarte aux pommes* with lashings of Chantilly cream, putting to rest my theory about her diet consciousness, but she had ensured that the meal was completed with the essential *café*, and was now heading conclusively for the cloakroom. She was an expert diner with years of practice, proficient in her art, knowing precisely when to nod for more bread or water and signal for the bill. This was a social occasion; she was alone yet comforted by the presence of like-minded souls. Communication with a waiter, a stranger, even a couple of tourists, struck me as a far more acceptable option than a lonely office sandwich or an aimless wander past shop windows, clumsily juggling an overstuffed *panini*. I felt alien, with no office to return to. I had no place here, could exert no influence, had no guidance to offer. These people were in the know, using food as a worthy excuse to chat, relax and share the events of the day. My work could not be done in Toulouse, Corsica or Paris. I was needed at home.

We returned refreshed and happy to be back. It had rained for the entire four days, washing away some of the city's beauty but helping us both to silently appreciate the merits of this visit. The shop was encouragingly busy with devoted coffee drinkers, cheese connoisseurs and those forlornly seeking a rare ingredient, essential for the success of their imminent dinner party for eight. 'So how was Toulouse? Had it changed? What did you eat?' they asked, sipping cups of *grand crème*, anxious for news from France.

At least I had trained my customers well; they were now asking about meals, talking about food in a typically French fashion. This is something that still amazes me when Stéphane's parents ring for news, spending the first ten minutes enquiring about what we've just eaten or what we are planning to eat. 'Have you eaten yet? What are you eating tonight? We've just finished the most gorgeous *sauté de porc aux olives*. I think it's the best your mother has ever produced.'

I remember having felt incredibly anxious when the phone rang, avoiding it for fear of these interrogations. I had churlishly suspected that they were trying to find out whether I was a worthy wife, feeding their son correctly with classic, respectable dishes. There was probably an element of truth in this in the early days, but I am now, not surprisingly, more relaxed about these matters and recognise this inquisition as innocent everyday chit-chat, a commonplace conversational topic and a genuine expression of their love of food. Splendid meal experiences are what they like to talk about best – those, and sometimes the weather!

I spoilt my customers that day with mouth-watering

descriptions of our meals, depicting the colours and aromas, portraying the scene, laughing at the unruly mous- tache of our waiter and describing the elegant simplicity of our wine.

'And what did you have for pudding?' This was a jolt back to reality – to the need to satisfy this English craving for cloying sweetness with sticky puddings and impressive, sculptured desserts.

I stuttered, momentarily thrown by this perfectly benign enquiry. What was so strange about asking about puddings? Nothing, I suppose – it was just another of my uncertain- ties, a familiar feeling of unease swelling from deep within, and all because I questioned my ability to dazzle on this front as I could with savoury flavours. The sweets we had sampled had not been impressive, rich or gooey but simple desserts made from pure seasonal fruit. We had indulged, sometimes sharing like children, coyly requesting an extra spoon, but all our end-of-meal treats had been fruit-based, an elegant refinement of nature's naturally sweet offerings. From the smooth, acidic sharpness of a divine *tarte au citron* to a classic *poires au vin rouge*, I had been captivated by the adaptation of fruit's natural sweetness into something offer- ing a more enticing succulence.

In autumn and winter apples abound. Even those that are bruised and not very pretty can be transformed into this aromatic pudding.

POMMES AU FOUR À LA CANNELLE
Preheat the oven to 190°C/375°F/Gas Mark 5.
 Wash and scoop out the cores of 4 apples and discard the contents.

Make an incision in the skins, sketching a circle around the centres. Place the apples in an ovenproof dish and sprinkle some cinnamon into the scooped-out hollows.

Mix about 25g of butter into a soft paste and add 25g of icing sugar, an egg yolk, 50g of almond powder and the zest of an orange. Put the mixture into the hollow of each apple and then sprinkle some brown sugar on top.

Pour 4 tablespoons of water into the bottom of the dish and bake for about 45 minutes. The apples should be tender when pricked with the point of a knife.

Delicious served with vanilla ice cream or crème fraîche scented with a drop of Calvados.

POIRES AU VIN ROUGE

Peel 4 just-ripe, unblemished Williams pears, keeping them whole.

Pour a bottle of good red wine into a large pan with 250g of caster sugar, 1 tablespoon of honey, a vanilla pod cut in two lengthways, and a pinch of nutmeg. Bring to the boil for ten minutes.

Place the pears in the hot wine (they should not be squashed one against the other) and let them poach, bubbling gently for a maximum of 7–8 minutes.

Take the pan off the heat, remove the pears and place them carefully in a large presentation bowl.

Put 200g of raspberries, blackberries or dark black cherries in a processor and blend, then push through a sieve and add to the wine. Mix well with a spoon and then pour the wine mixture over the pears.

Allow to cool in the fridge for 8–10 hours before enjoying.

I need not have worried. My customers were already capti-vated by the magic of simplicity, flavour and harmony. They groaned in delight at my descriptions, closing their eyes to imagine all the harder, relishing every adjective and exaggerated superlative. They were a rewarding audience, turn-ing to my shelves to be inspired, listening attentively to my cheeseboard recommendations, joking like intimate friends. For the first time I recognised my power to influ-ence and guide, and it felt good. Pieces of the jigsaw were coming together in my head as chance comments and casual remarks suddenly re-emerged in my memory. Restaurant regulars who had over time become close friends shared our love of splendid meals and frequently initiated their own *soirées découvertes* at home, flagrantly pinching our combin-ations, calling Stéphane up for last-minute advice about cooking times. I began to truly appreciate the extent to which our influence had won over these treasured few when the no-fuss menu concept was suggested as a dinner party option.

'I've got some really good pals coming for dinner tonight and I really don't want to spend the entire evening fretting over the food, sweating in the kitchen while everyone else is having a good time.' This was a lament from stressed, panic-stricken souls heard almost daily in the shop, as they clutched their lists, miserably planning unwanted dinners.

I was thrilled by the inspirational solution boldly proposed by one friend for their forthcoming evening. 'I'm doing a no-fuss menu, French Living-style, just as you have always recommended. This time I really don't care. I want to feel like a princess, laugh uncontrollably and have a spec-tacular time with my friends.'

I have always advocated the simple approach to casual

dinner parties, the less cooking the better. Many scoff and mutter under their breath, whispering things like, 'But that's cheating.' Sometimes a tiny amount of compromise is required to make sure you relax and enjoy yourself. I don't really think any compromise has been made in terms of flavour with this ready-made menu, courtesy of French Living.

> Canapés of *saucisson de rosette*, *tapenade* and *anchoiade*.
> *Foie gras* on warm toast.
> A jar of *sauté de canard* – a warming casserole of duck in red wine and *cèpe* mushrooms, ready made – just warm through. Served with a jar of *haricots verts* tossed in garlic.
> A selection of cheese from the French Living counter – a ripe Camembert, a couple of *caprifigues* (fig-shaped goat's cheese), one coated in herbs, the other in ash, a slice of extra-old Beaufort and a salty wedge of Roquefort.
> Six slices of *tarte au citron* expertly crafted by a French Living chef.

I began to listen out for evidence of our influence, the luring of dormant taste buds into acts of unaccustomed bravery, and would chuckle in childish delight when I found it. Young Saturday helpers were often excellent subjects for culinary transformations. One day a shy, quiet worker raised her head from the growing pile of stained *grand crème* cups she was washing and declared that she would be introducing her parents to an alternative cheeseboard that Christmas. 'Do you know, I'm tired of Cheddar and Stilton. We have them every year and they're just so predictable, even with the grapes, celery and vintage port. I'm going to buy my parents some French cheese this year.'

And she did. Nothing too pungent, off-putting or unusual: a portion of St Nectaire, a slice of Comté and some Bleu d'Auvergne.

And then there was *la salade*. This will always remain closest to my heart as my first triumphant food discovery, and it should come as no surprise that I experience the greatest pleasure when its charm is understood and extolled by others – such as this eighteen-year-old, in her first Saturday job, tossing salad leaves in thick peppery vinaigrette dressing, coating every leaf, building the creation with tomatoes, cheese and ham, sometimes egg, often *Niçoise* olives. Incredibly this therapeutic process leaves its mark, and my team of helpers walk away indoctrinated by the power of vinaigrette for ever. They even attempt to spread the word to those around them. 'Do you know, my parents have always made us eat salad. Every Friday. A slice of ham, some tomatoes, iceberg lettuce, celery, beetroot, and pickled onions for flavour. And I hate it.'

And so this girl took over the Friday evening salad preparation, tossing her creation wildly in the potent vinaigrette – a large bowl filled with coated leaves hiding surprises buried deep within. She was ready to break the established order of her household, like a rebellious teenager, intent on shocking. After years of solitary salad plates with each morsel clearly identifiable and certainly no fancy dressings, this revolutionary bowl was certain to cause stupefaction. She would need to give it time and probably adopt a softer approach.

'So how did the salad go? Did your parents enjoy it?' I enquired.

'Well, I'm not really sure,' she said. 'They just wanted to know where I work.'

267

So tell me again, where is it you go every Saturday? Maybe this question meant they liked it.

I watched many such questioning young minds, selfishly savouring their development and their burgeoning interest in the food displayed enticingly around them. Influencing and inciting change raised my spirits and filled me with a comforting sense of well-being. I seemed to be increasingly surrounded by individuals who were chasing their dreams, seeking novelty in their narrow, enclosed existence, and my negligible role in creating change filled me with immeasurable satisfaction.

A friend of a friend from Corsica had sent their son to us for work experience, a six-month stay to improve his English before he returned to his studies and to follow the path of most young Corsicans – getting a job in a hotel, a restaurant, anything tourism-related. Except the plan went wrong and he never returned. He's still here now, although not working for us, building a life for himself in England. Maybe one day he will go back, but for now he has escaped and relishes his suburban freedom. He often calls in, drinks his *café*, treats himself to a *plat du jour*, mysteriously drawn back to familiar territory and a comforting, distant reminder of home.

And then, of course, there's Celia. She's still searching for settled contentment and has also decided to look for it in England, close to us, her second family. All these attachments can sometimes seem burdensome, as if I have a kind of all-consuming parental responsibility for these evolving young people. And yet I know deep down I am proud that they have chosen my country, my people and my culture.

I decided it was my turn to start choosing. The more content I felt the more guilty and nervous I became, watching Stéphane gazing at glossy architectural photographs of dream homes and buildings, searching for inspiration and his own self-fulfilment. Our land, our island, our uncertainty. Where could we go next? I stared at him, still attracted to those dreamy, devilish eyes, his dark, thinning hair now lightened with flashes of grey, and contemplated just how far our relationship had come. We have been incredibly fortunate in being able to share our work and pleasure, to pursue our fascination with the power of food by surrounding ourselves daily with so many memories, scents and flavours. We've used the process of cooking together so many times to heal rifts and disagreements, always calmed by a heavenly meal, the triumphant result of our tense, silent effort. A delectable meal seems to work for us every time. Eating out, face to face, without the children, with a waiter to fetch and carry, are occasions for us to plan. We've used the restaurant table so many times to catch up and talk, without distractions, forced to face each other and listen. It was time to call Stéphane to the table.

I booked a table for two at French Living. For the first time we would dine together at our own restaurant, experience the magic of being transported back home to France, setting the scene for some decisions. Stéphane has always taken the lead with new projects, taking me by surprise, sometimes upsetting me with his forcefulness. This time I wanted to take control and avoid any surprises. I did not want suddenly to be confronted by one of his momentous announcements.

I had chosen a suitably quiet evening, having checked the reservations well in advance to make sure our night would not be ruined by Stéphane feeling obliged to tend to his guests and start pouring wine. There was a group of four chatty ladies sitting under the mirror I had bought specially when we first opened, and a scattering of intimate couples at the wall tables, snugly isolated. Soft, flickering candle-light helped remind us we were here to relax – to receive attention rather than give it.

We were predictable in our choice of aperitifs; I ordered my favourite kir and Stéphane his reliable Ricard. The menu, unsurprisingly, was as familiar as an old friend from Toulouse, and equally predictably, embellished with Stéphane's signature.

'This is strange,' he complained, looking around cautiously, fixed rigidly to his seat, not daring to move.

'No it's not,' I retorted. 'This is what we always wanted. A restaurant that feels like France – set menus, value for money, no themes, trends or pretence. It's yours to enjoy, you know. Sit back and relax a little.'

And that is what he did. He began to smile and visibly unwind, suddenly appreciating the value of this moment.

'This feels good, doesn't it?' I whispered. 'We've actually managed to make a Frenchman feel at home in England.' I looked at him, interrupting my efforts to accurately stab a snail in its garlicky parsley-butter sauce. 'Look carefully at what we've got,' I went on. 'Can't you see? All these people, some still strangers, others friends, and we've brought them together, given them some happiness, a taste of France. Some may have always dreamed of finding happiness abroad, wished they could live the French dream, but they'll never have the courage to do it. They come here and they don't feel so guilty about staying.'

Stéphane stopped eating and stared at me. My mouth felt uncomfortably dry, as if I'd had too much to drink the night before. My heart was thudding in my ears, adrenalin coursing through me.

I could hear myself babbling on, not wanting to give him the opportunity to respond with a torrent of French ideals. I so desperately wanted him to fully acknowledge the desirability of his creation, and at the same time consider carefully all the people he had met along the way – the strangers and friends who had gathered around him, provided support, love and happiness. These you cannot create in the search for some sort of idyllic home. And they are what matter. I've come to realise it's the people who touch our lives every day who count most, not the country, the house, the magnificent view. 'I don't want to run away and abandon all this, Stéphane, leave all these people who love what we've done and are here for us every day.' Finally I had admitted it.

He looked dumbfounded and fell silent. I was allowed to continue, to justify myself further.

'Don't you see, we're following the French plan. We apply the power of food and mealtimes to socialise, to be together and make sure there is some human contact during our busy, stressful day. We're living the French dream here, surrounded by friends and people we love. I understand both cultures better than ever before. I'm accepted now by your Corsican family, and we can so easily bring them together – here, in Paris or in Corsica.'

Our waiter interrupted, clearing his throat nervously. *'Dessert, monsieur dame?'*

I didn't really want to be disturbed now, focused as I was on persuasion, but I had already made my choice. 'Mmm, let me see. I think I'll have the *moelleux au chocolat*,' I said, for the first time ever selecting a *dessert*.

Stéphane peered at me again and laughed loudly. I grinned slyly and began to admit to my recently acquired taste for chocolate – the occasional late-night treat picked surreptitiously from the *ballotin* box, the devious licking of velvet-coated spoons before the children could see, and those feelings of irresistible temptation pulling me towards the sweetness of a dessert. I had no explanation for this sudden reversal, but I did not want to resist it .

He watched me eat the dark, moist chocolate sponge slowly, carefully, floating in sated contentment, relieved of all pent-up anguish.

We were almost the last couple in the restaurant, now neatly reset for the next day's lunchtime service. We ordered coffee. I decided I needed a hot, strong espresso to sharpen my senses and prepare me for Stéphane's response.

He didn't offer me any response. Perhaps he didn't have one at that time. He smiled affectionately and caressed my hair softly as he always did when he wanted to soothe me. He told me not to be afraid, to live for the moment, and not to run away from the opportunities.

We had never done that before. We were certainly not about to start now.

Epilogue

THE ISLAND ALWAYS finds a way to bring you back, to keep its grip on you. Our teenaged visitors eventually return once the city has drained them of their last pennies or their parents start making serious demands. We also return every summer, joining the tourists in their annual mission to revitalise themselves. The village characters, restaurants and bars are still there, nothing has changed, although the village sign deteriorates a little more each year, fading into illegibility. Perhaps one day I will take out my paints and boldly put our village back on the map.

The beach changes shape constantly. Last year it was perfect, ideal for lounging, building sandcastles and keeping an eye on the children while they splashed furiously in the waves. We often stand together on our land, excitedly checking the view, making sure we can still see the outline

COME TO THE TABLE

of the Ile Rousse. Here we feel invincible, ready to carry on with our lives. The island does its job superbly, filling us with strength and renewed determination to carry on our good work. Our field remains as it was, full of thistles and other weeds that we occasionally pull up, trying to make it look loved. Of course, there are plans. We have agreed that there is still lots more work to be done. A new purpose seems to have been injected into our lives.

Island family members now make more visits to us in England, no longer wary of the foreign intruder in their midst. They seem to have found the courage to travel and explore, to leave the confines of their island and discover another. I think they like it. They still bring mountains of gifts but in exchange allow me to settle the bill at a restaurant or two. I enjoy introducing them to a part of my culture, helping them understand better who I am. They love the crumbles, old-fashioned village pubs and classic Lancashire hotpot. I think they also now appreciate the work we do and do not consider us as just another couple of restaurant owners. French Living is more than that, and fortunately they understand this and are able to accept our choices.

Mum has also rediscovered fun and adventure, with a new partner to entice her away on day trips and holidays. She is living her life to the full again, which is just as it should be. My old excuse of needing to stay in England to be close to her and support her seems superfluous now.

We carry on working harder than ever to bring the French dream alive to as many as possible. And yet we often wonder how we could also bring the Corsican island magic into the lives of our customers and friends.

For now I'll continue admiring my quaint cottage garden with its baby green buds now waiting impatiently to emerge, ready to herald a fresh start. Nothing can keep us down – there will be a new purpose, a new dream. I munch contentedly on the last chocolate from our *ballotin* gift box and promise myself that I will never be afraid again.

Glossary

affineur person in charge of the last stages of the maturing process of cheese

anchoiade spread made with anchovies

artisanal cheese cheese produced using traditional farmhouse methods

assiette plate or platter

auberge inn or hotel

bain-marie (a) roasting tin containing hot water in which another dish will sit while the contents are cooking or (b) pan that is used to keep sauces warm or to allow slow cooking. A container is placed inside the pan which is filled with hot water (a tightly-fitting bowl over a saucepan would do)

ballotin gift box

banon goat's cheese wrapped in chestnut leaves, from Provence

bavarois mousse made with cream and gelatine

beignet fritter or doughnut

biscuits à la cuillère soft finger biscuits

les bises the French greeting of a kiss on either cheek. In

Paris they kiss four times, in Corsica they kiss only twice!

bol bowl

bonbons sweets

boudin blanc sausage made with bechamel sauce and minced chicken, served at Christmas as a starter

boulangerie bakery

brandade de morue French fisherman's pie made with cod, mashed potato and garlic

le brocciu Corsican ewe's-milk cottage cheese

brochette kebab or meat cooked on skewer

buche log

buche de Noel Yule log

calissons d'Aix diamond-shaped sweets from Aix en Provence made with candied melon and almonds

caprifigue fresh goat's cheese in the shape of a fig

caramel au sel de Guérande caramel made with butter containing grey coarse sea salt from Guerande

cassoulet speciality dish from Toulouse made with beans, duck confit, pork and Toulouse sausage

cervelle de canut Lyon speciality of fromage frais with added garlic and herbs

châtaigne chestnut

cocotte casserole dish

compote puréed fruit

confit de canard d'oie conserve of duck or goose

confiture de coings quince jam

confiture de pastèques watermelon jam

conger conger eel

coupe fruit or dessert dish

croquembouche pyramid-shaped cake made with prof-

iteroles filled with *crème pâtissiere* and glued together
with caramel. Served at weddings and christenings
croûtons small pieces of toasted bread
cughiuette Corsican sweet biscuit

demi literally means half. If you ask for it in a bar you'll
get a half of lager beer
dessert du jour dessert of the day
diabolo lemonade flavoured with a fruit syrup e.g.
diabolo grenadine is lemonade flavoured with pomegran-
ate syrup
dragées sugar-coated almonds

encornet squid
épicier grocer
épicerie fine delicatessen

faire chabrol expression used for finishing a bowl of
soup by adding some wine to the last drops of liquid
fermier cheese farmhouse cheese
fiadone Corsican cheesecake
fil wire (used to cut blue cheeses)
fougasse Provençal bread made with herbs
frisée spiky-leaved lettuce

gésiers gizzards
gigot d'agneau leg of lamb
goûter literally the verb means to taste. It is also the
term used for a snack given to children when they
return home from school to keep them going until
dinner
grand crème milky coffee like a cappuccino

grasse matinée lie-in
gratin de chou-fleur cauliflower cheese
gratin baked in the oven with cheese
grenier attic

hachis Parmentier meat dish covered in mashed
potato. In France, dishes containing potato are described
as Parmentier because they are named after the French
agriculturalist Antoine A Parmentier who was credited
with improving the production and popularising the
eating of potatoes in 1785

jambon de Paris cooked ham

Laguiole Laguiole is a well-known French brand of knife
that resembles a flick knife
lait cru unpasteurised milk
lardon cube of belly pork
lonzu cured Corsican ham

magret de canard duck breast
maquis Corsican moorland
marron entier whole chestnut
marron glacé sweetened chestnut
matelote d'anguilles eel stew
merguez sausage spicy lamb sausage
moelleux au chocolat individual chocolate sponge
cakes
mûre sauvage wild blackberry
murènes moray eel
myrte myrtle

onctueux smooth, creamy

pageots Mediterranean fish that resembles a gilt-head fish

pagres Mediterranean fish that resembles sea bream

Paris beurre baguette or sandwich made with cooked ham

petit crème small milky coffee like a cappuccino

pièce montée *see croquembouche*

plateau de fromage cheese board

plat du jour dish of the day

poitrine fumé smoked belly pork

pommes dauphines light potato dumplings that have been deep fried

rillettes like a spicy potted meat, usually pork or goose

rondelle slice

rosette de Lyon type of saucisson (cured sausage) from Lyon

rouget red mullet

rouille spicy sauce made with mayonnaise and hot harissa, spread on croutons and served with fish soup

salade composée mixed salad

santon ornamental figure often used to decorate a Christmas crib

saucisse en brioche sausage in pastry

soirée découverte discovery evening

soupe corse Corsican soup

steak haché French-style burger

tâche stain

tapenade spread made with black olives
tartine slice of buttered baguette and jam
tilleul lime leaves used to make an infusion
toile cirée waxed tablecloth
tomate farcie stuffed tomato
trompettes de la mort horn of plenty mushrooms
trou normand Normandy tradition of drinking a glass
 of Calvados in between courses to stimulate the appetite
 and make room for the rest of the feast

vendange tardive late harvest
verveine lemon verbena
viennoiserie pastries such as croissant, pain au chocolat
 etc.
vin jaune prestigious white wine from the Jura mountains

Index

PIATKUS BOOKS

If you have enjoyed reading this book, you may be
interested in other titles published by Portrait. These include:

0 7499 5034 X	Abba: Unplugged	Karl French	£16.99
0 7499 5051 X	Anne Boleyn	Joanna Denny	£8.99
0 7499 5067 6	Children's War, The	Juliet Gardiner	£20
0 7499 5065 X	Come to the Table	Louise Luiggi	£7.99
0 7499 5019 6	England v Argentina	David Downing	£8.99
0 7499 5057 9	Girl Next Door	Anne Diamond	£17.99
0 7499 5006 4	Jon Bon Jovi: The Biography	Laura Jackson	£16.99
0 7499 5052 8	Life and Limb	Jamie Andrew	£7.99
0 7499 5003 X	Lifting the Veil	Piers Dudgeon	£20.00
0 7499 5025 0	Neil Diamond	Laura Jackson	£16.99
0 7499 5027 7	Rod Stewart	T. Ewbank and S. Hildred	£8.99
0 7499 5029 3	Roger Daltrey	T. Ewbank and S. Hildred	£17.99
0 7499 5020 X	Simon Weston: Moving On	Simon Weston	£7.99
0 7499 5021 8	Sophie's Story	Vince Smith	£8.99
0 7499 5061 7	Surviving With Wolves	Misha Defonseca	£17.99
0 7499 5037 4	Willie John	Willie John McBride and Peter Bills	£8.99

All titles are available from:

Piatkus Books Ltd, c/o Bookpost. PO Box 29, Douglas, Isle of Man,
IM99 1BQ

Telephone (+44) 01624 677 237
Fax (+44) 01624 670 923
Email: bookshop@enterprise.net
Free Postage and Packing in the United Kingdom
Credit Cards accepted. All Cheques payable to Bookpost

Prices and availability are subject to change without prior notice. Please
allow 14 days for delivery. When placing orders, please state if you do
not wish to receive any additional information.